Just One *Cornetto*

London to Sicily in a Small Motorhome

Keith Mashiter

Published in 2013 by FeedARead Publishing

British Library C.I.P.

A CIP catalogue record for this title is available from the British Library.

ACKNOWLEDGEMENTS

Once more, thanks and deep love to my wife Gail, who continues to cheerfully endure my ridiculous ideas with great patience

Throughout the book I quote descriptions of objects, buildings, places and their history which invariably have been derived from our very battered copies of *The Rough Guide to Italy* the bible for our travels. If no reference is given then the *Rough Guide* is most probably the source.

Local guides and pamphlets, too numerous to mention or list, have added further information together with Internet browsing.

Michelin are our favourite maps and sat on Gail's lap throughout our drives and in the evenings reminded me where we had been. Whilst on the subject of maps please ignore my references to Italian road numbers as they will invariably have changed.

For information on Mafia activities I have relied heavily on Peter Robb's *'Midnight in Sicily'*; David Lane's '*Into the Heart of the Mafia'*; Roberto Saviano's *'Gomorrah'*; and John Dickie's *Cosa Nostra.'* I don't recommend reading these before you go.

HRZ Reisemobile GmbH in Germany built a superb van, Vanmaster of Wigan sold it to us with great courtesy, Going Spare Autos of Brentwood serviced it with friendly efficiency and stalwart Nigel and his team at East Coast Leisure in Basildon fitted the extras we needed and made sure they worked.

Cover design, artwork and photography by me.

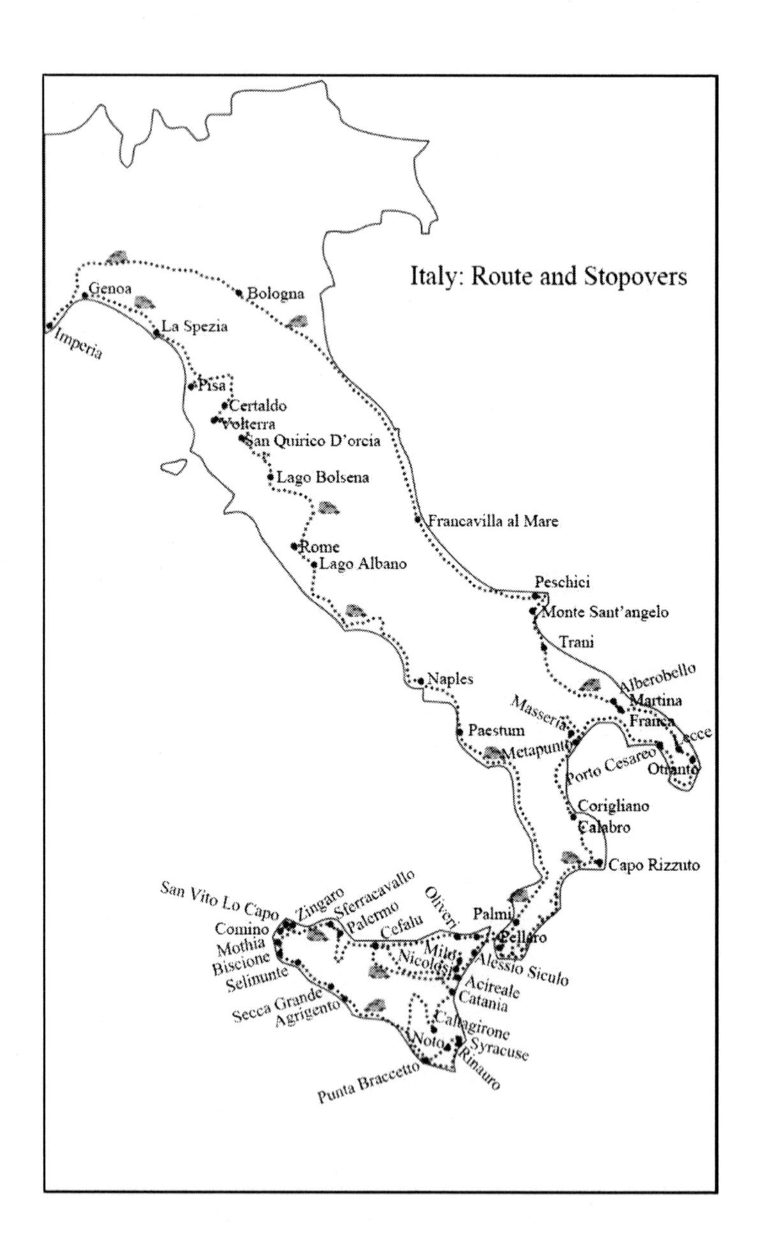
Italy: Route and Stopovers
Genoa
Bologna
Imperia
La Spezia
Pisa
Certaldo
Volterra
San Quirico D'orcia
Lago Bolsena
Francavilla al Mare
Rome
Lago Albano
Peschici
Monte Sant'angelo
Trani
Naples
Alberobello
Martina
Franca
Masseria
Paestum
Metapunto
Lecce
Porto Cesareo
Otranto
Corigliano
Calabro
Capo Rizzuto
San Vito Lo Capo
Zingaro
Sferracavallo
Palermo
Oliveri
Cefalu
Palmi
Pellaro
Comino
Mothia
Biscione
Selinunte
Milo
Nicolosi
Alessio Siculo
Acireale
Catania
Secca Grande
Agrigento
Caltagirone
Noto
Syracuse
Rinauro
Punta Braccetto

CONTENTS

BEGINNINGS 7

PICTURES FROM GENOA 12

CINQUE TERRE 20

LEANING TOWARDS PISA 29

AN INCIDENT IN THE DARK 36

A DICKENS OF A TOUR 45

ROME AND BEYOND 58

ROME TO NAPLES 70

NAPLES 76

SOUTH FROM NAPLES 83

NEARLY THERE 91

SICILY: FIRST IMPRESSIONS 96

ETNA 109

CATANIA AND CALTAGIRONE 116

MOSAICS AND ENNA 127

PUNTA BRACCETTO 136

TO NOTO: THE GOLDEN CITY 143

NO KISS! 159

SYRACUSE: IT'S HARD TO LEAVE 168

SOUTH THEN WEST BY AGRIGENTO 187

CHRISTMAS 195

TO PURGATORY AND BEYOND 207

ERICE: DOG BITES MAN 219

PALERMO 229

CORLEONE 246

FINALE 251

CARNEVALE 267
FINAL DAYS AT FINALE 276
LEAVING SICILY 283
ROUND THE TOE 289
TRUMPING IN THE TOWER 299
A BEAUTIFUL BOOK 308
NEW ITALIAN FRIENDS 315
TONY BLAIR'S FRIEND? 325
A QUIET NIGHT? 337
NEARLY A BULL'S EYE 347
IT'S OVER 358
POSTSCRIPT 365

Beginnings

Giuseppe leant forward in his chair, causing it to scrape on the tiled floor, put his hands round his coffee cup seeking warmth in the unusual chill of the café, and thought about what he was going to say.

‘I only want to do what is legal.’

‘But you said before that a local cartel was controlling planning permission for your house.’

‘It’s true. I went to the Mayor and he said you must have a minimum of five thousand square metres of land before you can build a house. So, I bought five thousand and applied for permission. Another man bought a five thousand plot behind me and straightaway built a house on it. So when nothing happened, I went to see the Mayor and he told me I would only get permission if I had ten thousand square metres so I bought the next land – it is a wasteland and of no use – but nothing happened. He told me I should be patient and I would get permission, maybe tomorrow.’

‘How frustrating,’ I offered.

‘Yes, but I wanted to do everything legally,’ said Giuseppe with an exasperated sigh.

'What happened next?' asked Gail, intrigued by the saga.

'Nothing, nothing, nothing,' said Giuseppe. 'I went to the square to play cards with the men as usual. That's all the men do here – sit in the square or go to clubs to play cards.'

'Yes, we wondered about that. Why are there so many men in the piazza*s* of every town we go to?' I asked between mouthfuls of my *cornetto*. 'What do they do all day?' Giuseppe shrugged.

'Play cards sitting in the traffic fumes.'

'What work is there for them?'

'Work? Nobody works. They sit in the square talking or go to card clubs. There are always deaths, but they live long lives because they have no stress – they get everything off their chests. It's a small community – lots of inbreeding.'

'But don't they get bored going every day?' I quizzed.

'I'll tell you a story. One man told his wife he didn't feel like going to the square that day. She pushed him out of the house: "If you don't go, we won't know what's happening."'

'And money?' Gail asked.

'Oh! They have loads of money and new cars every year – not just little cars – *big*, *big* cars. And all their children go to university. Yes, they have lots of money. They build houses they don't need.'

I was aching to ask how that could be, but felt we would be moving into forbidden territory. 'We've seen lots of houses with the upper floors not finished, looking abandoned.'

'Yes, in case a daughter or son wants accommodation later.'

'So, you went to the square…'

'Anything said in the square gets around fast,' explained Giuseppe. 'So, I told them the man behind me had built on five thousand square metres, as well as others – doctors and dentists.'

'And?' we chorused.

'The Mayor sent for me. He said he knew I had been talking in the square and it wasn't good if I wanted to get the permission.'

'Blimey. Sounds like tough talk. What did you do, back off?'

'No, I let them know in the square I was visiting a certain place, and I went on a day I knew someone from the Mayor's office would be there. So I would be seen.'

'A Mafia place, Giuseppe?' I asked, trying not to show my anticipation.

'*Si. Si...*' He lapsed into Italian for a few seconds. 'But, I have nothing to do with them – just to be seen there, you understand, would be enough.'

'So you didn't meet anyone?'

'By chance I did meet one man – we had a drink. He told me he knew about my problem. If I wanted permission, his people could get it. If they came to my town, the local's "hands would shake."' At which point Giuseppe gave a good impression of trembling hands, holding them out in front of him.

'So?'

'Of course I want nothing to do with them. Once they have you, then...' He didn't finish the sentence. 'Enough talking, we go now.' Our time was up. With many unanswered questions, we left the café and stepped out into the cool evening air.

'Ciao, Giuseppe.'

'Ciao, Luigi.'

'Ciao, Giuseppe.'

'Ciao, Federico.' Everyone we met knew Giuseppe.

'You want to follow me up to my place in your campervan now?' he asked.

The moment had arrived. I had been thinking hard about Lonely Planet's warning that kidnapping was prevalent in the mountain district. Yet refusal would be difficult, and wasn't that why we had chosen to travel thousands of miles in our new van to southern Italy and

Sicily? For the possibility that between the pretty hilltop towns, some of the most beautiful and important World Heritage cities, an active volcano and sundrenched beaches, we might brush up against its infamous, but normally hidden, darker side? Gail and I glanced knowingly at each other, climbed into the van and set off behind Giuseppe's immaculate new, *big*, *big* car up the unsigned mountain road.

Sicily is an island that boasts thirty centuries of history blooded by Phoenician, Greek, Roman and Norman invaders, who left behind temples, amphitheatres and castles and brought about some of the most beautiful and important cities and civilisations known to mankind. An island wrapped in its past, it has an enticing edge of unknowns, murderous crimes and political corruption. The island is large enough to explore, and topographically varied, with a remote mountainous interior and endless coastline. With a population of five million, it is profoundly influenced by its ten million descendents living abroad. Some claim it to be a land like no other, with parts closer to Africa than Europe. Inspired by Fallowell's book, *To Noto: or London to Sicily in a Ford*, I felt that Sicily was far enough to be different, and close enough to be feasible.

Gail, my wife, was happy to indulge my whim, but we were also apprehensive. The reality of us being confined for six months to the small interior of a metal box could easily prove to be a trial of our hitherto matrimonial harmony. Our previous exploits to France and Spain had been in a super-luxury, all mod-cons, ten metre American Recreational Vehicle (RV) with a car in tow, so you will appreciate the dramatic change our new, 5.6 metre Germanic conversion of a silver Mercedes Sprinter panel van was going to pose! Despite my initial reservations and heartache at losing my ten-tonne toy, I had to admit that the new van, aptly named

Holiday Dream,[1] was perfectly formed, with a four-seat dining area, pull-down full-sized bed, and a bathroom with separate shower – just as long as we didn't want to move around at the same time. It was September – Italy beckoned, and our challenge commenced.

[1] 'Holiday Dream' from the range of campervans made by HRZ Reisemobile of Öhringen, Germany. Ours was one of only two built with right-hand drive.

Pictures from Genoa

Shafts of sunlight pierced the tree branches and played across the platforms at Pegli station where we waited, along with morning commuters, for the train to Genoa. We had arrived late in the afternoon of the previous day after a ten-day tour across France including a drive following *La Route des Grandes Alpes* from Bourg-Saint-Maurice over the many 2,000-metre Alpine passes down to the Mediterranean. The van had behaved faultlessly and our only problem was a non-functioning laptop GPS. Crossing the border into Italy we had moved from peace and order to chaos, turmoil, disarray and confusion. We were surrounded by noise, fumes and people. Cars, vans and scooters hurtled in all directions and all at the same time; traffic lights swung from above or were hidden behind bushes or street furniture. There were mothers with buggies and straining children, cars parked in every available space at daft angles in narrow high streets with wing mirrors ripe for knocking off, overtaking vehicles, undertaking vehicles, swinging across your lane vehicles, delivering vehicles, crossing the road in 'deep gesticulating conversation without looking' pedestrians, and window-gazing shoppers and fashionistas. These were all watched by pavement lunchers, espresso-drinking café-counter standers, or beer-drinking bar loungers. In short, a seething mass of humanity simply getting on with their normal daily ritual – '*Bienvenuto a Italia.*'

We walked out of Genoa's Stazione Principe into the hubbub of Piazza Acquaverde. Like lost souls, all confidence gone, we stood in the elegant square and tried to orientate the map against the surrounding streets whilst Christopher Columbus looked down on us. Our frame of reference was our *Rough Guide Italy*, which quoted Henry James: 'The most winding, incoherent of cities, the most entangled topographical ravel in the whole world…'

'Would you like some help?' a Nancy Dell'Olio look-a-like asked me. Shiny black hair fell about her shoulders, her eyes were big, heels high, she had a deep tan, and the dress was, shall we say, more cocktail than business. Wary of female approaches at station exits, I must have appeared reluctant.

'I am an official guide,' she said, sensing my unease.

Oh yes? I thought, waiting for the hook.

'Where are you going?' We had to admit we didn't know, and plumped for the cathedral. She turned the map the right way up and pointed out that Via Balbi and beyond would take us into town, but we *must* visit Via Garibaldi, from where any right turn would take us to the cathedral and the Palazzo Ducale. She was indeed an official guide and we were glad she had suggested Via Balbi, as its parallel neighbour, Via di Prè, was described as 'busy and notoriously seedy.'

After two hundred metres our mental energy was expended and we stopped for coffee in an arcaded *gelateria*. The lady set up a table outside (thereby allowing her to charge more, we thought) and rewarded our first stumbling attempts at spoken Italian with delicious and free lemon-filled *cornetti*, thereby starting my addiction. We were carried along, dodging traffic and preserving life, when relief came in the pedestrianised Via Garibaldi. Here, a narrow street is bordered by a succession of elegant Renaissance palaces beautifully decorated with pastel-coloured stuccowork and medallions and concealing huge, fountained courtyards. Anxious to see inside one of the places, we followed a crowd up broad steps and into an airy auditorium. There was a big attraction to the right and a crush of young men had pushed forward to see it, with their mobile phone cameras held high to capture the moment. We fanned out to the side to a see a display of the World (Jules Rimet) Cup being watched closely by the smartly uniformed security man, his hands behind, his hat pulled firmly down over his eyes (but not so far that he couldn't see). It's rare in Italy to see a uniformed official who doesn't look the business. Gail was clearly disappointed by the display.

Finding our way to the sixteenth century Palazzo Ducale we entered the huge atrium to find a spellbinding display of Chinese warriors – the Terracotta Army had arrived. Only twenty made it to the British Museum and there were queues round the block, yet here there was more than twice that and it was free to enter and meander round. These were all painted with large white Chinese characters. At first sight they are a uniform army, but closer inspection reveals that the uniforms are different in fascinating detail, and each one with different body characteristics and facial features. The longer and closer you look the more human they become. Did they derive from the factories of a power-crazed dictator or could there be any truth in speculation that they are, in fact, body casts?

Via San Lorenzo, a pedestrianised street bordered by fashionable outlets, was a pleasure to walk down. Piazza Banchi, once the heart of the medieval city, had a tiny enclosed market square selling books, records, fruit and flowers. However, our misguided wanderings to get to the port also took us through a maze of narrow, seamy back alleys between six-storey buildings, with other buildings bridging between them. Many were deserted and abandoned and in others, men were lurking suspiciously. At an intersection the atmosphere changed – a crowd of African men were gathered outside the doorways of the near-derelict buildings, whilst in the few shafts of sunlight that had filtered through, black prostitutes were openly touting for business.

The port itself is a busy and modern area with opulent yachts, cruise ships, restaurants, congress centre, a replica galleon, and a futuristic machine that lifted us skywards in a glass bowl to provide a fascinating view of the city skyline and the motorway that sweeps above it on stilts. Being a tourist area, it is also heavily populated by pavement sellers of fake designer handbags and sunglasses and Gail was sorely tempted. At the rear and to the south of the port is an impressive, brightly painted stucco that Palazzo di San Giorgio built in 1260. It has a clock tower and golden statues in clamshell alcoves. And there, on the elaborate fresco, is St George killing the dragon. We were intrigued to find that they had an English flag flying, and the shields had a red cross on a white background. There were quite a few such flags in Genoa and although the guidebook had no explanation I am indebted to Bruno of Genoa and WikiAnswers[2] for the information that: 'The original St. George's flag, a red cross on a white field, was adopted by the Republic of Genoa in 1099, after the first crusade. Then it was adopted by England and the City of London, in 1190, for use on their ships entering the Mediterranean Sea to

[2] http://wiki.answers.com/Q/What_does_England's_flag_stand_for

benefit from the protection of the Genoese fleet. The English Monarch paid an annual tribute to the Doge of Genoa for this privilege. Since then, that flag remains as both Genoa's and England's flag.'

We wandered off into the alleys again, seeking a different way back to the station, only to find they got progressively rougher and scarier. Men loitered menacingly in shops and in stairwells; groups sat on stairs, and scooters buzzed past at speed. It was an alien environment and not one we would venture into after dark, but as time went on and no trouble ensued we relaxed and made a discovery – Chinese wholesalers of handbags, clothing (anoraks a speciality) and sundry goods. This was where the guys from the port bought all their stuff. Crates and cardboard boxes marked with Chinese characters were piled up to the ceilings of shop after shop. At the port, the African guys were negotiators supreme, but here it became obvious who ruled the roost. They bought their wares at the price they were given – the Chinese were implacable. We tried it ourselves and also failed (but Gail did get the handbag she wanted at trade rather than tourist price!)

Emboldened by our adventure, we walked the 'notoriously seedy' Via di Prè to find you couldn't get to the station that way, and retraced our steps.

'*Scusi. Va bene per Pegli?*'

'*No*,' replied a passenger sitting on the train we thought was ours.

'Which one can it be? I was sure it was ours,' said Gail.

'I think it is. But if it doesn't stop we're going to end up in San Remo!' We took a chance, counting stations and praying a little, but then the ticket inspector came and checked our tickets without comment. We got back to Pegli and wearily climbed the hill to the campsite.

That evening I delved into *Pictures from Italy* by Charles Dickens. He had arrived in Genoa in 1844 by boat from Nice with his large family, and was conveyed by horse-drawn carriage to a house at Albaro, two miles outside the city. But he went on a 'long-winded journey' through 'lanes so very narrow' rather than 'through the Strada Nuova, or the Strada Balbi, which are the famous streets of palaces,' and 'I never in my life was so dismayed.' He described 'the unaccountable filth (though it is reckoned the cleanest of Italian towns), the disorderly jumbling of dirty houses, one roof upon another, the passages more squalid than any in St. Giles or old Paris; in and out of which not vagabonds but well-dressed women, with white veils and great fans, were passing and repassing.' However, after living there he came to see it as a city of contrasts – 'things that are picturesque, ugly, mean, magnificent, delightful and offensive break upon the view at every turn,' such that on reflection, 'I little thought, that day, that I should ever come to have an attachment for the very stones in the streets of Genoa, and to look back upon the city with affection as connected with many hours of happiness and quiet!' From our own limited visit and experiences of Genoa I empathised with these thoughts, and retired pleasingly satisfied with our first Italian experience, and a new travelling companion in the form of Mr Dickens.

We departed the excellent, picturesque and park-like Camping Villa Doria in Pegli bound for La Spezia and the Cinque Terre, and the Autostrada was magnificent. We flew above the coastal towns and inland villages and dived through tunnels – some an inky blackness, others brightly lit. I switched the lights on, off, on, and left them on. I tried to tune the radio but, 'Oh bugger, another tunnel.' I switched it off. I donned sunglasses as sunshine burst into the cab then took them off again as another unlit tunnel appeared. It was a busy spell. At times solid buttresses supported the road, and then sections where the architect and engineers appeared to have taken leave of the laws of physics and installed spindly legs that challenged all-known wisdom suddenly appeared. We looked down on more red-roofed, seaside villages that had been dropped into a mountain cleft and smeared up the sides with a church spire popping up for cooler air. The Autostrada provided sweeping bends with dramatically flashing amber lights to heighten the Italian's motoring experience.

We pulled into the Servizio and Autogrill that everyone stops at for the obligatory espresso (after all, it was Sunday) – time to show off their latest clothes '*fare una bella figura*' and look good. A smart red convertible Alfa Romeo pulled in and parked close by. Dad, the epitome of casual elegance, tried to usher his smartly dressed wife and two children out.

'*Andiamo!*'

'*Papa*. I feel ill.'

'What do you mean, Federico?'

'Papa. I feel sick.'

'*Mamma*. Can you deal with your son? Oh no, NOT in my car! *Mamma Mia!*'

To say we took a wrong turning in La Spezia would be correct. Lack of simple preparation like reading directions to the *sosta*[3] combined with a gung-ho 'we're sure to find it' spirit found us parked by the pretty harbour walkway surrounded by people urgently seeking a table at the many outdoor restaurants bustling with early lunchers. It seemed unlikely that a *sosta* would be found in such a pretty setting, and having driven the length of the seafront up to the Naval Museum and Arsenale and back, we concluded it wasn't. Exiting in a southerly direction, we saw a motorhome sign and followed it and others through the dockyards, foundries, industrial complexes, over railway lines and bridges, round a supermarket car park and finally, to what looked like a piece of waste land. There was a barrier and a bell, but no one answered the call. A man who had adopted vagrancy as a clothing style emerged from an old caravan and pointed to a collection of corrugated iron buildings that Gail found to be

[3] An area for campervan parking - facilities may vary from very little, other than parking and perhaps water, to more comprehensive services.

an ambulance station with attendants in fluorescent orange, one of whom let us park.

'Shall I put the kettle on for tea before we eat?'

'Oh pleeeease.'

'There's no gas.'

'But everything's turned on,' I said desperately, and went through one of those 'panic-motivated-try-everything-twice' manoeuvres. Thankfully it worked, although I had no idea what had happened.

We sat outside, moving our chairs to avoid the shadow cast by the large asbestos dockside building, listening to the dog barking over the hedge and the hum of traffic, and reflecting on our arrival in supposedly one of the most beautiful parts of Italy. The unattractive neighbourhood we found to consist of docks, servicing rail lines, and a Zone Militaire. Incongruously, buried in it, was also an exclusive yacht club with row upon row of super yachts and wooden-masted sloops all jostling for space.

Cinque Terre

Gail had a long-held wish to visit the five tiny fishing villages stranded by rocky outcrops on the Ligurian coast known as the Cinque Terre, and to walk the eleven kilometre scenic path that linked them. Behind the villages, (Monterosso, Vernazza, Manarola, Corniglia, and Riomaggiore), the sheer cliffs and rugged mountain terrain with dry-stone walls holding back terraces of vineyards were said to be 'stupendous'. The entire area has been included on the UNESCO World Heritage List as well as the World Monument Fund's '100 List Of Sites At Risk'.

Vehicular access seemed nigh impossible ('trying to tour the area by car or motorbike truly isn't worth the effort…') and we were too far out to contemplate public transport. Seeking an easy day, we decided to try and find a place to stay that was closer, and headed for the village of Portovenere.

The drive was easy compared to the French Alps. We soon found that motorhome parking was banned in the village but available in a *sosta* on the headland for 1.50 Euros per hour. Walking back down the hill we were stunned by the jaw-dropping views of the village. Could any place look more perfect? The bright morning sun and clear blue sky had coloured the azure waters that lapped against a harbour full of small, colourful fishing boats with shimmering reflections. Umbrella-shaded tables crowded the tree-planted quayside, behind which rose a pretty terrace of tall, slim, rose-pink, blue, terracotta and white houses, restaurants and bars that had originally formed a defensive line. Two church towers, a crenulated grey stone castle and the village's stout defensive walls and towers angled up and fused into the rocky protrusions, crowning the scene. With the three offshore islets of Palmaria, Tino and Tinetto, it was picture-postcard perfect – and evocatively romantic for this birthday boy. I felt a shiver go up my spine.

A posh waterside restaurant provided a cup of froth for coffee, a glass of celebratory drink, and a stuck-up waiter. OK, so he knew the English for a glass of wine and I only know the Italian for a windowpane of wine. Exemplifying how well-protected this small village was, we entered through a towered archway in the main walls, built in the twelfth century with Latin inscriptions above and on the left, some Genoese measures of capacity dating from 1606. It had a narrow, flag-stoned medieval main street with shops set in pink-coloured buildings and flights of steps leading to the upper parts. Prodded by Gail on a particularly long set, we reached the Romanesque church of San Lorenzo, apparently founded on a site where a temple was dedicated to Venus (*Venere)* – and I feigned great interest in its striped façade as a ruse to catch my breath.

Keen to record our visit by way of postcards home, we found shopkeepers reluctant to accept a twenty-five Euros note, and after three attempts and much under-breath mutterings from them we were forced to go down to the harbourside bank to change it. Unfortunately for me (it didn't seem fair on my birthday!); this led Gail to discover a challengingly steep set of stairs set in the rocks ascending alongside the town walls. There should be a health warning at the bottom and an 'I knew you could do it' sign at the top.

The castle at the top has twelfth century origins and amazing views of the rocky outcrop, on which sits the church of San Pietro. Byron apparently swam out from a grotto below to see his friend Shelley on the other side of the bay. Just below the wall, on a rocky ledge, was the village cemetery. *A convenient position for those succumbing to post-ascent cardiac failure*, I thought darkly.

We ate at an atmospheric restaurant on the main street that had dark wooden benches and trestle tables; a raised, shop-like counter with bread waiting to be cut, and behind, racks of wine up to the ceiling. The walls had old black and white photos of a couple at various life stages in various locations – presumably the grey-haired grandmamma figure in a pinafore behind the counter and the old boy who emerged with the food from the kitchen. We then returned to La Spezia and sat out in the sun listening to the 5:00 p.m. dockyard siren sounding the 'down tools' and the end of a marvellous day for us.

The next day we headed for Monterosso – the furthest of the Cinque Terre villages. We selected Monterosso as there appeared to be road access, which we anticipated might mean an impossibly steep road down to a cove-bound fishing village. All went disappointingly well though – the hairpins were negotiable, as were the switchbacks that only narrowed as we approached the beaches. Yes, beaches. What we expected to be a cliff-side fishing hamlet with old men chewing on pipe stems, drying and repairing their fishing nets, or drawing their boats up impossible inclines to a safe harbour in the village street, was in fact a seaside resort. A large, concreted parking area beckoned, and they were willing for us to stay the night at 1.50 Euros an hour. A quick calculation along the lines of 'that's 31.50 Euros to stay until 9:00 a.m. tomorrow' made us consider whether there was any way to thwart the system, but the guard had a little box of a *Portakabin* kitted out with a bed and other items of domesticity so we decided to give it a go, and at least have a look around and have coffee or lunch.

The beachfront was seasidey in the Blackpool-Southend sense, with good mix of two-week tanned and newly-arrived-porcelain-white bodies disporting themselves in what was now the noonday sun. There were many hotels and rooms for rent (there are more here than anywhere else in the Cinque Terre) and a range of tacky shops. Behind them ran a railway – not a little tourist train, but with full-sized passenger and goods trains, whooshing or rumbling past on a line running from Rome to Paris.

We discovered that we were in Fegina and it was possible to stroll over the top (or risk walking through) a road tunnel to Monterosso Vecchio – the original village before people started sliding down the hill in the twelfth and thirteenth century. It was closer to what we expected, but still crowded with visiting groups who, on command, would move synchronously down to a landing stage to board a boat. Reflecting on our visit over coffees we registered some disappointment at the guidebook entry of 'Beaches, both free and toll, are broad and picturesque…' and the holiday tourist invasion (hypocritical perhaps, but we consider our travels to be more a way of life than a holiday).

We drove off in a westerly direction for Lévanto (not included as one of the five villages), and this time we did find the challenging road we had been seeking, and excellent views down to the coast, but were again disappointed on arrival. Lévanto was much larger than we had expected, with a resort atmosphere and that railway again. We followed 'P' signs up a narrow, one-in-five cobbled street, desperately seeking escape down a small cul-de-sac next to a castle.

'That was exciting. And the views are nice,' I said with satisfaction.

'Do you think you can get the van out again?' Gail asked uncertainly. A twenty-point turn and we were on our way back down, then off to the Autostrada and back to the La Spezia *sosta* – it was growing on us.

The next day we planned a full-frontal assault on the remaining Cinque Terre villages. Riomaggiore, the closest and most easterly, was the first in our sights – only to find that even out of season we were not allowed to park our van in their car park. Manarola, the next along, was more accommodating. As we walked down the steep hill into the village we discovered a series of tall pink, yellow and cream painted houses crowding out narrow streets and juxtaposed impossibly on a precipitous, dark, rocky headland. Above that ended in a sheer cliff – as though someone had sliced the end of the mountain off into a foaming sea. It was busy with hikers and other visitors. Small covered fishing boats were parked on the main street in town. Below the cliffs, others bobbed in the water, protected by a small rocky outcrop.

We bought tickets for the coastal walk, which started up the eastern flank of the mountain out of town on an ugly, viaduct-like arched concrete structure glued to the cliff face. Looking back down to Manarola, the view of the village huddled in the cleft in the rock was remarkably beautiful. Laid out before us was the series of coves and headlands that form the remaining three villages of the Cinque Terre round to Lévanto. We were soon surrounded by terraced vineyards tumbling down the mountain, and then I made a great discovery A miniature railway, similar to those that used to be at children's garden parties, but the single track on this one plummeted from the path and down the side of the vineyard in a series of roller-coaster dives – a gentle drop then a steep drop, a brief flat section to catch your breath, then dropping steeply again to finally disappear from view. The 'train' was a red plastic office chair mounted on a platform, with a foot support and a loop for a handlebar. Behind it was an alloy trailer, presumably for carrying grapes. The seat faced the 'engine' housed in an alloy cowl with red wheels underneath. As I tried to work out this remarkable piece of engineering, it occurred to me that when it set off down the unbelievable track the rider would be facing backwards, or more accurately, staring skywards whilst going almost vertically downwards. It was downright scary.

The coastal path was narrow, and cut into the rocky mountainside, the sea below it was well fenced in parts but absent in others. There were heart-stretching hills and welcome descents as it weaved its way round boulders, trees and occasional small plantations or along bare cliff sides. Views of Corniglia, the next village, came and went. Eventually we passed a rocky beach by the station and could see Corniglia high on a hill ahead. Thirty-three flights and three hundred and seventy-seven steps had to be climbed to reach it. I selected the hairpin road from the station as a gentler, but longer route.

Corniglia was buzzing, like most of the Cinque Terre villages, but perhaps more so for a village that is not connected directly with the sea. It has history of wine production going back to Roman times, and bottles of Corniglia wine were found during the excavations of Pompei. We found a village of tightly packed coloured houses on a terrace clustered round an open square busy with people sitting on benches eating pizza. We took one of the little cobbled streets up from the square to a coffee bar, but the lure of the pizza was too great. So, we went back to the pizza parlour and the grandiose chef in a curly top hat, and like the others, ate sitting in the sunlit square, Largo Taragio, below the Oratory of St Catherine and above the *Portakabin* toilets. (There was also a good display of ambulances, so the need must be there for unaccustomed walkers succumbing to the rigours of the climb...)

The section to Vernazza was more like a conventional hiking trail through vegetation with wonderful smells. We passed many people along here – some dressed for arctic exploration and others in beach sandals and shorts. Some were sitting and recovering while others marched boldly on. We kept a nice steady pace, only speeding up to play the game of impressing walkers who were struggling.

'Why do you speed up when we get close to other people? It's not a race!'

'I'm not,' I responded innocently.

'Yes you are. It'll be *you* that has the heart attack.'

Vernazza came into view and then disappeared in favour of Monterosso, the next village. The day had warmed up considerably and we came across a splendidly positioned, open-air restaurant with staggering view down the cliffs to the sea – and there were our Swiss friends from the car park. I was amazed.

'How did they get ahead of us?'

'I don't know – and it doesn't matter.'

The descent to Vernazza through a wooded area was long and steep, and seeing people (mainly portly Americans) puffing and panting their way up, I was glad we had chosen the south to north route. The town was spectacularly positioned on a rocky promontory – every inch of the scant space crowded with buildings. Along the edges were remnants of fortifications, and at the head, an ancient watchtower. All this disguised Vernazza's charming natural harbour, with small, colourful blue fishing boats bobbing in the protected waters, the fine surrounding buildings, Gothic creamy-pink church, and piazza. Of all the villages this was a jewel, but there were many tourists. We sat on the harbour wall eating ice-creams and drinking in the colourful scene as we watched a phalanx of people above setting off for Monterosso on the three kilometre, two hour trail (apparently the hardest section) and had a new respect for those I had ridiculed earlier quaffing champagne at their achievement.

We caught one of the frequent boats from Vernazza back to Manarola and got a whole new perspective – viewing each village as we passed.

'Is that a whale?'

'No, it's a fat person swimming on his back.' We pulled into the little jetty at Manarola and walked back through the town, once more stopping at the cellar café, where they were playing soothing music and had a small stage for live performances.

Reflecting on our Cinque Terre visit, it had been disappointing, yet satisfying – the 'wild roads' had been less challenging than anticipated, 'impossible to reach' villages had been reached, the 'remoteness' was belied by a railway station at every village, the pretty character villages were full of tourists and tourist traps, and the walk had been idyllic, but cluttered with humankind. In summer I imagine it could be hell. I felt we had ticked the box, but not fulfilled Gail's dream.

Back at the site we enjoyed a couple of days rest and relaxation.

'Hello. *Ciao, buon giorno.*' It was the camp's ginger cat, surprisingly nuzzling up for attention after a five minute display of stalking a plump pheasant that had landed nearby. It was life in the raw – a few minutes of bated breath fascination.

'Surely it must see the cat!' But we couldn't stand it any longer, and shooed the bird away. I was clearly bored, and the day was getting colder and cloudy so we caught the orange bus to La Spezia.

Ticketing systems in Italy were a mystery. Everyone got on, sat down, and did nothing ticket-wise.

'*Due, Centro, per favore.*' The driver had already pulled out into the road before proceeding to remove a wallet out of his pocket, take our money, and give us tickets and change whilst avoiding traffic, cars parked at odd angles, scooters scooting in and out, and pedestrians who thought that raising a hand before crossing the road would bring divine providence. La Spezia was, apart from the harbour area, in tune with the grey day.

That evening, examining a map of Italy brought home the wealth of treasures it was possible to see on the way to Sicily, and the conflict that all travellers must face between getting there and missing something en-route. I turned to

Charles Dickens's *Pictures from Italy* and decided that as we were already on his route, we may as well continue to follow in his footsteps as far as possible.

Leaning Towards Pisa

'Do you want me to fill it?'

'Yes, thank you.' We had pulled in for diesel at a filling station on the outskirts of Carrara in Tuscany after a coastal tour through Lerici and a crossing over the Magra river bridge (something not available to Mr Dickens, who had to endure a passage 'not by any means agreeable' in a ferry boat). It dawned on me that every vehicle in the garage was covered in white dust – as though someone had shaken icing sugar over them. Convoys of huge, white dust encrusted trucks drove by with massive marble slabs propped up in their trailers. The backdrop to everything was the snow-white mountainsides and caves eaten away by giant wire-cutters and excavators. You didn't have to be Sherlock Holmes to work out that Carrara was the principal source of Italian marble. (It has also been the world's largest producer and exporter since Roman times.) Michelangelo sourced his marble from here, and the Marble Arch in London is built from Carrara marble. In Dickens's day the marble was excavated using explosives, and the slabs brought down by ox-carts. Oxen were still used as late as 1929 when thirty-five pairs pulled the largest block ever cut (a gargantuan 300 tonnes) down the mountain on a wooden sled and along the road to the docks, using 70,000 litres of soap. We passed a car wash. *They probably use that amount of soap trying to keep Carrara's cars clean*, I thought grimly.

We pushed on to Lucca – an oval, wall-enclosed town. The ten metre high walls are intact, with bastions at each corner and a dry moat and large grassed area in front. Parking at the coach park, we crossed the busy roads to pass through the thirty metre thick walls at the gateway of Porto V. Emmanuele and into the open area serving as a bus station. The helpful tourist office provided a nice map, with all the buildings drawn in detail. Beyond this we entered into the relative calm of a mid-siesta, pedestrianised street, but not so quiet that everything was closed, and there were some lip-smacking pastry shops where we were able to lunch. One of the delights of Italy is the abundance of finger-food. A snack is no problem wherever you go, and if they don't have anything, they will soon rustle up a toasted sandwich for you. We wandered the chain-store-free medieval streets, peering into the beautifully presented window displays of the elegant shops and chic boutiques. It was a shopper's paradise (there are over eight hundred of these shops). The streets were spotlessly clean and the little mechanised street sweeper passed us many times.

We gazed at churches, down alleyways, and up at an ancient redbrick tower with equally ancient Holm Oak growing out the top that gave it an abandoned look (Toree Guinigi). The elliptical flagstone piazza almost enclosed by irregular, pastel-coloured houses, the sky a deep blue backdrop. The sunny side was full of chatting diners on shiny chrome chairs under cream umbrellas. It was not a touristic setting – these appeared to be locals at their favourite lunch spot. Many had their bicycles with them and in this respect Lucca seemed to be the Cambridge of Italy, a historic, lived-in town.

The square was the original 10,000-seater Roman Amphitheatre that over the centuries had become a fortress, a supply of material to build the houses, allotments, and a public slaughterhouse before Lorenzo Nottolino finally transformed it into a delightful area for alfresco dining and socialising. Close by was the pearlescent white church of San Michele. Begun in 1070 with a multi-tiered columned façade stuck on the end of the main building, its windows were open to the sky. (This design became a common sight as we travelled, and was probably due to the failure to complete the main body of the church to the originally intended height.)

Lucca is the birthplace of Puccini – he is commemorated in a piazza by an unusual, but nevertheless marvellous statue, sitting relaxed and smoking in a chair. We reluctantly left him there and returned along the grassed, mounded ramparts to the van. It was late in the day but we decided to press on to Pisa – a decision we started to regret when we couldn't find our turn, ended up in the back of a supermarket, found ourselves driving out of town in a different direction, and then decided to stay at a campsite that was closed. We had driven straight past the huge area Pisa had created behind the Tamoil garage for the hundreds of tourist coaches that arrived every day. Conveniently, they had also set aside an area for motorhomes.

The Leaning Tower of Pisa is known the world over, a symbol of Italy and a not-to-be-missed sight. At 6:30 p.m. the soft red glow of the disappearing evening sun on the white Carrara marble of the buildings on the grass field known as Campo dei Miracoli produced a magical scene. And, there was hardly anyone around. It was an exceptional but fleeting moment. The surrounding streets were atmospheric and many restaurants beautifully set up to catch tourists, but we were too tired to choose so called it a day and returned to a deserted coach park.

As morning broke, a procession of tour buses started to arrive on the park adjacent to us. Double-deckers, budget-tour buses, single super-luxury liners, some with so many facilities on board there was no more room on the back windows to put the stickers for aircon, toilet, video, radio, stereo hi-fi, TV, tables, drinks, coffee, ABS, retarder, courier, and some I couldn't even decipher! A guide descended ahead of his group. What would their talisman be? An umbrella? No. It was a giant yellow sunflower with fluorescent green leaves. As the group assembled, there wasn't a dark hair amongst them.

'Are they Swedish?' asked Gail, overhearing my murmurs.

'No. They're from geriatric land.' A budget bus, number ten, cream with a red flash, disgorges – the guide holds a crude board high in the air with '10' on it. But wait, eight black guys are racing across the car park, loaded down with armfuls of shiny belts and necklaces glittering in the morning sun. One has a tray of sparkling trinkets and finds it hard to keep up with his colleagues. They pick off their prey, a vulnerable lady, and swarm round her, draping necklaces on her and putting bangles round her wrist. Another pulls her husband aside.

'Good price. Very good price for your beautiful lady.' The passengers are saved by the call of their guide and snake off across the tarmac, following his orange sunflower. The sellers pick off a laggard at the end of the line, but still no success. They aren't worried – a superbus has pulled in and is starting to discharge its passengers towards a blue sunflower. As the sellers run over, five more buses arrive and they are split in all directions. A motley crew in jeans and orange, grey, purple and black anoraks and hoodies – they are indefatigable in the face of constant rejection. By 10:00 a.m. fifty buses are parked in neat, regimental lines, including Lorenzini, Giotti Bus, Galileo, Marcheschi,

Neapolis, Penning, and Maremma – the Italians seem to have the monopoly on using this park. Drivers go for coffee and return to wash their windscreens. But wait – who is on this bus? They look a fashionable, non-touristy crowd, with tight jeans, black boots, designer sunglasses and leather bags – and the women are smartly dressed as well.

When we reach the Campo dei Miracoli, it lives up to its name of 'Field of Miracles.' All humankind appears to be there – we should have known from the number of coaches. We recognise Japanese, Slovak, Chinese, French, Germans, and Scandinavians. They crocodile along behind leaders, or, without thought, step on the hallowed turf to get the perfect photo. Kodak and Fuji have lost a fortune to digital cameras in this one place. I am asked to take a photograph for a romantic young Italian couple, the leaning tower in the background – a straightforward shot taken a million times before.

The Leaning Tower and the cluster of eleventh and twelfth century buildings – the Duomo (cathedral church), Baptistry and Camposanto – do astonish and delight. They were beyond expectation and even more special viewed in the fading evening light when the day-trippers had gone. I had not expected them to be separated from the main town yet still within its ancient walls and so well displayed on their green sward. There is an unreality about the buildings – it's as though they have been dropped into place. The delicacy of their white marble construction is astounding. Admittedly, it is hard to ignore the mass of people and the line of vendor's stalls that runs the whole length of the pedestrianised road to the side, but the atmosphere is one of appreciation and enjoyment.

Without launching into a detailed description of each building (which you would find far more adequately done in a guidebook) there are a few points that interested me. The tower is a graceful and light building and provides a wonderful, if not strange view from the top. The round, red-domed baptistry has a magnificent pulpit supported by elephants, and light streams in from high windows. From the second floor there is a view down to an impressive font, and if you go higher, views of the other buildings to the outside. The Camposanto is reputed to be 'the most beautiful cemetery in the world' and this cloistered building carries the legend that Pisan knights brought back soil from the Holy Land so graves could be dug in it. Charles Dickens found that Pisa's buildings did not live up to the expectations brought about by pictures in his schoolbooks and thought it 'another of the many deceptions practised by Mr Harris, Bookseller, at the corner of St. Paul's Churchyard, London,' although he did eventually come to regard the buildings as 'the most remarkable and beautiful in the whole world...'

Wandering through narrow back streets, we peered in at two old silversmiths in white aprons, eyeglasses in place, working on intricate pieces, and passed furniture restoration shops piled high with materials and part-finished chairs, and bookbinders with huge manual presses. We had coffee in a café served by a midriff-exposing, perfectly tanned beauty of a signorina. I took a while selecting a tart with crosses on it so that those snaky hips stayed in view a little longer. And, she made a perfect coffee with a fern pattern in the froth – 'How did she do that?'

Three girls came in and indulged themselves in small V-shaped cups full of a gooey coffee creation that they ate with a spoon. They longingly savoured every mouthful of their Saturday treat and continued licking their spoons long after it had been devoured.

Italian cool in Pisa not only includes convertible Alfa Romeos, but iconic Fiat 500s. George Michael look-alikes can ride Dutch sit-up-and-beg bikes and still look cool, provided they have designer sunglasses and can ride the bike whilst smoking and talking into a mobile phone.

In the afternoon the temperature dropped so we went off to a Laundromat to do the washing before scuttling back to the van. The afternoon withdrawal had started. Yellow, black and blue sunflowers were being paraded along with boards displaying even numbers from two to eight. Our merchandisers were out in force to capture those who had failed to find a suitable souvenir. Bus engines were started to get the heaters going. Maybe, two hundred vibrating, polluting diesel engines sprang into life. Blue, red and orange anoraks moved in lines. Swathes of people milled about, looking for their ride back to the hotel. Air horns sounded to attract attention and crocodile lines set off across the tarmac when someone spotted the bus. People clambered up stairwells out of the cold and flopped into seats. It was after 5:00 p.m. – who would be the last away? But our sellers weren't leaving. They sat on the walls, and thirty minutes later, buses started arriving – it was the Saturday evening 'eat at a typical Italian restaurant' crowd. We decided to eat in.

An Incident in the Dark

Dickens went from Pisa to Livorno, back to Pisa, and then to Sienna and on to Rome. His route was probably the Via Aurelia, but he makes no comment about this other than to mention the many religious crosses on the road. We set off late morning after attempting to rinse Carrara dust off the van – it set like concrete. Our intention was to head east to Florence, but we took a wrong turn and were soon going north before turning east, and then at Montecatini turned south down the S436. It was not the prettiest Tuscan route – the scenery being constantly interrupted by industries. We were lured by descriptions of San Miniato, a medieval village on a steep hillside with a warren of attractive cobbled alleys, and were not disappointed. We did the tour right up to the tower of Rocca, which provided a splendid view and the history that Pier della Vigna, treasurer to Frederick II, blinded and imprisoned there, jumped to his death from the top. But we shall remember San Miniato for something else.

Because of the delays and diversion we were starving, and it was cold. Caffé Centrale appealed immediately. It had a worn and homely look and inside an old boy dressed in a rumpled, dark suit with open-necked white shirt nodded a '*Buon Giorno.*' Beyond the wooden counter there was an open area with marble-topped tables and wrought iron chairs. On the wall to the right a huge and complicated display of boxes of Ericlea and other teas were stacked. Pictures on the wall were old English signs of the type tourists buy in Portobello market, thinking them original. There was a games cupboard with *Pictionary*, an old radio and piano, and an aquarium. An old lady in a primrose-yellow pinafore shouted orders, and argued constantly with the old man. He annoyed her further by whistling and singing to himself. Finally it was our turn, and thankfully, she had a menu in English. We scanned the various dishes and she wrote our order on her pad and then left the menu on the table, shouting the drinks to the old man as she disappeared up some stairs. Gail had another glance at the menu that had been written in wobbly English.

'There's a service charge.'

'How much is it?'

'It's priceless.' I picked up the menu for a closer look. *Service and Breast ten percent*.

I wondered exactly how this would be delivered, and desperately tried to formulate a refusal tactic, but as it turned out, it was her good-looking daughter who served our meal, so my thinking rapidly changed to that of an unfulfilled fantasy as we left to drive the minor road to Certaldo. (Eagle-eyed map-readers will have noticed that we bypassed Florence, where we have visited many times as regular tourists.)

A flea market blocked Certaldo's main street, so we drove to the other end of town looking for a way in. We went up, up and further up a narrow steep hill (*Via del Castello*) until we emerged into a small, but magnificent square with no obvious exit that would accommodate us, so we had to turn and go back down again, squeezing past the surprised tourists struggling up. We eventually found a *sosta* surrounded by trees on the edge of a dried-up, but grass-growing riverbed. There were some flats opposite and behind us and I wasn't sure whether we should stay. I wandered over to talk to the only other occupant, an Italian who introduced himself as 'Marco'.

'Hello. I'm Keith.'

'Kate?'

'No, Keith.' (It was about here that I discovered there are only twenty-one letters in the Italian alphabet – and they don't include K. In addition, Italians can't say the 'th' sound. The closest Marco could come was 'Kate' since he had heard of Kate Blanchett). Marco confirmed that it was fine to stay, and also explained that you had a legal right to stop overnight anywhere in Italy, provided it wasn't marked as prohibited and you didn't put anything like chairs, tables or barbecues outside your van.

'Is it the same in England? We are thinking of visiting.'

'Probably best not to in England.'

It was a bitterly cold evening but we were warm and toasty in the van. The penetrating cold persisted the next day, and we had to don fleeces and anoraks to keep it at bay. Certaldo is typical of many Tuscan towns with a picture-perfect, walled medieval upper part for tourists and wealthy weekenders, and a lower modern town where people live and work in the industrial complexes. From the large open Piazza Boccaccio we followed a sign '*el tren*' through smoked-glass doors to buy a one Euro one-way ticket from the smartly uniformed ticket clerk before being led by the lady attendant to the glass cubicle of the upmarket, multi-person, Stannah stairlift. Two minutes later we jerked our way into Old Certaldo, or Certaldo Storico, to discover that Monday was closing day, and with the cold, nobody else could be bothered.

Originally an Etruscan-Roman city, it has little streets with redbrick, palaces, churches, castles, fortress walls, towers, patios, alcoves and arcades – many of which have been restored. There are gardens and views across the rolling Chianti region vineyards to the more famous towers of the hilltop town of San Gimignano. Certaldo on a warm summer's day would be idyllic. Home to Italian writer and poet, Giovanni Boccaccio (who died in 1375), there are many remembrances, including a Casa Boccaccio (which of course was closed on Mondays). We climbed up to the twelfth century Palazzo Pretorio, the residence of the Florentine governors, which was recently restored to its original condition. It has a picturesque façade with heraldic shields (and probably an interesting interior – viewable on any day but Monday). Then, a moment of excitement.

'Wait a minute – someone came out of that deli.'

'It's got a couple of tables and chairs inside.'

'I'd love a coffee.'

'Let's give it a try.'

'*Due cappuccini?*'

'*Si.*' It was so good to get out of the cold. I wandered the 'we sell everything' emporium, eagerly anticipating my coffee, but there was no sound of the Gaggia coffee machine coughing and spurting hissing steam. Instead, the little old signora had disappeared through the curtain into some dark recess beyond.

'I know what she's doing. She's boiling up a pan of milk on her stove. I can smell it.'

'No she's not! What Italian would do that?' hissed Gail.

'Well, where's the shiny coffee machine? Have you heard her banging the old coffee grounds out of the filter thing, or grinding the beans, or clicking the filter back into place? No, and there's not a steaming hiss to be heard! Uh-oh, here she comes.' We sat up guiltily.

'Grazie.'

'*Prego.*'

'I knew I was right, this cup of milk has never seen a coffee bean in its life – it's ghastly!' And thus ended our tour of Certaldo.

With the van heater on full blast we took an even smaller road across country to Volterra, enjoying Tuscan scenes that make inviting travel brochures when the sun is shining. San Gimignano, always tourist clogged when we've been there, fluttered in and out of our vision. As we wound up the narrow approach road to Volterra, the view was wondrous. Another neat, hilltop-fortified town with red roofs, domes, castles and towers. Up at 1,170 metres on a plateau impregnable to attack, the cold had become more penetrating – D.H. Lawrence is quoted as writing 'it gets all the wind and sees all the world – a sort of inland island.' Despite the weather, the town was there to be explored. We passed through the walls and ascended a long run of steep, broad steps which soon joined the main street. Like Certaldo, this was a well-preserved town with a medieval heart, but there was more life here. Inviting restaurants, cafés, and shops lined the paved, pedestrianised street. Alabaster is the main feature, having been mined and crafted in Volterra since Etruscan and Roman times and we were initially intrigued by the beautifully presented windows with predominantly colourful bowls of fruit, garlic, nuts, biscuits, cakes (and even raw and fried eggs) all made of alabaster, but it soon became wearisome.

Nosing around the town I found some stairs going down to a cellar workshop. A bald-headed man in a white coat and luminous green sports shirt noticed us and waved us down. He was a lone alabaster artisan and we craned forward enthusiastically, feeling privileged to be the only observers of his skill as he started to carve a new two-inch square block of alabaster. The block was fixed on the end of an electric rotating lathe, and as it spun around he got to work with his impressive set of chisels. Five minutes later he had carved a mushroom – and judging by the blocks remaining, had another thirty to do. Impressive enough to make appreciative noises but not so much to as to encourage the passage of money. Can't they think of making something that isn't food related? He is one of a dozen or so artisans working in the central area – the dust problem pushing mass production outside the town.

We walked into the piazza and onto Via Lungo le Mura del Mandorla, which provided one of the best views down to an impressive first century BC Teatro Romano. I wasn't sure how the Romans had managed in their togas, but we were frozen in fleeces and anoraks, so cold-footed it back to the main street, diving into *L'Incontro* – a restaurant, bar and gelateria. Reminiscent of an All-Bar-One at home, it had a backdrop of dark wood floor-to-ceiling cupboards full of wine bottles, dark wood tables, and counter with marble tops, bentwood chairs, arched ceiling and rough-brick walls. We thawed out with coffees, wrote postcards home so we could linger longer, and then stretched it out with more coffees. Thoroughly warmed up, I even contemplated the glass-encased *gelateria* section. My impression was that Volterra had a vibrant feel – people lived there normally and it wasn't abandoned when the last tourist bus had gone. We tried to tour a little more, angling up towards the castle (intrigued that in such a place it was used as a maximum-security prison) before heading past the Museum of Torture and down to the van.

That evening it got colder. The gas heater fan was working overtime so I ran the generator to keep the battery topped up.[4] When Gail started cooking, the gas hiccupped, but with the generator off it coped. When the cooking and washing up was finally over at around 10:00 p.m. I wanted to run the generator again to make sure the battery was topped for nighttime heating but there is etiquette to not running them late and disturbing neighbours. Our only close neighbour was a man in a new German van that was duct-taped up at the rear where he must have hit something. With a noisy wind howling round and a generator that is quiet but still audible, I decided our need was greatest.

---

[4] The generator is permanently fixed on the underside of the van and can work automatically: it is an Italian Gasperini Self-Energy 20 LPG generator.

Less than two minutes after starting the generator someone thumped hard on the side of the van. The van suddenly became very small, and we sat paralysed. Should we open a door, a window, even a blind? Was someone trying to speak to us, or just remonstrating? They had knocked very hard! Maybe someone (or more than one) was standing there trying to trick us into opening up…

'Must be the man next door complaining about the generator,' said Gail.

'But we've only been running it two minutes!' She drew a blind a little.

'I can't see anyone outside. Mind you, it's pitch black out there.'

'Well, I'm not going out in this cold to discuss it. How intolerant. Doesn't he realise we wouldn't do it if we didn't need to?'

'Perhaps he thinks you're going to run it all night.'

'How did he get to that conclusion – we've only just started it! He must have run round the instant he heard it.' The man next door became more and more vilified in my mind, and I finally decided he was in a bad mood because he'd damaged his new van, and was taking it out on us. My thoughts churned over and over, preventing sleep. I decided I would settle it with him in the morning. We survived the night, but as we breakfasted the next day I planned my strategy with a little less enthusiasm.

'He might be a big bugger!' When we drew the blinds, our neighbour was just settling into his driving seat. He mouthed a smiling 'good morning' to us, and waved cheerily as he drove away.

'I was thinking – it was probably someone having a bit of fun on their way to their parked car,' said Gail. I had missed a night's sleep for *that*?

No longer in the mood for more Volterra sightseeing we dumped the contents of the toilet cassette and drove round to the supermarket for shopping before setting off once more into the Tuscan countryside with the cab heater on boost. Rather than being verdant with crops of glowing wheat, maize or oat fields bending and swaying in the breeze, brilliant yellow sunflowers so abundant in this part of the country and vegetables such as artichokes and cauliflowers, the land we were passing had been deeply ploughed, leaving furrows with great sods of earth to be broken down by the winter cold. Old-fashioned crawler tractors with triangular tracks rolling round, one wheel at the front and two at the back, toiled up the steep hillsides, dark smoke puthering out of their chimney stacks in the cold air. The agricultural landscape had been sculpted by the days of the *padrone*, who sharecropped with local peasants. Only the reforms of 1979 ended the feudal system, but there is still the satisfying feeling that this is a land that is being worked – man and nature in conflict and harmony.

We selected route R68, where the soil changed to an earthy brown and vineyards began to appear on the roadside. There was a fascinating approach road up to Colle di Val d'Elsa, a hilltop Tuscan town famous for crystal glassware. We completed a road tour of the town but finding nowhere to park we pushed on to the even more minor road, R2, to find a stunning view ahead of the completely walled thirteenth century town of Monteriggioni. It sits on a low hill, surrounded by vineyards and olive groves off the small by-road to Sienna. It is the smallest of medieval fortified towns, completely encircled by well-preserved, ten metre high walls, and fourteen towers. Entering from a car park outside the wall we passed through one of the two gates into a gem of a sleepy town (siesta time) with just one large piazza and a pretty, simple, Romanesque church, some restaurants offering local produce such as wild boar, shops, a delightful hotel, ancient houses originally owned by nobles, gentry and merchants, a tourist office, and, surprisingly, an Internet Point.

Walking the town's cobblestone streets took no more than half an hour. It was a strategic Siennese military garrison protecting the road from Rome to Europe (which runs right through it) and fought over constantly by Florence and the Bishop of Volterra. The only medieval reference to Monteriggioni comes from Dante, who used it at the heart of his *Inferno* to compare the towns 'ring-shaped citadel crowned with towers' with giants standing in a moat, thereby emphasising their gargantuan proportions, immobility and bellicosity. The fortress withstood almost permanent siege conditions, the public gardens of today providing crops to feed the populace, and fell for the first time to the Florentines in 1554 – not by breach of the walls but by betrayal. Because of its proximity to Sienna, Florence, and the Autostrada, I suspect it suffers a different kind of invasion today: coach party tourists.

A Dickens of a Tour

Pressing on to Sienna, we had to decide where to stay for the night. The Sienna *sosta* had received mixed reviews and we'd visited Sienna before. (I am conscious that I have written much about the places we visited and stayed between Pisa and Sienna, whereas Charles Dickens simply wrote 'we travelled through pleasant Tuscan villages and cheerful scenery all day.' Later, after a small digression about roadside crosses, he writes, 'On the evening of the second day we reached the beautiful old city of Sienna.' He takes no more than a paragraph to describe his short visit: 'It is a bit like Venice, without the water.' Like us, he passed on.)

We were not cruising motorways, but on the road which is labelled on modern maps as Via Cassia, and links Rome to Florence. I was enjoying the thought that Dickens and his family had travelled the same road, and enjoyed a landscape that has probably changed little, although he makes no comment about that stage of his journey. Following *Roma* signs we arrived at San Quirico d'Orcia mid-afternoon and soon found a well-ordered tarmac car park *sosta* at the southern end of the town, with the sun emerging to greet us.

It may not surprise you to learn that San Quirico d'Orcia is a hilltop Tuscan town and also has fourteen towers, although some have been incorporated into other buildings.

The *sosta* was situated off the road heading out of town to Rome, below a modern block of flats and adjacent to a small play park for children. The park was fabulously equipped, with no litter or graffiti anywhere, and had wonderful views across the Tuscan countryside. Alongside was a large area laid out amongst the bushes and trees with walks for dogs and their owners, and below it lay olive groves and vineyards. A worker buzzed in on his green three-wheeler *Piaggio Ape* loaded with yellow plastic crates, bumped over the curb, and disappeared down the hill.

Because of the new warmth we were better motivated to explore the walls, and then enter through a wood of Holm Oaks known as the English Garden. Beyond it lay a sixteenth century, box-hedged formal garden with a central statue of Cosimo III de' Medici, a calming, serene atmosphere, and a view of the town's rooftops and bell towers. Old men played cards in the square and interesting little shops were being opened after the siesta. At the top of the main, flagstone-paved street was La Collegiata – a super, honey-stone, rustic-tiled church mentioned in the eighth century, and next door, a massive palace (Palazzo Chigi Zondadari). Opposite that was another (Palazzo Preorio), which houses the clean and helpful tourist office. After coffees in Piazza della Libertà we spotted some trestle tables groaning with produce. Behind the display was a tiny and enchanting, crypt-like shop full of bottles of wine and thousands of jars of gooey honey, jams, figs, pestos, funghi, and mustards. We examined packets of pasta with every shape and colour you could think of – ocean fish as though you had picked up an aquarium, or, a bag of butterflies. There were shelves stuffed with round cheeses, olive oils from every region, more wines, *grappa*, *limoncello*, herbs, risotto and arborio rice, liquorice allsorts, chocolate bars, *porcini* mushrooms, another counter of hams and soft cheeses, liqueurs, strings of sausages, and somewhere amongst it, a diminutive lady in a pink-check housecoat. She waved us in.

'*Prego*.' We commented on the amazing aromas of the cheeses. She immediately cut small pieces for us to taste, together with two different sorts of jam. Everything was delicious, so we agreed to buy. She took out a knife the size of a sword and proceeded to cut off about two kilos of cheese and select two large bottles of jam.

'*No*, *piccolo*!' we chorused. What a sales lady. To this day, I am a lover of Myrtle jam.

San Quirico was an interesting place to be – and off the tourist track. As we wandered back down the main street we came to a twelfth century hospital, hidden behind a brick archway. There was a small cobbled courtyard with an ancient (sixteenth century) well that had a stone arch supporting the iron bucket mechanism. Stairs led to a loggia on the first floor, where potted plants had been placed along the top of the wall. It was a time warp experience – I doubted that much had changed here. It was a place that gave succour to pilgrims on their way from Canterbury through France to Rome on what became known as the Via Francigena or Via Roma, depending on which way you were going.

Standing in the main street outside the hospital and across the road from a simple Romanesque church and bell tower and looking down the road to a sun setting on the chalk plains and rolling Tuscan hills, I felt, unusually, the romanticism of history. Not only had Charles Dickens and his large family trundled down this street in their coach in January 1845, but centuries of pilgrims had followed in the footsteps of Sigeric the Serious, Archbishop of Canterbury, who walked it in 990.

I turned over the map the tourist office had given us. 'There is an enchanted place in the Valdorcia where all things take on a magical touch, senses are heightened and you are carried away into another world. A world full of good things, simplicity and beauty. Where your way of looking at life changes, with no need to hurry or worry, until the wisdom of a slower pace of life is understood. Senses, locked away in our memories come forth once more and penetrate this idyllic living painting. The golden grain, the red of terracotta…' So – there was the explanation for my moment of reverie.

As we returned to the van I did feel that what we were doing was working out in the way we wanted. We were enjoying a freedom of movement that wouldn't be achievable on the flight-hotel-coach, or even the hotel-hirecar plan. The choice of our small van had liberated us – the places to explore were inexhaustible. We could take whatever time we needed. We were off the beaten track and staying where we wanted, without reference to others (except that every two to three days we needed to find somewhere to empty the toilet cassette.) However, I (and perhaps you, the reader) had begun to wonder how this unbridled pioneering spirit could be balanced against the overall objective of reaching and spending time in Sicily. *Shouldn't we just get on the Autostrada and get there?*

With a 'let's get on with it' spirit, we set off early the next morning, but covered no more than four kilometres before we stopped at another hilltop village – Bagno Vignoni. Down by the motorhome park is a huge spa resort. The main piazza of this small medieval village was a surprise to us – we didn't find the characteristic paved or cobbled square, but instead, a giant sixteenth century rectangular thermal pool, gently bubbling and steaming away in the chill of the morning. It was surrounded by stone buildings that had been turned into restaurants and gelateria, and at one side, a covered way so you didn't get wet (unless you went in the pool). Cloudy, grey sulphurous waters run in channels out of the village and down the hill to multi-baths. A stopping point for pilgrims to ease their aches and pains, it was also frequented by famous dignitaries, and has been known since Etruscan and Roman times. But we had to push on – we were on Mr Dickens's trail.

He described how the landscape 'gradually became bleaker and wilder, until it became as bare and desolate as any Scottish moors.' And, as we drove the remote road over the hilltop, we agreed. We were looking out for La Scala. Dickens had noted that, 'soon after dark, we halted for the night, at the osteria of La Scala: a perfectly lone house, where the family were sitting round a great fire in the kitchen, raised on a stone platform three or four feet high, and big enough for the roasting of an ox.' With no other house for twelve miles, things 'had a cut-throat appearance' with 'rumours of robbers having come out,' but then they were fed well, and made light of the robbers. Could the place still exist? Our map showed a La Scala. (Google 'La Scala, Castiglione d'Orcia' and their maps will show you the same.)

'Probably a large village, town or even an industrial complex by now,' I said to Gail. But there was nothing – we had clearly gone past where it might have been.

'I'm going to turn back.'

'Does it matter that much? We were hoping to push on.' I crawled back.

'Look! There are old, boarded-up buildings at the side of the road, but no village.' We pulled in on the rough ground behind a large, stone building with a pitched roof of straw-coloured tiles. I scouted round: there were derelict outbuildings and an enclosed yard that looked as though it might have housed animals. The main building was rough stone, buttressed in places, and had few windows. Whilst I toured round, Gail sat in the van and re-read Dickens's book: 'a perfectly lone house' – it had to be the one. I walked round to the front. The wall had been plastered and there were two great, arched doors and a barred window, above which was a plaque: Scala P.B.[5] We had found Mr Dickens's

[5] It is more than likely that P.B. would stand for Poste e Bagagli or Post and Baggage, or it could be Poste e Bivacco i.e. bivouacs in its more archaic sense of resting place, B&B in modern terms. Hence, Scala was a post-house, i.e. staging post and post office.

hostelry. Nothing had changed! It lay shuttered and boarded, but in ostensibly sound condition – it simply needed the plaque, 'Charles Dickens slept here January 1845.' I could imagine their carriage setting off for Radicofani.

In case you do have a map – the road we were on, the Via Cassia, goes over a raised section before entering a tunnel in order to avoid Dickens's Radicofani, which sits atop a steep, steep hill above. The twelve miles was in every way as he described it – 'over country as barren, as stony, and as wild, as Cornwall in England.' As we drove up we could see the tower of a castle poking above the trees and we stopped to allow an old shepherd, wrapped up against the cold, get his flock across the road. We drove around the town to park at the lower end and then walked up Via Roma, the main street that Dickens would have travelled on. It's a narrow, stone paved street and I wondered whether they would have had difficulty getting through. The stone of the houses was dark and heavy, and the street like a northern English mill town (although that may have been the cloudy weather). On closer examination, it has all the palaces, churches, arches, alcoves and alleyways of an integrated medieval town, and an important one, since before the modern road workings it was a controlling stronghold. Red and white flags flew from every house.

'*Buon giorno.*'

'*Buon giorno.*'

'*Deutsch?*'

'*No, Inglesi.*' I was in conversation with a white-haired old man standing outside a house on the main street.

'Why do you come to Radicofani?' He spoke good English, so I explained to him about Charles Dickens. He knew nothing about it. He reluctantly told us his name was Aldo. I told him my name was Keith – he tried it once then:

'Who cares?' Aldo told us he was ninety, was born in Radicofani, and had bought his house for one dollar. As a younger man he was known for his wild boar hunting. Nowadays, the youths did the hunting and brought him the head for boiling so he could remove and mount the tusks for them. He persuaded us to go into his house. Downstairs, the three-storey cottage was one room, and on the white walls was a huge array of hunting trophies: stag horns, large horned skulls, tiny skulls, and mounted wild boar tusks, along with his gun and water bottles. He offered us coffees and we looked around – the one room had been completely restored – it was modern and comfortable and equipped with an excellent kitchen and breakfast bar. There was a fourteenth century pillar with iron rings 'where the horses were tied.' He had been working at planning drawings on an easel, and I suspected there was more to Aldo than we'd first thought. I asked if I could take a photo and he posed with his arms out like he was holding a gun and pretending to shoot me, his eyes twinkling.

'Where do you go next?'

'Roma, then Sicily.'

'Sicily? Pah!' he spat out.

'Why do you say that?'

'Beyond Roma, Italy is another country.'

Our route then took us out of Radicofani, where Dickens 'was obliged to take my other half out of the carriage, lest she should be blown over, carriage and all, and to hang to it, on the windy side (as well as we could for laughing), to prevent its going, Heavens knows where,' to wind down the hillside to the Via Cassia, and continuing Pilgrim's Way. The landscape here was scrubbier, with few trees, and for the most part had not been ploughed, although an occasional crawler-tractor and plough was seen toiling away up a hillside, leaving deep furrows with enormous sods of fissured earth in its wake. As we went on, Acquapendente looked interesting, with mighty walls and rounded bastions, but offered no accessible parking, and then below us an inland sea appeared – the mighty Lake of Bolsena and the town of the same name – a fortress of a place with walls and a square tower on the top of cliffs. We ate at a lakeside eatery then started looking for a *sosta* along the edge of the lake.

Behind a rusty iron gate was where we thought it should be. Gail jumped down and tried, but it wouldn't open. Beyond the gate and in amongst some olive trees we could see a primitive brick building with terracotta ridged tiles, so Gail went round the corner and squeezed in past another gate. The door to the building was open and the inside looked like a cave and smelt like a cattery. Sitting at a small table was a scruffy little man in an old blue Barbour jacket and corduroy trousers and peaked cap, sorting olives. She exchanged words but was unsure whether they were meaningful, and the old boy seemed unphased by events so she assumed we could stay and unlocked the original gate from the inside. I drove in and took stock of the idyllic, but grubby olive grove. A welcoming committee of cats of every species and colour (the ginger gene predominating) made their way over. I counted nine before giving up because I had to slam the van door to so they didn't get in. All the equipment was there, but not in an assuring way. Whilst I fiddled with the connections the stockily built, unshaven little man started to limp over to us. What seemed like fifteen minutes later he arrived in front of the van and started, very slowly, to write down its number. It was painful to watch. He looked at the number plate (first letter 'P'), the pen hit the paper and I saw a 'P' slowly forming on the pad. After an eternity he looked up and then down and an 'N' started to form. *Should we stand and watch or make tea?* I thought, wondering what would be the least embarrassing for him. When it felt like early evening he had finally finished, and handed the paper to Gail. She handed over thirteen Euros and he shuffled off back to his building.

I took a tour round the site. It was more extensive than it first appeared. Beyond his building was a new drive-over dump, a water tap for rinsing and a separate one for filling tanks, and globe lights were hidden amongst the many olive and fig trees. The neighbouring fields were also olive groves and the lake was across the road. There was an older motorhome parked near to us, but it didn't look occupied.

'Where do you think he sleeps?' I asked Gail.

'I don't know. There was nothing inside the building – only a table, chairs and the black plastic buckets with olives in that he was picking the leaves off.' We walked along the lake to Bolsena, the distant grey islands floating like giant hippopotamuses in the ripple-free water. The town is perched on a massive rocky outcrop and dominated by the castle. When we entered it, I felt heaviness from the tall terraced houses, the stones of which were blackened, and many shuttered and even padlocked. Tunnels off the side streets ran into blackness, and not a living soul was about. Old ornate gas lamps were fixed on the corners of buildings but their light could never penetrate the little alleys and snickety stairs. We tried one signed to '*Il Castello*' and Gail raced ahead and disappeared from view into an inky blackness, only to discover it was bricked up. We climbed steep cobbled pathways and stairs under tunnels created by scaffolding for restoration work, past newly roof-tiled domes, under a final archway topped by buildings at Via delle Piaggie, and finally into a square – the sole occupant an old, beshawled lady sitting on a bench outside a bar. A lady came out of the gift shop to greet a man with the customary kisses, but after a moment's pause they kissed again with passion, and clinging onto each other, moved inside the shop. Struggling higher up, we came to the castle (now a museum), but eschewing this, clambered up the spiral staircase onto the battlements for magnificent views across the rustic-tiled roofs to a cloudy sky penetrated by the rays of a fading sun. Each was a different hue and ranged from whites through orange, terracotta to red. We tried a few more streets on this upper level – they were narrow and cobbled with flagstones, the buildings tall and their dark stones worn smooth. The doors were heavy, with great iron knocking knobs, and the window shutters closed. Old Bolsena at five in the afternoon is closed. On a fine, sunny day, it would probably match a Provençal village, but certainly not on a gloomy day in late October.

The following morning we saw the old boy arrive at the gate dressed in a quilted blue jacket, brownish trousers, and his peaked cap. The white plastic bag he was carrying must have contained cat food for they had soon surrounded him, and like a pied piper he led them, limping slowly to the hut. It had rained in the night but the sun bravely tried to bring some light and warmth down on us. Various people started to arrive in cars and the old man emerged, slowly, until they surrounded him. He was like a child in their midst, beaming away. They were olive pickers, and soon had an array of green plastic nets spread out on the floor under the trees, and buff-coloured ones draped over the hedges and hanging onto the floor to meet the green ones. They looked more like city people on a weekend break, and I wondered whether they were family. Whilst most busied themselves with stripping the olives from the trees by hand, one produced an extending pole that he plugged into the camp electrics. Two blades at its end oscillated violently and shook the olives free from the upper branches. We had seen olive pickers in the Alpujarra region of Spain use long sticks, but had never seen any mechanised poles (although in the Jaen region, where olive groves stretched for miles, we had seen tractors with a mechanism for gripping and shaking the trees). It was a hive of activity, and our small friend wandered about beaming, but unable to contribute because no branches were low enough. (I have always wondered why the nets couldn't just be tied between the trees so that olives falling of their own accord would be collected!) He indicated to us not to drive over the nets and opened the second gateway, which we took as a hint that we were in the way, and left for Viterbo and Rome by way of Ronciglione.

Ronciglione is now off the main route, but wasn't in Dickens's day, and he stayed a night there in what he described as 'a little town like a large pigsty.' I couldn't wait to see it. The road from Bolsena to Viterbo was in poor condition, and produced little of interest: new housing, scrubby hills, umbrella pines, patchy vines, and an abundance of scrapyards and *zona industriale*. In Viterbo we edged our way west when it should have been east, and then grabbed at a road to San Martino al Cimino, but in so doing we missed some warning signs which we thought were '4 metre height' limits. As we are 3.1 metres high, it wasn't a concern, but as the road climbed a steep hill it soon became apparent that the sign had meant the width between what had now become steep-sided earth walls topped by hedgerows. We hoped that nothing would come the opposite way, and as we passed a beautiful, lemon-yellow villa we realised that this was the main purpose of the road, and it suddenly narrowed even more. Out of the blue, we came to a railway level crossing signed 'left to San Martino S.S. or right to San Martino'. Why we chose left I don't know – I think the road just looked that bit wider. It went a hundred metres to a station, so we had to reverse back. After a series of mistakes, we finally admitted that our 'way finding' faculties were exhausted, and parked in a square outside one of the main arches through the walls into San Martino.

'Why you wanted to find this place, I'll never know. Even Dickens said it was a pigsty!' Gail declared.

'Well, he said he went past a lake, in one part very beautiful, with a luxuriant wood in another, and volcanic hills!'

'But we don't know how we're going to get on in Rome – we should allow more time so we're not hassled.'

'We'll have to ask someone. It's a 'no parking' place so I'll stay at the wheel and you go.' Gail got into conversation with a man in a blue and white tracksuit in a black VW Passat.

'That man says his girlfriend is buying bread, but he wants us to follow him when she comes out.'

A girl emerged from the bread shop, got into the car, had a conversation with the driver as he revved his engine, and then the equivalent of *The Italian Job* got underway. We followed him under the arch (height OK), up the cobbled main street, dodged down a side street to the left, then the right to avoid the arch at the other end of town. We climbed a steep hill out of town, and negotiated hairpin bends through woods. The pace was frenetic, and fortunately the road was without traffic. At a T-junction he suddenly stopped and came back to tell us that we should turn right as he was going left.

'Why you want to go to Ronciglione?' he asked doubtfully. I tried to explain my addiction to Charles Dickens and showed him the book – whether he understood I'll never know. Gail was convinced he was an Olympic athlete on winter training in the woods.

When writing my notes later, I checked other visitor's experiences to San Martino on the Internet. From *Trip Adviser*: 'Getting there was a nightmare… But from Viterbo city centre to the hotel was a complicated task (no relevant signposts). After a couple of laps in the city centre, we surrendered and a very kind Italian guy not only pointed out the right direction, but also drove directly ahead of our car nearly all the way to the hotel!' So, guiding lost tourists seems to be a local occupation.

We drove through more woods and down a steep hill to the Lake of Vico, which was pretty in a dead sort of way (Dickens alludes to a buried town that rises up occasionally). After climbing more hills we finally got to Ronciglione, avoiding the by-pass and driving straight into the town, as did Dickens. We could see all the rooftops below, but as we entered the elaborate gateway and descended through the town, didn't find anything to hold our interest (which may have reflected our mood) and were soon out of the archway at the lower end, stopping purely for a call of nature. Beyond Ronciglione it rained and the scene deteriorated, with depressing industrial estates and blocks of flats, unrelieved by plantings of umbrella pines or yellow-globed lighting on the ring road. The increasing industrialisation continued until we reached Rome's ring road, the Grande Raccordo

Annulare, and almost underneath it, our next stop – Planet Camper, 'a green oasis on the banks of the Tiber River.'

Rome and Beyond

We took the short walk to the river – it brought back memories of Salford waterways, with dark dank waters and derelict shopping trolleys buried in the muddy banks. Across the campsite were large pylons, their cables drooping overhead and zizzing and humming in the rain. Neon signs reaching high into the sky flashed their message to the cars and trucks negotiating the gloom of the Annulare. A flashing rooftop sign on a building tried to compete for attention. Police and ambulances, their emergency lights spread by the misty rain, sirened their way through backed-up traffic. Spears of light fell from the amber street lighting and the restaurant behind us had wrapped fairy lights round the trees to guide people in. Ranks of motorhomes, looking sad and dejected, were parked up for the winter awaiting their warm-weather owners. Others optimistically had sale signs on them, but were probably stuck there until spring. Rivulets of rain ran down the windscreen and there was a gentle patter of rain on the roof followed by a deluge, obscuring everything. It was a *Quatermass* scene (for those that remember it) – we were alone in an industrial complex – you could die and no one would know. But, we were in the Eternal City and snug inside our van.

The rain persisted through the night and we woke to grey clouds and chaos on the anti-clockwise Grande Raccordo Annulare, with emergency vehicles once again threading their way through the gridlocked traffic. We resolved not to do anything, whereupon the sun emerged and the sky brightened. Cognisant of the problems we had experienced with our map, I got our handheld GPS out from the back of the glove compartment (where, non-functioning, it had been thrown in frustration). Switched on, it showed us stuck by the lake at Géraudot (day three). On a whim, I changed the batteries, hooked it up to the external GPS aerial and the laptop, and stared unbelievingly at a map of the Grande Raccordo Annulare with a red triangle blinking to the side. Things were looking up.

To celebrate, we decided to lunch at the smart pizza restaurant behind us on the campsite, so we tarted ourselves up. The pizza section was closed and we were guided to the main restaurant nicely set out with blue and white tablecloths. The waiter, in long black apron, black pants, white shirt and slicked back hair, informed us that pizzas were off there as well. Then he went away while we struggled with the menu. A group of lads in hoodies and working boots arrived from a building site, sat at a table close to us, and gave their orders immediately without consulting menus. Two other tables occupied by office workers did the same. We finally realised there was a 'Menu of the Day' at the front. You selected one dish from each of two sections. In the first we recognised: 'Minestrone, Pasta, *Coniglio*,' but no others. In Section Two: 'Salad, Spinach. Pepper, *Patatas Fritas*, *Patatas Rosta*.' A strange setup. Gail got tasty rabbit stew after she'd finished a salad. I got pasta with bacon followed by peppers. And the cost? Seven Euros each.

We walked back in the sun, and sufficiently motivated, I washed the van of a combination of Carrara dust, the swirling dust from Volterra's car park, and the rain-borne industrial pollutants from Rome. Although it was hard work, I was entertained by a young couple from the restaurant whom, having returned to their car, proceeded with increasing states of anger to have an argument. Gail vacuumed and polished inside and then helped me to finish drying off in time for the climax of the couple's show (our intuition said he was married) of slamming doors and the girl driving off with a dusty wheelspin, leaving him to walk.

Our van was spotless and we had everything we needed: we ate dinner, dozed, read books, nobody knew where we were, and we were alone on a huge one hundred and fifty pitch site. Well, not entirely.

I woke the next morning to realise that something had bitten me on the forehead and I resembled the Elephant Man.

'Are those fireworks?'

'No – someone's shooting by the river.'

'How do you know? There's a mist everywhere.'

'I made it up. Okay for Rome today?'

'Sure. How do we get there?'

'Camp brochure makes out it's easy-peasy.'

'What's that in Italian?'

'I don't know. I made it up.'

With no time limits, we could stay anywhere we wanted for as long as we liked – a strange sensation. I am someone who needs limits and boundaries (even if they are there to be broken), goals and objectives. With Rome on our doorstep, but not in sight, we were motivated to go, but not sure in what context – the avid tourist, the historical eager-beaver, the culture-vulture, the dining experience gastronome, or the fashionista shopper?

'Let's just have a wander round and see what happens – soak up the atmosphere. I don't want a big guidebook chase-around. I didn't sleep very well, and my back is killing me.'

Getting there was easy according to the colour leaflet provided by Planet Camper. At any time between 9:00 a.m. and 12:30 a.m. they would minibus us the three hundred metres to the bus stop for the 302 or 334 to whisk us north in five minutes to the Saxa Rubra station. Here, an efficient train would speedily carry us into Rome in fifteen minutes, to Piazzale Flaminio station close to Piazza Popolo, and the Eternal City would be laid out before us.

'Could we have a lift to the bus stop to go to Rome?' Gail asked in the office. It was 10:30 a.m. – well within the time parameters allowed. Consternation ensued. The girl asked the man but he seemed more interested in getting the red and blue balloons tied on to the motorhomes he had all set out for an end-of-season sales extravaganza. Reluctantly he agreed, and his little van careered the three hundred metres under the flyover and round to a lonely looking bus stop by a dirt lay-by where he wished us '*arriverderci!*'

'*Un momento!*' I said, hanging onto the door. I established that the stop on this side was the one for the 302 and the 334. The engine revved.

'*Bigglietto?*' Well, I had to ask! A hand pointed irritably to the *Tabacchi* kiosk across the road and he was off to tie on more balloons. For those whose only experience of public transport is the Docklands Light Railway, bussing in a foreign country is a forbidding prospect. What system operates, what protocol should be observed (front door or back door), buy the ticket on the bus or off the bus, where will it stop on the way back, what's the name of the stop, 'look, the notice has two names on it, what do we ask for?' – all these need to be considered.

We skipped across the road. The *Tabacchi* kiosk was dark and locked. An old man stood waiting patiently and shrugged, indicating (I thought) that the owner was having a drink in the café kiosk next door. A young aproned lad was busy cleaning the windows, then he brushed the steps and pavement, emptied the rubbish bin, and arranged the chairs and tables outside, but no-one emerged to open the *Tabacchi*.

'What a great start this is,' I moaned.

'Patience,' said Gail, 'someone will come eventually.' The old man went to peer through the café window to no effect.

'If the *Tabacchi* owner is in there, why doesn't he tell him customers are waiting?' Finally there was a rattling at the *Tabacchi* door and it was opened from the inside.

'Probably having a crap.' The old man bought his paper and moaned a lot, but he probably did that every day.

'*Due bigglietti per autobus*,' I demanded.

'*Due Euros*.'

'Okay, so we've got them, but what do you do with them? We don't even know how far we can go or come back!'

When a 302 finally appeared round the corner I waved and it stopped, but the driver couldn't have cared less. There was a yellow ticket validating thingy on a post halfway down. Gail got her ticket in, but as it came out the bus was away, and she was thrown to the back. I hung on as though on a ship floundering through momentous waves, and in the same fashion of grasping for steadying rails, we gained seats facing each other. There was one other passenger, a lady. The bus careered round corners and up the ramp to the Grande Raccordo Annulare, speeding straight on with little regard for the stream of traffic it was joining, and then gave the same disregard to those joining at subsequent entry points.

'Geez, let's not miss the stop,' I said, craning round in my seat to look forward from a rearwards facing seat – the motion and rattling of the bus making me feel quite queer. Some Saxa Rubra signs whizzed past.

'I hope we haven't missed it,' I volunteered, hanging on as we dropped down a ramp and veered round another corner.

'Look at that,' said Gail. It was a huge gypsy encampment in the station car park. Motorhomes and caravans were parked at every angle. New black Mercedes four-by-fours and washing lines full of clothes shot past. We pulled up in front of the station and disembarked.

'I feel sick,' I groaned.

'Me too.'

Saxa Rubra is a modern looking station, if you like modern concrete. We waited for the super express, wondering whether it would be one of those double-decker affairs. There was a shaking, a zizzing of electric overhead cables, and then something resembling a train pulled into the platform. Was it a goods train? The driver seemed to have sunk down below the cab window, so ashamed was he of what he was driving. In fact, the whole train seemed to have sunk below the platform. It was a wreck of a passenger train – filthy and with graffiti that would outdo anything seen on the New York subway. On board, things got worse. There were green plastic seats to our left ranged along the wall. Elsewhere they were bus style. Going into Rome, the big city had persuaded us to dress up in the sense that we had made an attempt with the limited clothing we travelled with. I immediately wished we hadn't. The guy opposite had a large, soft travel bag and wore a black New York baseball cap, black leather jacket, and jeans. The young fat guy one seat from him was also in some sort of trouble, continually putting his head in his hands, rubbing them through his hair, lowering his head to his knees, lolling back in his seat with his eyes closed, and all the time muttering under his breath. Was he going to be sick? The lady next to me soon left. The train had no windows other than in the folding doors that opened automatically at each station, but they didn't always close automatically. A passenger would occasionally help by thumping the doors, which I noted were almost rusted through at the bottom. Deep, discomforting black filth and grime accumulated over years sat in every crevice and yellowing corner. Apart from our close neighbours, there were many bowed heads – they seemed a done-down group – and who wouldn't be, subjected to transport like this? What did it say about a people who accepted it – and a governmental organisation that imposed it? I felt quite depressed.

. We arrived at the Terminus Flaminio and obediently discharged along with our fellow travellers and a very noisy group of young ladies wrapped sarong-style in Spanish flags. Apart from their enthusiasm, the scene outside was not encouraging – the station approach was occupied by numerous stalls selling cheap handbags, scarves, jewellery and other tat – all manned by black guys keenly watching for anyone showing the slightest interest.

We crossed the road and entered the city by the Porta del Popolo, just as Charles Dickens had done in January 1845, except that another couple of arches had been added in 1879. 'A cloudy sky, a dull cold rain, and muddy streets, I was prepared for but not this: and I confess to having gone to bed that night, in a very different humour, and with a very considerably quenched enthusiasm.' But we were soon of the opposite view (as was he the following day) as you will hear from my impression of our day's visit.
In Piazza del Populo, we circled aimlessly round the central obelisk, not realising its 1250 BC antiquity. The atmosphere, enlivened by sunlit cafés, restaurants and fountains, was energetic and good-natured, and the populace young. We spun naturally out of the large oval towards the beckoning twin-churches of Santa Maria in Montesanto and Santa Maria dei Miracoli, and the famous Via del Corso, home of plush shops and big banks. The shady side streets had high-fashion boutiques and, fortunately, many cafés for our morning coffee. Revived, and assuming the 'here for a day' tourist role, we found the Spanish Steps and jostled with other Canon and Nikon-wielding tourists to take the obligatory photos at the sparkling fountain side, with a backdrop of steps overflowing with young humantide. Not far away, and almost by accident, we came on the Trevi Fountain, and were pleasantly surprised, expecting this to be in a large open square and not realising it is the back end of a building and composed of a large, elaborate Baroque frieze

of Neptune and other statues set upon rocks, with more statues over which the water flows. We didn't tempt fate by throwing any coins in over our left shoulders and wishing we could come back to Rome again, because at the rate we were travelling that could slow us down even further.

The Piazza Venezia was mayhem, but we were determined to cross to the Il Vittoriano, an immense and overwhelming marble building and monument built on the side of the Capitoline Hill and dedicated to Victor Emmanuel II, the first King of Italy. It dominates the square in an impressive but incongruous way, and rings to the sound of traffic and piercing whistles of the guards, who take delight in preventing anyone who has struggled up the many steps sitting down or consuming food or a reviving drink. It houses the Tomb of the Unknown Soldier – guarded by two soldiers. The views from the top onto Trajan's Forum, and in the distance the Colosseum, made the climb worthwhile.

We were anxious to find our way safely through hectic traffic to the Colosseum, 'perhaps Rome's most awe-inspiring ancient monument,' surviving after 2,000 years of ravage. It is a massive structure, about fifty metres high in a pink travertine stone that housed fifty to eighty thousand spectators. When opened in AD 80, they partied for a hundred days and killed 5,000 animals. Although quoted as 'the largest in the Roman Empire,' we preferred the one in Nîmes in France, as it appeared less ravaged – the Colosseum has lost the top part of the wall on one side due to stone raiders taking it to build new houses. (This was stopped in the eighteenth century by Pope Benedict XIV.) One remarkable feature I learnt about the Colosseum was that it had a sunroof that could close – and the anchors are still visible. Wembley stadium may be new, but not that new...

We ascended the Palatine Hill and its buildings (where Rome was founded in 752 BC) to look down on the Forum, situated in the valley between the Capitol Hills and the Palatine Hills. It was more than we had imagined. The commercial, cultural, political and religious centre of the ancient world with the first paved road (Via Sacra), said to be built around 600 BC, was recognisably laid out below us. We walked unfettered in the hot sun through the paved streets, past partially-intact villas, temples, churches, basilicas, columns, fallen ribbed stones and carved stones, and our imaginations needed little stimulation to recreate Roman daily scenes from Hollywood movies. The climax was the intact classic Arch of Septimus Severus (AD 230), one of the most important triumphal arches in Rome. We walked around, through and round again, admiring the remarkable friezes and statues depicting Roman triumphalism, and imagined Mark Anthony delivering the speech about Caesar's death from the adjacent low brown wall, or Rostra. A quick glance at the Temple of Emperor Antoninus Pius and Faustina to see the rope marks worn into the top of the pillars, and we climbed up the steps at the end, where a dynamic young American tour guide caught our attention as he re-enacted Caesar's life story in an enthralling and captivating way to bring ancient history to life for his group.

We went on to visit the Capitoline Hill and a visit to the Church of Santa Maria in Aricoeli at the highest point, requiring a perspiration break. In this church was a wooden figurine of Christ carved from the wood of a Gethsemane olive tree that was rushed out to the near-dying in a coach so they could avail themselves of its healing powers. We did not see it (the original was stolen in 1994) but Charles Dickens went to great length to describe it being shown in the church with much reverence by two monks, who then made a 'small charge' and 'all the money collected, they retired…' He tells of it being taken round the city – 'It is most popular in cases of childbirth…' but a 'near relation of a Priest, himself a Catholic, and a gentleman of learning and intelligence' wouldn't have it in his house when his wife was ill because 'it will certainly kill her.'

We passed the Marcus Aurelius statue in front of the Municipal building, then descended the Cordonata, a beautiful staircase with statues of Castor and Pollux at the top and Egyptian lions at the bottom, to cross the busy traffic on Via del Teatro di Marcelloto to the theatre (17 BC), itself another area of remarkable ancient history adjacent to the former Jewish ghetto. Beyond this was a momentarily quiet area with Sunday pavement diners, and then, unexpectedly, a vegetable market with three-wheeler *Piaggio Apes* loaded recklessly with giant orange pumpkins, gourds and squashes.

It would be hard to visit Rome and not see the Vatican. We followed the river round to join the throng crossing the bridge and those being discharged from coaches to make our way through the phalanxes of street vendors selling unbelievably irreverent tat to arrive in Vatican City, St Peter's Basilica – a colonnaded piazza with many thousands of empty plastic chairs. It left me feeling flat. I wanted to be overawed but wasn't. That such a centre of world religion, a beacon for piety in a materialistic world, should be handling itself like Disneyland with long queues, high prices, hawkers and a 'fleece the tourist' attitude, was disappointing. But then we were tourists like all the others pouring in – we simply hadn't the patience to queue and visit the interior. (The statues on the colonnades did catch my attention.)

We returned by way of the incongruous, rusty-brown Castle Sant'Angelo, a solid lump of a place that looms up like a giant water tower. It was built by Hadrian and came to be a place of retreat for popes under attack. From there, we crossed on the delightful pedestrian Sant'Angelo (AD 136), modified and now embellished by ten wonderful seventeenth century statues of angels by Bernini. Wandering even more aimlessly, but trying to do a sweep to the station, we ended up in a large square – Area Sacra del Largo Torre Argentina, created around the second century BC. The buildings were found in 1926 when clearance work was undertaken. In the Teatro Argentina, Rossini's *Barber of Seville* was met with such booing that he took refuge in a pastry shop that used to be next door. We went through some alleys to a huge, oval, three-fountained piazza (I assume this to be Navona) full of students with banners, and a stage with a rock band packing up but with their adrenalin still pumping, not being able to resist another occasional roll on the drums, a crescendo on a guitar, or a toot on a trumpet.

The square is surrounded by elegant buildings, one of which is the church of Sant'Agnese in Agone, built on the site where, according to legend, St. Agnes was stripped naked but was miraculously saved from disgrace by an extraordinary growth of hair in answer to her prayers. A wedding party dressed for a *Tatler* magazine photographer waited patiently on the steps for the black Mercedes bringing the gorgeously dressed bride. With the many restaurants and cafés, this was the gathering ground for the local population. Feeling weary, we found our way the short distance to the Pantheon (27 BC, rebuilt AD 125) and Piazza della Rotonda. It seemed too real for a 2,000 year old building that has been in use throughout its life. Being dedicated as a church and burial ground (a function it still fulfils) probably saved it. A round building with a massive forty-three metre high dome, a portico of three rows of eight Corinthian columns copied by so many town halls, it was not exempt from being raided for building materials, and even the British Museum houses capitals from some of the pilasters. In the seventeenth century, the Pope (in whose care it was) ordered the bronze ceiling of the portico to be melted down and the bulk went to make cannons for the Castle Sant'Angelo. The interior, despite the crowds milling about in the doorway, had a sense of harmony, and with the dome, a sense of proportion. Strangely, the nine metre hole in the dome, the oculus, lets in daylight, but when it rains, water cascades through and slowly drains from the floor. With a couple of centurions posing for photographs outside, it was a fitting place to end our day in Rome.

The train and bus journey back we hoped would be trouble-free. However, the driver of the bus we boarded hadn't the decency to tell us that he was clocking off and we only realised when he drove to the bus garage and departed without a '*buona sera.*' After fifteen minutes another driver appeared and drove back to the railway station where we had started. It all made for an exhausting, but enjoyable day. Rome had exceeded our expectations.

Rome to Naples

We set off with a working GPS on the laptop. A red triangle following the pre-determined route added a new, confident spirit and we were soon leaving the Grande Raccordo Annulare at Exit 23 onto the Via Appia and passing the airport. Our target was a modest thirty-five miles away – but it was not Marino, where we found ourselves, and we had to turn back towards Castel Gandolfo, catching a wonderful view of Rome, and weave our way down the hairpins to the lakeside (Lago di Albano).

Thinking there might be a *sosta*; we tootled down a no-through road on the western side and discovered one behind a locked gate. A few enquiries of a neighbour and we soon had the waiter from the restaurant along the road opening up just for us. It was an orchard and we had electrics and water. We set up and walked back along the lakeside watching a sea-plane landing then taking off again. The lake was pretty, and surrounded by hills on three sides and cliffs where we had come down. The town was at the top of the cliffs. Each of the lakeside pizzerias or trattorias had a grassy area and then a shale beach. Empty white umbrella posts stuck up everywhere like some giant garden game. Little bars were being tidied from the weekend's activities, and it wasn't hard to imagine oiled bodies disported on sunbeds. There were a number of people in stretchy Lycra doing stretchy things themselves, making us feel guilty for sitting and eating lunch. Gail must have felt particularly guilty, because she walked to the top of the cliffs while I sauntered back with the weak excuse that I'd been driving. At the top is the Pope's Summer Palace, with a fine view down to the lake and our little *sosta*.

After rain in the night and persistent backache on my part we left the next day, making our way back onto the Via Appia to pass through Albano, mad with people, traffic, a rain of autumn leaves, and more tremendous views back down to Rome and the plateau. How must returning legions have felt coming upon that sight? Ariccia, Genzano di Roma came and went and then we stopped for supermarket shopping in Velletri. As I sat in the van and the skies darkened I observed the urban life around me. Workmen asphalted a stretch of road: one man with a pickaxe, two telling him how, and another to inspect. A fire engine arrived at speed and the firemen rushed into the supermarket, emerging ten minutes later with their shopping. Then a police car drove the wrong way down the road, just to show that he could.

The Via Appia from Velletri and beyond Cisterna di Latina is as straight as can be. It was a blur of initial high cliff views across the flat Roman plain, mountain villages like Sermoneta and Priverno to the east perched impossibly on cliffs of the Monti Lepini range, stinking chemical plants, scrapyards, more scrapyards, and angular umbrella pines leaning into the road, gradually replaced by plane trees, quarries, scrubland, and flat agricultural land with rows of cabbages. We were diverted towards Borgo San Donato, and close to the sea, things changed. Everything was '*borgo* this' or '*borgo* that' (district, quarter, neighbourhood). There were few houses, just buffalo-like cattle and horses. The sea on our right was bright and sparkling as it broke onto the shore and to our left more water and locks to keep it in. Sand blew across the road from the dunes and the beaches were perfect – golden and empty. Only an occasional car passed. Here and there we spotted a restaurant shuttered for the winter and in danger of being buried in the drifting sand. Then ahead, poking out of the sea, was the 1,700 metre limestone crag known as the Circeo peninsula. Mussolini built the town of Sabaudia for Italian worker's holidays – it took two hundred and fifty-six days, and included a large anti-aircraft gun and surface-to-air missile in the main square. As we drove past it was a ghost town – neat and clean, but empty. Beyond, there were more and more smart, but boarded-up, villas. Finally, when it looked like our road would crash into the mountain itself, we entered San Felice Circeo.

We drove up and up, and worryingly, up again – and finally parked to allay Gail's fear of us getting stuck. It was a perfect spot and we headed for a bar-restaurant that we found had an awning-covered terrace with a perfect view of the lower town and more distant beaches. My memory though, is clouded by the coffee (that was hardly warm) and the two sandwich-wraps. Gail's was warm, but only on the outside, and of indeterminable content. Mine, we guessed, was tuna. The medieval old town had a pleasant square with an information office. We drove out to discover we were on the longest cul-de-sac in the world, and going along the peninsula to the lighthouse.

Still following Charles Dickens's route, we drove round the bay and Terracina to take the small road up to Fondi: 'Take note of Fondi, in the name of all that is wretched and beggarly,' he wrote. Unfortunately, we were diverted away to the right so I was unsuccessful in getting to the main street, 'a filthy channel of mud and refuse…' or see 'hollow-cheeked scowling people…, all beggars…' What we saw was the backs of houses and some towers.

From Fondi we climbed the long hill to Itri and as we did, we passed a brown sign – Appia Antica. The original road bore away from the one we were on – a sandy cart track between olive groves and across an old stone, humpbacked bridge, then away and out of sight to return over another bridge with a ruined stone building, and then it was gone – down the river valley and out of sight. By using the original Roman roads (that were now often no more than country lanes) and following Dickens, we had certainly been brought closer to history.

Itri smacked us between the eyes as we entered – a huge stone fort appeared below the mountain with a rounded bastion at the base, a long castellated wall climbing up, and then square towers and high walls at the top. We tried to park for photos, but the cobbles were immense and probably from Roman times – it was a rock-and-roll moment.

Like Dickens, who headed inland to Capua ('hardly seductive to a traveller now…') for a rest before reaching Naples, we decided to focus on our night's accommodation and diverted through Mondragone – a big mistake. The road was rough and the scenery was rough – not simply 'boarded up, seaside out of season' but 'gone forever, irretrievable' buildings that would never be attractive. Mondragone, where we thought we might stay, appeared – and what a hole it was – like some Mexican frontier town (and that's probably doing the Mexicans a disservice). The buildings were decrepit, and the people looked as though they were on the make, hanging about outside bars or playing cards. The traffic was chock-a-bloc, and when we did turn off to try and find the place for camping we ended up at the back of a supermarket in an area that made us feel uncomfortable. The town had us looking in all directions at once. We got back to the main road and decided to head for the Lido instead. Stopped at a traffic light, a down-and-out took a small tissue from his pocket and wiped the headlight of a waiting car, then demanded money from the driver. As I was mentally preparing my response, the lights went to green. Nearly through the town we dived down to the sea to find the next place, and it was even worse – derelictus horribilis. A gang of youths advanced on us, so already feeling uncomfortable, we turned back.

'I don't like Italy,' announced Gail, out of the blue.

'But what about Tuscany, Rome, Genoa, the Cinque Terre, Portovenere?' I reminded her.

'Well, except those.'

We found our way back to the main road and set off south again. The traffic was like a dodgem-car circuit with death wish overtaking manoeuvres.

'Why do they do that?'

'God, he's not going to make it!' The oncoming car had to give way. Two trucks came close to colliding in front of us as one pulled out to overtake a car moving unusually slowly – the driver was on the phone, smoking and waving his spare hand at his passenger to emphasise a conversational point. The landscape deteriorated further – the road was on stilts across a barren, flat land, occasionally tilled, more often the home to rusting trucks or cars piled high. Few lived there. We flew over it, determined to make our next site before dark. Did I mention it had started to pour with rain?

With the aid of the GPS, we eventually entered the outer reaches of Naples heading for Quarto. The roads narrowed, the traffic intensified, and the rubbish was stacked high on every corner and spilled out onto the road. Every two hundred yards saw another pile of rubbish leaching in the rain. We went under a tunnel unexpectedly.

'That shouldn't have happened,' said Gail, peering hard at the laptop glowing in the darkness. We came to a roundabout besieged by traffic from five directions, and unsure of the right exit, did two circuits, brushing off attacks from incoming cars that gave no leeway. The road we exited on was a channel between rubbish piles. Black bags bursting open, white bags untied, open bags, non-bagged stuff – all getting soaked in the rain.

'What is going on with all this rubbish? It's third world.' We picked off our left turn to enter a narrow road bordered by houses, passed over a railway bridge, then found our next turn was very narrow and climbed steeply round the back gardens of the houses until the housing stock improved and we got to an ending (in the sense that we couldn't drive any further). A black guy hailed us from across the road and led us up a steep hill through a heavily fortified gate. We had found the *sosta*, a haven of calm in an uncertain world of noise and filth. We were in a garden and we were set up and snug. Our relief was palpable.

Naples

The drizzle of rain developed into a thunderstorm in the night, with lightning and heavy rain beating on the roof. As Gail peered out of the small bedroom window there was a thunderflash of lightning so intense she reeled back. By breakfast all was calm again and the only decision to make was what to do with our day. I was all for going to Pozzuolli, a short distance away, but Gail was keen on Naples and bought two all-day-all-travel tickets from the *sosta* office for three Euros each. The station was a short walk away, but it didn't have an entrance on the side closest to us and we struggled to find one on the roadside.

'Hey! Johnny.'

'Is someone shouting at us?' Gail asked.

'Ignore them – they probably want to sell us something.'

'Johnneeee! Hey, Johneeeee!'

'It's the man at the newspaper stall.' Eventually acknowledging the caller, he smilingly told us we had walked right past the station entrance (and here we thought we'd dressed so as not to look like tourists). The station had a simple platform, an unmanned office with nowhere to buy a ticket, and the concrete building had been painted and then sprayed over with graffiti. Another waiting passenger helpfully looked at our tickets and pointed out that the train we needed would be the next one.

An impressively sleek train arrived with a smart interior, and slid noiselessly out of the station and into a long tunnel to arrive in Pozzuoli. We went through another tunnel, emerging with pleasant views of the sea and offshore islands soon replaced by graffiti-painted concrete blocks of flats next door to a rusty, Bessemer-process industrial complex with a spewing chimney. City railways inevitably look into the backsides of houses, warehouses and less salubrious areas, but our vista continued to deteriorate. It was daunting, depressing and worrying – the stations seemed to be joined together and were as bad as their surroundings. Only when we pulled into Mergellina did things improve – and then we were in a tunnel until Montessanto, our destination.

'Centro Storico' conjured up images of a historical centre – palaces, churches, cathedrals, and squares with restaurant tables and chairs spilling into them and bathed in the morning sun. We live in the heart of London and are used to the hubbub of city life, but nothing could have prepared us for our exit from the station: filth, graffiti, noise, people, buzzing scooters, battered cars, more people, tat sellers, and dark alleys and passageways that assaulted our senses. We were swept uncontrollably down narrow streets like a football crowd leaving a match – scooters squeezed past and horn-sounding, people-crushing, accident-damaged old cars criss-crossed the streets. We stepped over, and inadvertently into, piles of rubbish and goods from small shops as they spilled out into the street, handbag and jewellery sellers with their wares spread out on the floor as they tried to protect it, beggars hustling, men lurking in doorways, and stinking rubbish bins overflowing. I was confused and conscious of warnings about false bag carriers, pickpockets, distraction thieves, scooter-borne bag-snatchers, gun-toting muggers, three-card tricksters, sellers of high quality merchandise who switch it for a fake (or even a brick) as you get your money out, and hassling street sellers who know every English word but 'No.' They could all have been there. The side streets, flying flags of washing from the high buildings, were a rabbit warren of forbidding, dark, narrow, slummy alleys with feral cats and stray dogs. We couldn't escape.

'See Naples and die?'

We were disgorged onto a main street. My head was spinning and aching from the tension and we pounced upon a free table at an outdoor restaurant, relieved to have entered some form of normality. We enjoyed what everyone does when they get to Naples – a pizza. I reflected on Dickens's image of Naples: 'But, lovers and hunters of the picturesque, let us not keep too studiously out of view the miserable, depravity, degradation, and wretchedness, with which this gay Neapolitan life is inseparably associated!' Nothing had changed.

Steeling ourselves to find the picturesque, we started our tour by walking to Piazza Dante. The pedestrian crossing lights changed immediately the button was pressed. It made no difference – cars and scooters continued through the red light at high speed. Eventually, after watching the locals I learnt the technique of simply stepping out. For emphasis, I raised my hand high as though I owned the place, stepped out confidently, averted my eyes from the traffic and prayed for safe deliverance. It worked – I think they admire anyone with the chutzpah to have a go.

I will make only fleeting reference to the architectural masterpieces we passed, as the details are available in any Rough Guide, and to be frank, our walkabout, although extensive, was not a relaxed one. Rubbish and graffiti was inescapable in Naples. Everything lay about in front of national monuments, churches, cathedrals and palaces. Tourist information boards were obscured by graffiti.

Elaborate, historic wooden doors and arched entrances to elegant courtyarded palaces were graffiti-painted to oblivion. Corner walls, once blank, invited a mob of design freaks with spray cans and messages for those passing by.

From Piazza Dante we passed into streets full of youngsters spilling out of small back-street cafés, eating gelato and sitting astride scooters in groups. Round into Piazza Gesù Nuovo we paid five Euros each to see some disappointing cloisters of the Santa Chiara Convent, 'truly one of the gems of the city,' and round the corner, more dark-haired Italian beauties on scooters and motorbikes. Via Bernadetto Croce had a multitude of brightly lit caves acting as shops, blazing wood-fired pizza parlours and many historic churches and monuments obscured by the rubbish bins in front of them. Pasta shops with large barn doors opened out, dripping with dangling spaghetti, clear plastic bags of pasta shapes and shelves of lemoncello bottles all glittering from the bare-bulb lighting. This was a pedestrianised street for nimble scooter riders. No one seemed to mind. (Did I mention that there was rubbish, litter and graffiti everywhere?) And, in the midst of it all, young couples sat on graffiti-painted benches oblivious to anything other than the love of their life as they held each other fondly. Others not yet paired up sat and read books. Groups of girls in tight jeans shopped madly.

In Piazzetta del Nilo there was a strange, angular church that looked as though it could have been part of a castle but was a mess, with small windows, ornate balconies, and odd projectiles. It reminded me of where a terrace house had once been torn down from a row, leaving brickwork and old fireplaces exposed. (I would tell you more of Sant'Angelo a Nilo but the signboard was covered in graffiti). The walls of buildings around the square were covered in posters all stuck on top of each other but carefully placed below stone plaques: 'Vietata L'Affissione – Art 446 C.P.' (Prohibited the Posting – Article 446 C.P.)

The street changed to Via San Biagio dei Librai and narrowed and darkened, being overhung by balconies to the right and wooden-jettied upper storeys on the left. Daylight hardly penetrated and the crowds were hemmed in. We danced around a gay couple in front of us – a young man with his arm tightly round the shoulders of his bearded companion. Further on, in a cave of an alleyway, we saw a fruit and vegetable stall seller in a yellow T-shirt, all twenty-five stone of him, holding fervent discussions with two Mafioso men in sunglasses. They wore 'we've heard all that before,' expressions. Old, arched double doors led through alcoves and cloisters to the courtyards of wondrous buildings with elegant porticos, embellished window surrounds and armed guards. In contrast, others entered by the same arrangement housed shops below and flats above.

We entered a street that I now understand is called 'Christmas Street', or the Italian equivalent. Every small shop front opened into a huge gallery of nativity, with thousands of figurines. Some displayed the nativity scene, others figures such as the Pope, Mother Theresa, Pavarotti, a footballer, Charlie Chaplin, Hitler doffing his hat, Roman gladiators, and even clowns and marionette figures. The shelves groaned with the weight. There were so many that the man in one shop appeared to be one of them. We probably ended up on Via dei Tribunali. Some of the streets running off here to the south were the narrowest we had come across.

The Gothic thirteenth century Duomo we found to be unprepossessing, somewhat tucked away, and closed, so we missed the opportunity to examine the phials of blood of the patron, San Gennaro. Three times a year his blood taken at the time of his martyrdom in AD 305 near Pozzuoli mysteriously 'liquefies' in the bishop's hands. If it doesn't, (a rare but not unknown event), disaster will strike the city. This apparently happened in 1944 when Vesuvius erupted, in 1980 when there was an earthquake, and in 1988 when Naples lost at football to Milan. The ceremony, when it occurs, is a boisterous affair and the blood 'liquefies' in front of everyone. Paul Daniels and Derren Brown – eat your heart out.

We took in the nearby, much-restored white Castel Capuano, residence of the Norman King William 1, and now a courthouse, before taking Via Pietro Colletta to Corso Umberto 1. Back streets running off here were wider, but jammed with pavement parked cars and scooters below crumbling apartment blocks. In older days, with kids playing, washing flying, ladies sitting out chatting, and Sophia Loren side-saddle on a scooter, the film makers made them characterful. Today they were uninviting – particularly as they are known to be the haunts of the Camorra, or local Mafia. The same guys who have control of the city waste disposal (an oxymoron, if ever there was one). No authority could control what goes on in those back streets. I read of 'people being captured or pulled into some houses in these narrow streets.'

Corso Umberto gradually improved as we walked its length towards Piazza Bovio and we decided it was time to get back to the station. It was at this point that my normally superb sense of direction malfunctioned. We ended up in a slum quarter, a maze of alleyways – everything looked the same by then. Each time we tested a new street, it went steeply uphill, and after a long day it was getting exhausting. When we decided we had made a mistake, we had to re-pass the corner men, who eyed us up rather strangely. It was plain for all to see that we were lost tourists. Momentarily out of control, and the adrenalin starting to rise, we had no choice. Gail emboldened herself and asked one of the corner-street men for assistance – we thought it less confrontational. He gave us directions, but after a while we realised he had sent us the wrong way. What was initially a small concern had grown to be a big problem. We had been reluctant to get the guidebook out for fear of looking touristy, and when we did, it simply showed a chequerboard of streets with no names, only 'Quartieri Spagnoli.' Somehow we were finally released, and the mucky station approach was a welcome sight. When we got back to the UK I read a comment about Naples from a resident: 'Quartieri Spagnoli? – There are times when a stranger is killed there every week.' Quartieri Spagnoli was a battleground for clans trying to control criminal business!

The train ride back was a blur. As we left the station it was raining hard. There was a greengrocer's stall across the road and we needed a few potatoes for the evening meal so we joined the queue. The man serving in the white coat was joking with those waiting, and when he saw us, he called into the back of the shop, and a man I took to be the boss emerged.

'*Patates – no problema! Quanto?*'

'*Tre.*'

'*Tre*?' As he selected about a kilo of potatoes despite Gail's protestations (she only wanted three), he said something to everyone else, and they burst out laughing. With the potatoes in the bag he grabbed hold of Gail.

'*Andiamo*!' and led her into the shop behind. Ten minutes later we left with potatoes, ham, and buffalo mozzarella cheese – after experiencing one of the best displays of good-humoured salesmanship I had seen in a long while. We skipped over the rubbish bags and made our way back to the van in pouring rain. Our day in Naples was over. It had left a lasting impression.

South from Naples

A number of motorhomes arrived in the night, and owners and friends were noisily shouting parking instructions and letting their kids run around late. More vans arrived in the morning and the *sosta* was getting fuller. We decided that Thursday, 1st November, must be the start of a holiday stretching into the weekend. As the places continued to fill, Mr Africa, in his green wellingtons and blue waterproof, stalked about waving his furled umbrella in a colonial way. Then he would lean back on it as he checked that his instructions were being carried out to the inch, in the same way he had with us when we had arrived. Then out of the blue, he tapped on our window with his umbrella and jerked his thumb at me in a 'Move your motor' sort of way. I was working on my computer with cables everywhere, Gail had washing up in and around the sink, and we were generally in the sort of disarray that a 'lazy, do nothing day' provokes. I ignored him – he had put us there and it was inconvenient to move. He squeezed another van in next to us and stared through the window, went to talk to the owner, and then came back and rapped on our window again.

'For goodness sake! Look, if we're going to have to clear everything up, we might as well push off,' I said to Gail. 'And there was a lot of noise from kids last night – it can only get worse!' We cleared up and I went to use the loo in the van. The next thing I knew the alarm was going off – Gail had opened the sliding door and didn't know how to stop it. There I was with my pants around my ankles, Gail yelling for help, and Mr Africa running over to see who was making all the noise. Carry on Camping!

I told Mr Africa (in French) that we were leaving.

'*Pourquoi*?' he asked.

'*Je ne l'aime pas ici.*'

'*Pourquoi*?'

'Oh, forget it!' The boss man didn't understand why we were leaving, but with thirty-three Euros in his hand and vans queuing to get in, he shrugged it off.

The Autostrada was jammed with cars – small Fiats that only did town driving were muscling with big black Mercedes and BMWs. Cars straddled lanes, drivers were on their phones and talking animatedly to passengers, with no hands on their wheels. Lane-joiners didn't bother to look at all and caused sharp braking and near pile-ups. The roads were wet and dangerous. It wasn't long before we came upon a multiple accident with cars, people and police everywhere. Manoeuvring our way round, we crawled along, tracking north-west before turning south. Naples was below us (we couldn't seem to shake it off!) and then it had a final say. At the entrances to the tollbooths were gangs of the menacing type, jumping from lane to lane and selling tissues, toys and other tat. As we queued for the booth they pushed their goods and faces against the windows. Ignoring them, we crawled to the tollbooth. But they didn't relent – even as we moved forward they stayed with us until we had to wind the window down to pay the fee, at which point they risked being crushed between the vehicle and the booth. We were wary of two potential problems: the tollbooth attendants are known to overcharge because no fees are posted, and the tat sellers might get their hand inside to nick the purse you're paying out of. We survived, but Naples still clung on to us – cement blocks of flats were everywhere.

Vesuvius appeared dimly through the dark clouds and pouring rain, and there was no great majesty to tell you of. Nothing appealed – we wanted to escape. The traffic was manic in contrast to Dickens's, who on a day trip from Naples was '...carried pleasantly, by a railroad...' We entered road works signed at fifty kilometres speed limit and nobody did less than one hundred – until the man in front slowed suddenly to twenty to take a phone call. Pompei came and went and we saw nothing. We decided to turn off to Castellammare di Stabia. It looked better, but not that much better, despite being on the bay and a few kilometres from some of the most beautiful scenery in Italy at Sorrento and along the Amalfi coast. It would have been a dream to drive the roads along the coast to Positano, Ravello, and Amalfi, but it was pouring with rain and would have spoilt the memories we already have of wonderful holidays there.

With mountains inland and the islands of Ischia and Capri off the coast we pushed on as the road flew over Salerno, its container ships and a marina full of yachts. Closer to us were never-ending grey concrete blocks of flats. After stopping for refreshment served by a grumpy barman, we turned off the Autostrada at Battipaglia onto the SS18, but were diverted through a small town to drive in and out of deep craters in the road. We had driven only seventy-seven miles, but it seemed twice as long. We arrived in Paestum and a barrier across the road, outside the complex of buildings opposite the Greek remains. It was still raining, and I was through with driving for the day. I asked the car park attendant if we could stay overnight.

'*No problema*,' so we gratefully parked at the back of the car park. People who had been to visit the remains as a holiday treat returned to their cars drenched. We took a sneak preview of the remains over the fence – a caterpillar of raised umbrellas snaked in and out across the Roman forum, amphitheatre and Greek Cerere temple. One by one, cars disappeared from the car park, night came on, and we were finally alone next to a deep, dark wood.

A utility question raised its head. With our unscheduled and rapid departure from the Naples *sosta* we hadn't emptied the toilet cassette, and it looked full. I went out to pee in the woods and we went to the Museum café so Gail could use their facilities. I debated a walk in the woods with the cassette and a spade, but it was pitch black and eerie. We shouldn't have rushed off in the way that we had.

'Can you hang on until morning?' I asked.

'I certainly can. It's you who gets up in the night!' With all the security devices on we went to bed. It's true that if you're asked not to think about something, that's the very thing you do think about. I woke at 5:00 a.m., 6:00 a.m., and again at 7:00 a.m. When the alarm finally went at 7:30 a.m. I was bursting for a pee and prepared to risk a cassette overflow, but fortune smiled on the brave and the sun was shining brightly.

A black ruffian of a dog appeared at the door of the van with a sorrowful look on its face. As we stepped out, it adopted us and followed us over to the small ticket office of the archaeological site, settling itself against the wall to soak up the morning sun. The lady collecting tickets knew the dog well.

'*Bella, Bella.*' She directed Gail to the public loos at the back of the building but had nothing else to do, as the girl selling the tickets was across the road having morning coffee. Tickets finally obtained and checked, we entered the site – that is, Gail, me, and our new canine friend. We had it to ourselves – what a privilege.

I have found it hard to write about our visit without descending to well-worn clichés. We were ignorant of the place prior to our arrival, and had come upon it by chance. We were on a site with three magnificent, near intact, golden-stoned, fifth century BC Greek Doric temples standing majestically on the plains leading down to the sea.

Attributed to the mythological Jason and the Argonauts, Poseidonia was founded by the inhabitants of Sibari in the sixth century BC. In between the Temple of Cerere at one end and the Basilica Temple and Temple of Neptune at the other, there is the complete, second century Roman city of Paestum, with the Amphitheatre, Forum, and Temple of Peace. But it is more than these magnificent structures, although I was amazed at their ability to construct them. Because the remains of the houses, shops, markets, streets, swimming pool, and other functional community buildings remain for you to walk through, you can let your imagination run riot. There are only walls to knee height and occasional brick-red pillars of a portico entrance, but this allows you to envisage the plan and to peer over into rooms of the houses, where in a corner might be a sizeable remnant of an intricately-patterned mosaic floor, in another a complete floor, pillars from the heating system, or a water channel.

The living and shopping areas, probably full of daytime bustle, are separated from the more formal areas by the Sacred Street or Street of Processions. Idyllic as living there must have been, it also called for defensive measures against the Etruscans camped across the Sele estuary, and the whole area is surrounded by well-preserved walls. As we approached the defensive walls at the southern end our canine friend, bored of our slow meanderings, wandered off. Inside the walls we found a restaurant, The Nettuno, not an eyesore or incongruous, but sympathetically in tune with the environment. In the grassy meadow in front, and amongst the ruins, the chef and two women assistants in full whites were picking herbs.

Following the fall of the Roman Empire, declining buildings in Paestum were stripped to build Christian churches, and malaria and Saracen incursions finally forced the few remaining there to flee to the surrounding hills. This left Paestum abandoned, until rediscovered by an Italian road-building gang in 1752. Then the new breed of eighteenth century post-Napoleonic 'Grand Tourers' like

Shelley and Goethe began to visit and proclaim their discovery, thereby influencing neoclassical architecture throughout Europe. Much is made of the visits of these scholars and poets and Shelley describing it as 'inexpressibly grand.'

Visiting the site had been a magical experience, but not so magical that we were drawn to follow the legendary superstition that 'Childless couples flock to the temple of Hera to copulate beneath the night sky, in the belief that making love within the shrine of the goddess will call forth her fertilizing influence and thereby insure pregnancy. At Paestum, Hera is not only a goddess of fertility; she is also a goddess of childbirth.'

We left the site to cross the road to the modern (1950s) museum. I am easily bored in museums, but this one astounded us. Exhibits were presented with Italian flair. The lower Greek section had a profusion of intricately-decorated clay vases and metal urns with beautifully-crafted handles from as early as 500 BC. Everything for daily living was viewable, and it made us wonder how little we had advanced from those times. Their city was ordered – they had pride in the smallest vase or utensil, the largest urn, or the grandest statue, all beautifully decorated and sculpted. Their lives are portrayed on these vessels, captured for all time. In the rear of the museum there are tomb paintings with a shocking and unexpected vibrancy of colour – they came one after the other until we reached the 'Divers Tomb.' This depicts a graceful diver in flight from a diving platform and supposedly passing from life to death. (*How is this known? Perhaps he was simply a good diver!*) Close by was my favourite – a rosy-cheeked, winged, Boadicea-like figure in a chariot flailing the two prancing horses.

We departed with embedded memories to find a *sosta* or campsite and ended up a short distance away at Villagio dei Peine, where for eighteen Euros we could have everything. It was our first campsite since Pegli. It was wooded with tall pines, and we found a sunny pitch facing the archway to the beach and sea, dumped the cassette, filled with water, walked the seemingly unending beach, and watched the sun drip into the sea as the redness spread out along the Amalfi coast to the north. The intensity of our own 'Grand Tour' meant that three relaxed days and nights at Villagio dei Peine came as a relief. Touring had become hard work, the senses were overloaded, and my fitful 'don't think about your bladder' sleep needed replenishing. Sitting in the hot sun, I soon dozed off. I woke dreamily, imagining a black rabbit hopping across the pitch in front of me. It stopped and looked back at me. I wasn't dreaming.

After a beach walk halted by some aggressive dogs, we decided to lunch at the campsite restaurant. Mamma welcomed us effusively, but the interior restaurant was empty and laid out with long tables in a wedding-style arrangement, white tablecloths and bottles of drink. We felt we were intruding into a privately booked room, but she would have none of it so we compromised and agreed to sit at one of the three outside tables. As we were eating, cars started to arrive with guests, for what was clearly a private family occasion – smartly dressed, they all greeted one another and fussed over their children. Everyone hailed us: '*Buon Giorno*.' Moments later the chef came out to greet us, afterwards the cook brought us pieces of pizza and added her own welcome and ran through a long menu of dishes. We made a stab at some of the recognisable ones (lasagne and fish) with salad and a carafe of wine for Gail.

We thought service would falter as the large number sat down for their meal, but no, the cook was out again to bring us fresh Buffalo Mozzarella and Ricotta cheese with bread, and then coffees. (Buffalo Mozarella is made only in Campania following centuries-old traditions. Apart from the Caserta province, the only other place where this product is found is the Sele plains, particularly south of the Sele River, where Paestum is found. Gail loved it; I found it bland, even rubbery.) The total bill for the meals was just thirteen Euros. A thunderstorm erupted and we lingered. Back at the van, two rabbits popped out from underneath to say hello, and later, fellow German campers insisted we go to the beach 'immediately' for the sunset. A fitting conclusion to our stay – the next day we would explore the Cilento coast, south of us.

Nearly There

'Hello. Hello. How are you?' Signor Mario greeted us cheerily in the sunshine. We followed him into his jumbled office to settle our account, where I discovered he had a computer with 'Internet' written on a slip of paper above it (I had been looking in the village for two days.)

'You have Internet here?' Signor Mario pointed to his Olivetti typewriter and back to himself and shrugged, then turned to the computer keyboard and pressed every key in a random fashion but the screen stayed blank. He flicked every switch on the wall, the screen stayed blank.

'I know nuzzing. Where you go now?'

'Sicily,' we chorused.

'Please stop on the way back.' Although I previously expressed regret at not driving the Amalfi coast road, being frustrated by bad weather and a tense post-Naples atmosphere, the Cilento coast more than made up for it. Its remoteness added to the beauty. Steep cliffs dropped into a crystalline sea, the coast was dotted with idyllic beaches, coves, and grottoes waiting to be explored, and the sky was a near-cloudless, iridescent blue. Every corner turned brought a new and exciting vista with small villages nestling in mountain folds, morning shadows from higher peaks playing across the valleys and small harbours, their fishing boats idle in the calm blue sea.

We sat in the sun at a pavement café in the lovely old village of Acciaroli. A market was in full swing alongside the port and all was overlooked by an old fort, a pretty church, and new works to beautify the place even more. It is rumoured that a local fisherman was the inspiration for Hemingway's novel, *The Old Man and the Sea*. We did a little market shopping then continued along the winding and twisting coastal road. Orange and green nets had been spread under the hillside olive trees or on the ground, but higher up the trees disappeared and the mountainsides were devoid of vegetation, providing a majestic backdrop to the rolling Cilento hills below. We dropped into Palinuro on the spit of land that pushes out into the sea and through the little town to the harbour, where we had an alfresco lunch alongside the fishing boats tied to the harbour wall. The sea was so clear we could see the fish idly swimming by, safe in the knowledge that it was the fishermen's siesta time. Everywhere was a delight. There were signs of tourism, but they didn't intrude.

Arriving in Marina di Camerota, we did three circuits and drove up to the mountain village of Lentiscola before we found the *sosta* we had been searching for. It was in an olive orchard and a young, tubby guy and an older man were busy spreading their olive collecting nets. No one else had intruded on their work space, and it was hard to park without spoiling their endeavours. Around 4:30 p.m. they set off in their beat-up red Transit van and left us to it. I walked down the hill to the town past a huge pile of rubbish that spilled out into the narrow road causing traffic chaos. It seemed out of character with the rest of the day.

We were woken by frantic and noisy activity towards the lower end of the site. The rubbish clearing crew had arrived in a mother truck and a fleet of smaller ones, and soon scooped up the plastic-bag mountain and tipped the green bins into the white, chomping-compressing monster. Job done, it reversed up the hill followed by a cavalcade of bumper-to-bumper small cars with impatient Italian drivers held up by the work in the narrow one way street. Our own campsite crew arrived shortly after and set about spreading more olive-catching orange, buff, and green nets on the ground under the olive trees.

We were off by 9:10 a.m., heading into a bright sun. Knowing we couldn't get under a low bridge in the village of Lentiscola, we backtracked towards Palinuro to take the small road inland through Centola and Foria. It ran through an exquisite, steep-sided gorge, and as we started to take the first hairpin we began to wonder about the rest, climbing precipitously up the mountain ahead. Luckily our road turned away to join the coastal road to the lovely Sapri, surrounded by wooded slopes with bare purple mountains in the background. The next section would challenge anything on the Amalfi coast in the beauty stakes. The scenery was stunning, with the road teetering on the cliff edges as it worked its way round the mountains. Small hamlets perched precipitously on the edge or nestled down by the water. In Fiumicello we made a coffee-stop by the harbour. A group of old men with walking sticks sat on the harbour wall watching us park. One of them wandered over and made a close scrutiny of our registration plate.

'*Gran Bretagna*,' he shouted to his colleagues, and there was much knowledgeable nodding of heads. It was an idyllic moment, sitting at a small table outside in the sun. Time could have stood still for us, like the old boys. Gail bought grapes from a travelling van and we wrenched ourselves away, although I'm not sure why – Sicily was our objective, but could it be any better than at that moment? We did a couple of circuits of Maratea and admired a statue of Jesus Christ on the hillside, like Rio's Corvacado, before deciding that Porto di Maratea, Marina di Maratea, and other Marateas might all be the same place and so extricated ourselves. By the time we reached Amantea, the landscape had changed and become more barren. Anxious that we might not find a place to stay, we made the decision to drive the seventy miles to Palmi, where we had good information for a campground, but being reluctant to leave the beautiful coastline, stayed with it until the airport near Lamezia Terme and then joined the Autostrada. It was a shock after tootling along twisting coastal cliff roads.

There were many road works near Palmi, and exits were blocked so we had to go past then return. It was a huge disappointment to find the barrier to the site entrance down and no signs of life. Gail went over to the restaurant and emerged with a cheery man in tow. It was all,

'*No problema*,' and soon we were bumping down a rock-strewn and muddy road in the dark to follow his directions to park in the '*panoramica*' and pine woods. We soon realised we were on the edge of a cliff, but couldn't see what was below other than a few twinkling lights. There were rockpools of water on the road and the odd mossy caravan shoved under the trees, but no other motorhomers. After two hundred miles and a tiresome search for the entrance to the site I suggested we see if they would serve us in the restaurant.

'*No problema*!' Strangely, we were served in a bare back room close to the kitchen rather than the main restaurant. We chose a table but each one we selected was apparently reserved, until finally we took the one allocated – but who was coming? We opted for the dish of the day for twelve Euros.

The young chef came out to tell us that we would be having '*antipasto*, *risotto mare*, *frittata*, *pesce and insalata mixta*.' Marcello, the owner, told us his wife was Spanish and we swapped Spanish words back and forth. With things on a roll I asked,

'*Il tempo?*' (The weather?)

'*Buono. No problema.*' (Later I picked up the newspaper lying on a windowsill and saw lightning flashes predicted for the next day.) As the mushroom *antipasto* arrived and was consumed, Marcello and the chef stood at our table and waited for compliments: We nodded accordingly.

'*Ē buono.*' The *risotto mare* arrived and was consumed. Expectant faces lingered by the table.

'*Ē buono,*' we said again. The *frittata pesce* arrived and was consumed.

'*Non é buono.*'

'*No*?' Crestfallen faces. I grinned.

'*Si, é buono.*'

'Ah! You make joke!' Browsing the newspaper again the front page showed photos of police arresting a Mafia suspect.

'Very bad in Sicily, Calabria, and Naples,' Marcello explained.

'Wait a minute – we're in Calabria and going to Sicily!' I whispered to Gail. At that precise moment, three men arrived. They could not have looked more Mafia than if central casting had sent them. The chef came out and fawned over them. Giuseppe was rubbing his hands in an obsequious manner. They wanted the TV on and it was switched on. We all watched a programme about healthy eating, fruits and vegetables, and jogging and exercise in an area where the Mediterranean diet was endemic and the epitome of healthy living. Another man arrived in a leather jacket. If he had taken a gun out and shot the other three I wouldn't have been surprised. A young couple looked in, and seeing who was there, didn't stay. We paid our twenty-nine Euros and left. The other 'reserved' tables remained unoccupied. Was my imagination running riot? We stumbled our way back in the darkness, watching our backs and simultaneously trying not to trip over stones or plant our feet in the deep puddles. The next day we would be in Sicily.

Sicily: First Impressions

Stromboli and its sister islands popped up on the seaward horizon as we breakfasted in the van. With the clouds and rain fest of the previous evening, we hadn't realised they were there. Perhaps we were in for some better weather. However, we were still surrounded by large pools of accumulated pine-needle-browned rainwater in the naturally rocky surface or, where it didn't exist, a quagmire of peaty needles. In a vain attempt at keeping the van clean I tried to thread it through the worst of them in first gear, but the juddering rocks spun the wheels where they wanted to or we squelched through the pine-soaked surface.

A few minutes later we were on the SS18 driving towards Palmi in the morning traffic. Then, having seen the mud-strewn road ahead, we turned onto the Autostrada. Massive works were underway at the side of the motorway. Deep-brown earth was being clawed away by giant earth movers, rusty but hopefully trusty girders were being craned into place, and tunnels were being excavated – a discontinuum of orange, plastic-netted and protected construction and deconstruction. We caught the briefest glimpses of coastal villages below, Sicily across the Straits of Messina, the green of the mountains rising to our left, and those falling to the sea on our right. We were released onto the most impressive of arch-supported flyovers, so high it was impossible to see the bottom of the supports on the land below, before flying out to sea with no visible means of support at all, and finally entering another dank tunnel, taking the exit for Villa San Giovanni.

The road into the port has been a bone of contention for truckers for many years – it was clearly marked, but narrow and pot-holey poor, particularly under the railway bridge where trucks necessarily slowed, not sure that the marked height was sufficient for their loads and where an unforeseen bounce could make a nonsense of it. I used the opportunity, as we waited to be loaded onto the ferry, to fiddle with the seat adjusters in order to allay the continual backache I'd been experiencing. Faces of hawkers selling DVD's or Kleenex packs appeared at what they thought to be the driver's window only to find a woman laughing uncontrollably at a man alternately lying backwards as though in a carrycot or with his nose pressed against the window in a standing crouch, like one of those 'eject you up and out' chairs advertised in the *Daily Mail* along with stair lifts and incontinence pads. Further endeavours were halted by the speedy approach of a large green and white ship with its rusty loading ramp already being lowered. It clanged down on the dock and was pushed along like a giant snow plough whilst masses of black smoke emerged from the funnel as the ship was presumably slammed into reverse to avoid the inevitable collision with the dock wall. Loading was prompt and efficient, we were on the ferry (crossing one of the busiest waterways in Europe – the scene of forty-four collisions in a fifty-year period), and Sicily was in sight.

No discernible signal was given for disembarkation, but engines were soon revving and everyone working out how five lanes were going to coalesce into two with no official to indicate priorities apart from one brave soul on the ramp waving vehicles to pass each side of him. We were moving when an old man with a walking stick took his life in his hands and launched himself across the deck traffic. (We don't know whether he made it, because we were damned if that little Fiat was going to squeeze in front and bring a row of cars with him.) The Messina dodgem car circuit was not too dissimilar to Dover, except that allowances had to be made for those double parking against the flow of traffic to pop out to buy their morning paper, get their bread from the shop, chat to a friend, pull across the road ignoring all traffic signals and then pull back into traffic without a glance, or overtake when to do so was asking the impossible of St. Christopher. The Autostrada south provided mountain tunnelling par excellence, and tunnels appeared with such frequency that the GPS simply gave up. Exiting at Roccumalera for the coastal road, we were soon in a narrow high street jammed with another crowd of people going about their morning business, and taking it all in a good-humoured way – after all, why not just park in the only traffic lane, jump out and go and have a chat in the car showroom, leaving your girlfriend in the car so she can chat to the lady who's passing? No reason whatsoever not to – except that everyone else is, too!

Signage was good for the campsite at Alessio Siculo and with a friendly welcome from the young lady in the office and some negotiation on prices we were soon sited overlooking the sea and a rather grey and boring beach. It was only 11:00 a.m. but the sun was shining, we were drinking tea, and we were in Sicily. A boy stopped to talk to us through our open door. With a thick Irish accent he explained that he and his mother had been touring in their new motorhome for eight months and they had arrived in Sicily the previous night. His mother kept a journal and wanted to write a book about their travels – she had a friend who 'could put in the full stops and commas.' He cycled past us a few times and then, when we had closed up for the evening, knocked on the door to see if we would like to swap some DVDs. He was clearly bored. (We later we learnt his name was Harry and he was fourteen).

We woke to bright sunshine and revving engines somewhere in the locality. On a walk to town we passed the dusty, concrete-forming plant at the back of the campsite – massive drainpipes, public seating, washbasins, Doric columns, or soaring eagles seemed no problem. There was life at the Heaven Bar, where the older men had quaintly gathered to drink coffee, or maybe something stronger, and play cards. There was life further on at some of the smaller main street shops, and a lot of life at the open-air fishmonger, where he and his assistant vigorously swatted at the flies to keep them off his proudly displayed and freshly caught swordfish. We stopped at the coffee bar opposite for cappuccino and a *cornetto* as traffic buzzed along the main street. The seaside promenade was a brilliant piece of work running the whole length of the town, above the gravel beach and strategically placed black lava rocks, with a patterned pavement, iron railings and ornate lamps. Small, freshly-painted, pretty red, white and blue fishing boats were drawn up off the beach onto cradles with wheels to aid subsequent launch. Developments, mostly painted flats or hotels, were restrained and rarely went above the fourth floor, and the only leanings to commercialism were a few signs to pizzerias. With a clear, transparent sea, a cliff at the southern end crowned by some ruined fortifications, and further inland, the mountain backdrop dotted with small villages perched precariously on the edges, it had a picturesque panorama.

But oh, Alessio Siculo, what a difference a little effort would make! Is this the Sicilian way? Not just faded in a genteel way, but literally rusting away, the iron railings had never seen a coat of paint. Their rust had run down and penetrated the disintegrating concrete supporting them. Grey blocks of unfinished and abandoned flats pointed seawards, protective polythene sheeting blowing gently in the light breeze and rusty orange cement mixers with grass growing through their wheels parked below. Some that had been finished already showed signs of concrete rot, with gaping holes appearing on the balconies. The lamps were only on one side of the street – on the beach side cables simply poked up out of the square holes that had been cleared for them. The pavement changed patterns about three times – supplies of the diamonds or the wavy rectangles had presumably run out to be replaced with plain paving slabs. Did the situation opposite the *Police Municipali* station give a clue? What had been planned appeared to be a grand semi-circle with palms and maybe seating, or even fountains. As the patterned pavement reached the semi-circle, it stopped and dipped down to a plain concrete base, but then resumed on the other side. There was no sign of further activity to come. Perhaps the money had run out, or perhaps it had gone to fund other causes? We spotted a tourist office.

'*Autobus* timetable?'

'*Autobus ora*?'

'Si.'

'No.' On the wall by the door was an impressive map showing camping sites in Italy.

'*Ha un mappa*?' I said pointing to it.

'*Finito*.' She thrust a brochure for a hotel into Gail's hand and we left.

'There are real rally cars, trucks and tents and things, real close by. Subarus, Poojohs (sic), Mitsubishis –it's awesome,' announced a breathless young Harry arriving outside our van on his bike. 'You gotta come, I know a path.' He led us out of the site down into the dry riverbed, through a copse, and up the bank the other side. The revving engines were the result of the *Rally Taormina*, a full-blooded professional event with fire-suited and booted drivers and navigators taking instructions or posing, and race trucks with generators humming to power lighting for the crew setting up service points for their cars. On the Friday evening, chaos reigned as the cars were jacked up on ramps under their team canopies, tuned and re-tuned, and then launched, exhausts spitting and sparking, down the *lungomare* (beachside road). Although barriers had been placed to prevent interaction with local traffic, at least around the pit area, the system had failed – after all, this was Sicily. Everyone had a perfectly good reason to be there – they always came this way. It was a maze. In the half-light of the setting sun, throbbing beasts of cars accelerated in all directions with shotgun-sounding backfires. Into the maelstrom drove trucks delivering more cars, semi-official cars, friend's of friend's of official's cars, boys explaining all to their girlfriends, two trucks carrying tarmac-laying equipment, and another carrying two huge boulders for coastal defences. I saw a small and worn 'once upon a time red' Fiat Panda go round the trucks and trailers three times as the aged driver unsuccessfully sought exit, but when a snorting rally car got up his backside he gave up, pulled over, and got out, leaving it behind a trailer unloading four blue and white Poojohs. For all I know he ran off screaming. Another old gent in his three-wheeler Ape appealed to me for direction, but I was unable to help and had to give him a Sicilian shrug. The noise went on into the night and through the whole of Saturday.

On Sunday, with better weather, we were anxious to do something and decided to hike to Savoca, a mountain village about four kilometres away and three hundred metres above us. Not having any local maps, we had to keep to the tarmac road that dives under the railway and Autostrada, and then winds itself up the mountain through a series of sharp hairpins, the severity increasing as you get close to the village. With a view in all directions, a purple-flowering roadside, and mountainsides covered in fruiting prickly pears, it was delightful – until shortly into the walk, when there was suddenly a tremendous roaring and shooting noise and one of those blue and white Poojohs screeched round the corner, followed by a red Citroen. We were on the rally route. Sunday drivers out with the family were driving up and down the same road, along with men on puttering scooters, the ubiquitous three-wheeler mini-trucks struggling up the steep hill, young men with arms around their girlfriends and phones to their ears, and delivery vans anxious to finish the morning's work. As we climbed the road we jumped from one side of the road to the other so as not to be on the apex and vulnerable to a sliding rally car.

'Oh, what's happened here?' A rally car had come to a squealing, dust-raising halt, and the white-suited navigator leapt out.

'I don't believe it – he's gone for a pee in the bushes!' I said to Gail. 'Here's another following, he's going to overtake. No, he's stopped as well, they're having a chat. This is the funniest rally – some are going like hell and others like they're out on a Sunday drive!'

'Apart from the noise they're making,' Gail said grimly.

'That one's on the phone. That one's smoking a fag. That one's got his elbow resting on the window. Gees, look at that – he nearly smashed into that car coming the other way!' Gail got more anxious as we progressed to the final section near the top, as the curves were tighter and the places of safety fewer. We ran from insecure to secure and paused before checking and then running to the next point. Finally we could see a small group of spectators looking down from the village's balcony, rounded the final corner, and much relieved, headed for the garden of a delightful looking bar across the road with tables shaded under a grapevine arbour. The waiter sat nonchalantly at one of the tables waiting for some customers.

'*Due cappuccini, per favore*?'

'*Si.*' We made some phone calls home and Gail told her mother we were going to try and find the restaurant where the wedding scene from *The Godfather* was filmed. A sudden thought struck me and I turned to the waiter, now back in his chair after serving our coffee.

'*El Corleone restaurant é qui*?'

'*Si.*' We were sat in Vitelli's Bar – where the reception was filmed after Michael's wedding to Appolonia, the daughter of the padrone. Savoca was used because the village of Corleone was deemed less photogenic, and the Mafia weren't keen on the film being made there. Inside is a 1950s time warp, with a few faded photos from the film making. Opposite the balcony is a small town square with palm trees and views down the green mountain valley to the coast. Walking the old village road, two memorable events occurred.

'This is a beautiful old village, and the scenery is spectacular,' Gail remarked.

'Yes, but look! There's Etna,' I exclaimed.

'Where?'

'Over there, behind that range.'

'Fantastic! And so clear.' A snow-capped Etna could be seen clearly to the south-west – was that smoke or steam coming from it, or just passing white cloud?

'But Keith, can you hear that?' Exquisite choral music drifted across the valley from a convent or monastery on a far ridge. It was overlooked by a ruined castle on another. What a romantic place.

Searching for the Catacombs I smelt cooked food – not boiled vegetables, but seared meat. My juices were flowing. Our friend at the Vitelli Bar had closed but we found Nino and Olga's Ristorante Del Parco below the SR19. Arriving in walking shoes and rucksack got us a look of disdain from the two white-shirted, full-length black-aproned waiters, but we persevered and got a table for two (which seemed to be harder and harder to achieve as time went by) and it was interesting to see how they treated later arrivals. As most tables were set for six, those for the couples arriving were at a premium, and they got lots of shoulder shrugging and were shoved off to some other place outside the main restaurant. That is, until one couple arrived – when the whole thing suddenly went into reverse. 'She of the young blonde' and 'He of the Mr Hunk and dark glasses' were ushered to a table for six and the waiter sat with them, ignoring all pleas from his colleague that food was ready to be delivered. The owner came over and was about to deliver a basket of bread from the antique table by the door that had previously held ours when he realised (as we had) that it was stale, so went to the kitchen to cut up a fresh loaf, and served it personally. Gail (who was able to observe activities in that direction) noted that they were having 'mountains of food'. To infer that they were being fawned over would be correct. We watched in amusement as more late arrivals in twos then continued to be excluded. We enjoyed our meal (mussels for Gail and a mixed grill for me), that together with a salad and chips and a glass of beer and coke came to twenty-four Euros – inclusive of cover charge and stale bread. It was an honour to have been served.

By the time we came out, the Catacombs (which contain thirty-two ancient mummified monks) were closed (or had yet to re-open, or weren't going to open). As the rally continued, the walk down proved as equally challenging as the way up. We dodged from one side to the other, hid behind barriers, and ran for unfenced openings. When two ordinary cars stopped side by side in the road to have a chat below us on a blind hairpin bend, I couldn't believe it! A rally car was coming down on full throttle, and a collision inevitable. I frantically waved him down and he screeched to a stop on their bumpers and then tried to overtake them as they started off and another car came round the bend up the hill. Four cars were trying to fit on a road for two, but being in Italy, somehow it sorted itself. There was a near miss on another corner, and then a whole cavalcade of rally cars mixed with ordinary cars and an ambulance, blue lights flashing, appeared and charged down the hill as though joined together.

'This rally is crazy,' I said. 'What on earth sort of rally runs on narrow hairpin mountain roads along with the normal Sunday traffic and young guys who think they'd like to be rally drivers? I think it's some sort of timed event – you have to arrive within a certain time window – but then you get someone in one of those three-wheeler Apes and he could blow your chances. In fact, you could arrange that so as to ruin your competitor's lot!' We laughed, and an old boy on a scooter experiencing a serious shortage of hill-climbing ability stopped next to us to give the engine a breather. A box on the back carried a large plant that dangled into his face. We tried to communicate, but without luck, and as soon as his scooter had recovered he set off again, blowing blue smoke.

We were glad to get back to the van where Alison, Harry's Mum, told us she was bored with the site and would leave in the morning.

'If God exists, why did he create mosquitoes? Give me one good reason,' I asked as we spent the first part of our evening attacking the little blighters. 'Did you see the blood in that one when I squashed it? Got that from somewhere – I hope it's not mine.'

Peering out of the van in the morning, we were conscious of new neighbours across from us with a white Sprinter van, a small yellow tent, a young child, and a baby that Gail was woken by in the night. Our original neighbour, also across from us, had parked with the front of his car tight against my rear doors. Probably peeved that his normal spot had been taken by the new arrivals, he thought he'd share his upset with someone else and succeeded. We decided to leave along with Alison and Harry, who were going to drive up to Savoca to see 'the mummies.' Harry, however, had yet to rise so Alison manoeuvred her van alone whilst Harry slept in the upper bed. Our target was Taormina, the medieval hill village about thirteen kilometres south along the coast and 'Sicily's best-known resort,' where the Greco-Roman Theatre with Mount Etna as a backdrop had entranced D.H. Lawrence and Goethe. The approach road itself was a construction marvel, with hairpin bends and flyovers curving over the hillside and back again. The village hung from the cliff top, and higher still another (Castelmola) looked even more precariously perched on a crag. At the top of our road was a subterranean car park that we knew we couldn't get into, but were hopeful of the open area in front of it where a number of non-motorhome vans were parked.

'Oh no, we're getting the official finger,' I said as an auburn haired, black puffa-jacketed lady walked towards us wagging her finger side to side.

'No parking.'

'*Dové*?'(Where?)

'*Il Mare*,' she suggested, with a 'couldn't care less, just doing my job' shrug.

'What's she saying?' asked Gail.

'Wants us to park in the sea,' I replied.

'I'm sure she doesn't.' We turned round and examined the flying flyovers from another viewpoint before we reached the coast road and headed for the *Funiculare* (cable car) station to find that the parking also excluded motorhomes. We continued further along the road, hoping to approach Taormina from another angle, but on turning up a promising hill found a red-circle sign banning motorhomes. I did a three-point turn and descended again, unsure what to do.

'I'm going to the cable-car station to plead with them. If we pay for the ride, surely they'll let us park?' I said, exasperated. We parked, and in a mood to do battle I marched off to the ticket office, but soon returned. 'It's closed. There may be a bus down on the main road but it looks like the next one isn't for another hour. Let's go for a coffee – I've seen a cheap little place. At least we know we'll get what we want there!' The old lady was hardly discernible sitting below the counter, but she soon swung into action as we walked in.

'*Due cappuccini, per favore*.' She came out to the little pavement table with a tray and two of the hottest coffees we'd ever experienced, and watched over us, her only customers, like a grandmother would her favourite grandchildren.

'This is hot, you'll need to let it cool,' advised Gail about the same moment as a bus pulled into where we had parked the van.

'Bugger! He's just pulled out again.' We finished the coffees as fast as we could. 'Look, a minibus has just pulled in – he's dropping off some tourists and might give us a lift. I'm off. Pay for the coffees.' Gail appeared five minutes later.

'What's happening?'

'They've also realised the cable-car is closed and have all got back in the bus.'

'Guess how much the coffees were?'

'A Euro each?'

'Five Euros for both.'

'Blimey, she saw us coming!' A taxi pulled in and six minutes and fifteen Euros later we were at the tourist office of the motorhome-hating village.

It had been worth it. Taormina was enchanting, smart, and more like a Provencal village. The main street, Corso Umberto, is a succession of smart shops housed in ornate palaces. Each shop (and they are mostly clothing or jewellery) is an Italian lesson in how to display goods in such a subtle way that everyone will marvel, but non-purchasing sightseers will pass by – 'please don't enter unless you have the money'. I was fascinated by a shop selling large, colourful confectionary fruits and other items (including a plate of fried eggs), which I assume were made out of marzipan. The detail was amazing and on the shelves above were delicious, mouth-watering nougats and pistachio pastries. Each side street had inviting panoplies of beautifully laid and 'come eat here' restaurant tables perched on ascending or descending steps or hidden in a shady corner, the large number of tempting restaurants a testimony to the crowds that must besiege the place in peak season. However, being a Monday, trade was slight and waiters and owners stood outside hoping to catch the attention of the passing American and German tourists. The street eventually opens up at the glistening-white Piazza 1X Aprile, where there are sun-drenched sit-out eateries, a balcony view down to the sea, and west to a white, fluffy-cloud-swirled Etna. The street continues further to the Piazza Duomo, and along the way we found an Internet shop. After we had handed over the obligatory identification and descended to the cellar the lights cut out and that was the temporary end to our communications. The Teatro Greco was a joy and a disappointment. The backdrop view to the coast and Etna across the stage was quite stunning, but diminished by the workmen hammering hardboard for a forthcoming performance. After Internetting, we decided to walk down past the bus terminal, and discovered a delightful set of flower-bedecked stone steps running the whole way to the coast road and affording fantastic views of the crystal-clear waters, rocky outcrops, and beaches. It was unmarked at the top, but at the bottom, to the west of the cable-car station, enthusiastically signed '*Taormina*'. I was glad we had walked down rather than up.

Back at the van we found Alison and Harry's van next to us, and I left a note about our plans. We decided to head for Etna and the campsite at Nicolosi via the Autostrada. As we climbed away from the motorway we joked about Etna and the possibilities of an eruption when, coincidentally, there was a lot of smoke about and a fire engine appeared behind me, blue lights flashing and siren sounding.

'You don't think?'

'Surely not.' Camping Etna was deep in gloom beneath the tall pines and after the hot sun of the day, shockingly cold. The black, lava-grit sand gets everywhere. A small, non-descript guy, his face wrapped in a puffa-jacket hood, eventually answered the buzzer and looked at us in our T-shirts like we had come from outer space. A discount negotiated, we set up for the night. A text from Alison and Harry asked about the site and later, that they had decided to stay in the car park at the cable-car station.

Etna

Soon after we had crunched our way out of the campground and set off for Etna Sud we were in awe of Etna. Extraordinary Etna. I'm not sure what we expected, but it was exceeded. Through the foggy, damp, low cloud mist that had descended overnight all we could see on each side of the road and over the lava-brick walls were fields of crystalline black lava. In some places rock grasses had managed to get a hold or there was an occasional derelict and broken building, but mainly it was great boulders trapped in huge black slag heaps. The cloud drifted across like steam emanating from the blackened surface, obscuring any views to the coast below or of Etna's peaks above but creating a surreal lunar landscape. We were the only vehicle making the ascent and it was exciting, but concerning. All that we were seeing had been spewed out of the still-active volcano above us. The awesome power of nature smacks you in the face and leaves you momentarily breathless and thoughtful. What we were viewing was so different, but not necessarily permanent – it could change in a moment. What remarkable power could push these masses so far? The volume of material spewed out was immense – in the last eruption in 2002-2003 a five kilometre long lava flow had run down the southern slopes to Catania, twelve kilometres away, and covered it in a fifteen centimetre ash deposit. We climbed higher into the clouds – would we ever see Etna?

When we arrived in the Refugio Sapienza car park it was enveloped by cloud. A roly-poly guy dressed for arctic work pointed out where to park and when I got out I realised how sensibly dressed he was – it was freezing cold. He asked for a 'donation' for the parking service.

'What is normal?' I asked.

'Fifty million Euro.' We hovered between the café and ticket office, but decided on the latter, where we were told the cable car wasn't running and the only option was a 'jeep' ride at forty-eight Euros each. It seemed a bit steep (no pun intended), so we moved to go to the café with the intention of discussing it.

'What time is the next one?' I asked as we turned to leave.

'Now, or ten-thirty.' Ninety-six Euros and three minutes later we were boarding a 4x4 vehicle to join a group of about a dozen middle-aged Italians on a day trip. When I saw the vehicle I knew it would be worth it: a Unimog, one of my unrelinquished desires – the ultimate Mercedes 4x4 Dakar Rally support vehicle. We set off up what I imagine a South Wales slagheap would be like. We tipped round bends, bounced over ruts, climbed precipitously and occasionally dropped steeply on the way up the lava mountain, but the Unimog never faltered in its pace.

'Have you seen the smile on your face? Now will you look out of the window? You're missing everything!'

'But you can't see anything with this cloud.' We did see a man working alone on the cable car. Was the cloud lifting? No, we still couldn't see Etna's peak. The Unimog climbed continuously over the lava, weaving round hairpin bends where the track was marked with poles to avoid black rocky outcrops. Then, without warning, as though it was a plane taking off, it broke through the cloud to a clear blue, untainted sky. Etna's peak was now visible, and excitingly, smoke issued from below it. Everyone had seen it – then a big plume occurred.

'Oooooh!' exclaimed all in nervous unison. We passed two snow-covered peaks, and still we climbed, tipping over slightly on a particularly sharp bend, dipping down, and then climbing powerfully up the hill.

'Doesn't that engine sound great?' Then we were on a black, lava-crystalline sand plateau and pulled up next to a boarded-up hut at the base of the smoking peak. As we descended from the jeep I felt we had arrived somewhere very different. It was a monochrome of black ash and white snowfields. White-grey clouds rolled past below us, and above it all was an intense blue sky. Surreal lunar landscape doesn't do it justice – indeed, it is hard to find the superlatives that do.

The guide explained the various peaks and showed us an excavated roof of a building that had been completely covered in the last eruption – steam still issued from the bedroom windows. We walked to craters that had spewed out ninety million tonnes of material when they erupted, and were still smoking. I realised that not only had the chill gone from my feet, but they were warming up. We saw the yellow sulphurous trail where the eruption had run down the mountain towards the towns and villages below. Competition winning photos were available in every direction. It was beyond imagination, and I envisaged that walking on the moon probably wasn't too different. Why had it just suffered some cratering and not imploded? As we moved away through the snow, the cold became bitter again. A lady in front, dressed more for a Sunday outing than our fleece, anorak, glove, and walking-shoe combination, was paralysed on the frozen snowfield so I grabbed her elbow to prevent her from slipping. (She should have paid attention to the instructions from Gruppo Guide Alpine Etna Sud who 'do not guarantee for the safety of people who do not have *haking-shoes.*') Finally, satiated but reluctant to end the experience, we were back on the jeep and bouncing controllably down again. We passed a brave, lone soul walking up. The Italians, relieved that nothing untoward had happened, broke out into Boy-Scout type songs, led by the startlingly red-haired lady at the front. Although initially she engendered only a low-key response, as we neared the starting point the relief was overwhelming and everyone joined in the clapping and laughing, until finally a huge *applausa per guida Franco* erupted.

We found Alison and Harry parked next to us on our return.

'Was there fire and flames?' asked young Harry. 'Was the lava pouring out, could you walk round the rim and look down inside?'

'No, there's smoke and steam and it's hot under your feet, but you can't go up to the active rim.'

'Oh.' And, after a momentary pause. 'Do you think you could do it by yourself, or pay them to let you go?'

'I don't think so – but there was someone walking up the jeep road.'

'Mum, we could do that it if we wanted!'

'Yes, Harry.'

We left Alison with the difficult task of satisfying Harry's continual questions and wild imagination and drove east towards Zafferana Etnea, into a welcome clear patch of blue sky that changed five minutes later into something out of a horror movie. With mist swirling just above us, the narrow and deserted mountain road took on an ethereal quality in the strange light. Gritty black lava had been blown over the perfunctory lava-brick walls to partially cover the sides of the lighter-coloured road as though the tarmac crew hadn't cleared up. To our left, the barren black mountain with occasional brown grasses that had managed to root themselves in oval mounds disappeared up through the cloud. To our right a lava plateau with more grass mounds, lava rocks and a rare bush gave way to occasional glimpses of distant ridges and small peaks between the dark clouds steaming up from the surface. Further descent led us into pine forests, dense clouds, and rain – like some primeval forest scene, until worsening visibility and hairpin bends forced us to use dipped headlight and wipers. Entering Zafferana Etnea brought some relief, revealing what to me was akin to a northern UK industrial town, where the buildings are made of large stone bricks that have since blackened (but in this case were black to begin with). The continuing rain seemed appropriate.

We spotted a sign to a supermarket – it was an 'ARD' on Via Alcide de Gasperi, the same chain that we used in Alessio Siculo, and timely for us to stock up. As we drove out up Via Roma we saw that every lamppost had a basket with abundant yellow flowers in full bloom. The town of Zafferana Etnea was not a typical Sicilian town (at least not of those we had seen thus far) and was taking a pride in itself. It was smart and the buildings and piazza were impressive. We were tempted to stop but continuing rain was a suppressant, so we found the intended campsite at Milo, where Stephania kindly came from the restaurant in the pouring rain to open the gate and make us feel like we were her only guests (which we were). Our spot was in a copse below vine-covered hillsides that on another day would have been delightful. We stayed in the van – the rain was unrelenting.

Waking to clear skies, we decided to drive the road that circumnavigates the perimeter of Etna's base. It criss-crosses the small tourist railway (aptly named the Circumetnea) that does the same one hundred and fourteen kilometres, and has often been ruptured by lava flows, which adds to the excitement. A wrong turn took us away from the more northern access area at Refugio Citelli and along the lower slope towards Linguaglossa. With a clear view of Etna above on our left we passed through an occasional small, bleak hamlet, with depressing tumbledown black stone houses, small old cars and tiny wizened people dressed in black doing menial tasks. Linguaglossa was a concentration of black stone buildings and jarring black stone sets in the road and did not entice us to stay. Beyond, there was open country, but more tumbledown buildings of grey-black lava stone with lava grit everywhere. Eventually vineyards started to spring up each side of the road – many terraced into the lava, and the north face of Etna had more snow than we had seen before. The little railway line competed with us for the route, first one side and then crossing to the other. We had hoped Randazzo would bring something of interest but looking down on it, we saw a gloomy grey town built of lava. Even as we entered we were uninspired to explore its 'dingily authentic streets', however, a 'Post Office' sign caught our eye so we followed in the direction indicated round block after block to a point where there were simply no more signs. Unsure of what to do next, I pulled into a small car park in front of some shops.

'Well, I think we've missed a sign somewhere,' I said, switching the engine off.

'I don't know how we could have – I was looking out all the time.' (It was one of those many 'map, GPS, route selection discussions' between driver and navigator with a hundred hidden agendas.)

'All this hassle for a couple of stamps.'

'Well, there's a SPAR supermarket at the end of the road and we need some breakfast cereal, so at least we won't have wasted our time,' said Gail, seeking salvation. 'It's across the road – that huge grey concrete building – we're parked outside,' she said on her return. As she went to get the stamps I kept an eye on the van, but couldn't help looking in the window of the car dealer behind. The young salesman, seeing me peering through his window, went into overdrive and opened the door of the showroom.

'*Prego. Prego.*' I spent the next ten minutes being shown a beautiful new, white, baby Fiat Cinquecento. When Gail returned from getting the *francoboli* I took her in. The poor lad must have thought a sale was imminent. Gail, with apologies to Boris (our existing small white car) loved it, and sat behind the wheel as she tried it for size.

Climbing beyond Randazzo, we passed through lots of olive groves, but the topography apart from the constant presence of Etna was unexciting. When we got to Bronte, we hoped with the historical links to Nelson (in 1799 King Ferdinand bestowed ducal estates on him as a thank-you for English help saving the Bourbon monarchy from Napoleonic revolt) for something of interest, but it was intensely busy with traffic, and again, somewhat gloomy. Only when I spotted a slot being vacated outside a café-bar and swooped in, did we change our minds. At an ultra-modern bar with restaurant behind, and adjacent to a new park overlooking a valley, we sat in the sun and indulged in coffees and a gorgeous pistachio-filled *cornetto* for me as we watched near-accidents occurring in the road outside. (Bronte apparently produces 85 percent of Italy's pistachio nuts).

We completed the rest of the circular tour via a giant new Carrefour at Etnapolis shopping centre and an ERG fuel station near Paterno (where we hoped to find a *sosta* but it didn't exist and had probably been replaced by bays of a car wash of sufficient height for a tall camper van). A good wash later we set off for Catania, Sicily's second-largest city, and despite the mayhem of traffic, managed to negotiate our way smoothly and without incident to Camping Jonio on the sea at Ognina, where Alison and Harry were already parked.

Catania and Caltagirone

The bus stop for Catania *Centro* was outside a small parade of shops opposite Ognina port. While waiting for the bus in the morning sun we entertained ourselves guessing which of the many hair-raising driving manoeuvres would cause an accident, and watching a prostitute soliciting the city-bound traffic. The orange 535 arrived and we and the prostitute (no business) boarded. As it moved into Catania, it soon filled up and there was only standing room available. We were unsure of which way it would go.

'Can you see where we are on the map?' I asked Gail. The lady opposite our seat asked us something that we supposed was where we were going.

'To the cathedral,' we chorused in reply. She proceeded to try and explain to us where to get off, but the man next to her interrupted and obviously had a different opinion, as did the young girl standing between the seats, as well as the man alongside her and the woman behind him – and soon we were an irrelevance as the whole bus began an active discussion as to the best plan for us. There appeared to be as many best plans as people discussing them, and the volume of sound increased worryingly. Just when I thought that violence was imminent, everyone burst out laughing and the young girl in the aisle explained, as best she could (and with much pointing from those close by), that the lady who had been the first to speak to us was going to the right stop so we should simply get off with her.

There was an anticlimactic silence, broken only by a woman mouthing-off whilst pushing roughly through those jammed in the aisle. Standing by Gail, she continued her tirade and appeared to be complaining about something. A Neanderthal lady and her husband were sat a couple of seats down and I noted her already ruddy features increasing in redness. She tolerated the abuse for a few more minutes and when she could no longer contain herself any further, she launched a verbal onslaught. Once more opinions started flying from one side to the other, but the complainant was unrelenting until the toothless man opposite us spoke directly to her and she suddenly stopped.

'What do you think happened there?' whispered Gail.

'I think the woman was complaining that she was ill and going to hospital and yet no-one had given her a seat.'

'What did the man opposite say?'

'That if she knew she was that ill, she should have used a taxi.' It's great to speculate when you know nothing.

The bus turned away from the port down Corso Italia. We knew it was Corso Italia because those around us told us many times over. The toothless man got out to be replaced by one with a full set of dentures, then we passed Bellini gardens, and then Bellini's statue (we knew because the dentured man had turned into a speaking information point). The young lady in the aisle got off at the university, which she told us was beautiful, but reassured us that we should stick with the lady opposite. What a busy route – there were mass movements on and off. The lady opposite finally rose and indicated we should follow.

'*La proxima fermata.*' A short walk later, we were in the Cathedral Square. On one side is the *Municipio* (Town Hall) and in front, and blocking views of the elephant fountain, was an extraordinary display of dustcarts ranging from rubbish-munching monsters to tiny Ape three-wheelers for the narrow backstreets. The operatives in their orange, green and silver day-glo boiler suits were all milling about, and more and more trucks were entering. It was a strike, a demo, and the *Carabinieri* were there to keep order, although they just congregated in the doorway to the *Municipio* protecting each other but looking cool in their sunglasses, crisp dark-blue uniforms and white leather belts shining brightly in the morning sunshine.

We set off to the south of the square to find the open-air market that we'd heard so much about. It was in full swing. The first part we came to was down some steps in a small square of its own and wholly for fish. Each stall comprised a weighing machine and boxes of fish stood on bright blue, bucket-like containers. The men serving were uniformly dressed in jeans and anoraks – the only variation being the headdress of hood-up, beanie hat, or baseball cap. All wore sunglasses and shouted their wares as they traded insults and jokes with their neighbours while other men stood around conspiratorially in groups. It was noisy, busy, and wet underfoot as stallholders continually splashed water over the displays of fish to make them glisten as though they had just been unloaded from the boat. The area seemed to be devoted to smaller fish and shellfish, with bigger fish being sold on stalls in arches under the railway. Back under the arches and around to the right was a rabbit warren of narrow streets of dilapidated balconied buildings. Jammed into these were bigger stalls with awnings and cave-like storage in the buildings behind. Because of the intense competition, every man was shouting his wares or joshing with competitors or passers-by. Fish, meat, vegetables, fruit, and cheeses of many varieties were available. Men with bare hands and axes wielded them freely, hacking off chunks of tuna and swordfish or hunks of meat from animal carcasses hanging in the refrigerated rooms behind the stalls. Others stripped leaves or trimmed vegetables to lay them out in impressive displays, or cut black, spiky sea urchins open, scooping out the orange flesh with a teaspoon, or de-bearded mounds of mussels. Things in buckets of water wriggled and blew bubbles, ugly fish stared back at you, amazed at being caught, and large, undulating animal entrails and stomach linings were being hung, stretched, stripped and sliced. We peered at what appeared to be goats severed perfectly in half from head to toe (wondering at the accompanying *castrato* at three Euros a kilogram), and at an unknown, black type of cake that was apparently made from the prickly pear cactus. Every stallholder was a tanned, swarthy, hard-working, not to be tangled with, boisterous, bargaining, money-making, skilled artisan – a readymade extra for a Hollywood Blockbuster follow-up to *The Godfather*.

Back into the main street, and hurrying back to the Duomo, we found the police had sealed off the surrounding streets to encourage a flow of traffic away from the demo in the square. But the opposite had happened. Cars were centimetres from each other across junctions, two police cars were trapped, everyone had tried every angle to get through, no-one was willing to give way, there was shouting and cursing, and horns were permanently sounding. Scooter riders squeezed between cars up kerbs, along pavements, and down steps. A dustcart forced its way along a side street in an attempt to get to the demo – sympathetic drivers giving it room. The policeman on point duty waved him away, but the truck drove on and the policeman had to leap aside. To save face, he chose to take it out on a car driver who tried to follow the truck.

The Duomo's grey and white façade is a complex and ornate Baroque style incorporating, on two levels, granite columns from Catania's Roman amphitheatre. We gained entrance through the main door only to be ushered out through the side door as it was closing for lunch. Wandering off to the north-east with the same thoughts of food, we ended up in another square with a huge market selling fruit and vegetables, clothes, sunglasses, handbags, and household goods. It was populated by many Chinese and African stallholders with good value eateries in the vicinity. After lunch we covered other attractions highlighted in our guidebook, but only the church of San Nícolò, the biggest church in Sicily, is worth noting. It was a nightmare of an unfinished façade, with columns stopping half way up, lower oval and higher rectangular windows unfinished, holes in the stained concrete brickwork like it had been used for shooting practice, weeds growing out of the roof, dark-green doors with peeling paint, and bizarrely, on top it looked like an unrelated, black, round, turreted mini castle had been dropped on it by helicopter. The unfinished building defied explanation, and my immediate thought was that it epitomised Sicily. In the scruffy square below and on the church steps sat similarly scruffy bearded students, dressed 'Bob Dylan 1960s style' and strumming guitars. Despite being ugly and unfinished (it had undergone a partial restoration in the eighteenth century), there was a functioning interior. At a table in the entrance sat three men looking more like nightclub bouncers than church wardens, but they waved us in, pleased that anyone should be interested enough. Alone inside, we found the interior to be a vast, barren, crumbling, unfinished nothingness.

After an evening trying to come to grips with the Wi-Fi Internet system at Camping Jonio and finally overcoming it the next morning by sitting outside the restaurant in the rain (don't ask) and sending photographs home, we decided to leave. Fearing Catania traffic, we used the computer to get a route and followed it slavishly with the GPS out of the city, being forced through red lights by incessant horns behind and, frighteningly, five kilometres back along a motorway bound for Catania before turning in the right direction on the S417 to Caltagirone. The rain started once more, and intensified from intermittent, to steady, to thrashing wipers and a miasma of poor visibility. Mud rivers flowed across the road from gateways and side roads, and the spray from the frequent heavy trucks came over as inundations of soaking brown filth. The poor road surface gave rise to deep, water-filled craters, and I wished I had the water-wading vehicle I had considered buying in moments of 4x4 euphoria. Slowly the mountains started to appear through the mist, but retained a shroud of dark clouds. A large tanker aircraft circled low in the sky and then dipped even lower, disappearing from sight as though going in to land, although no airfield was marked on the map. In fact, very little was marked on the map. Infrequently, small barns and dwellings were visible through the mist, giving a semblance of Tuscany without the cypress trees, but it felt remote. It was, therefore, surprising to come across a couple of ladies sitting roadside at a table sheltering under a colourful parasol. I thought they might be selling fruit and asked Gail whether we needed to buy any, but after passing a couple more, it dawned on us that these 'ladies' were selling fruit of a different kind. (Why this remote section had become a red-light district was not apparent, apart from speculating that as a truck route it was far enough from base and destination to be discreet.) In that rain, you had to admire their determination.

As we got closer to Caltagirone, the computer took us off the road to an even smaller country road, which had become a major river with filthy tributaries emptying in from the side. We saw Caltagirone rising up on a peak: a collection of neat, yellow stone buildings surmounted by a profusion of church bell towers and domes – and how grand it looked. We started climbing up round hairpin bends, the town off to our right.

'Oh no,' said Gail, seeing that we had entered a nightmare situation. A normally charming, black-lava brick street of tall, balconied buildings that disappeared skyward to nearly touch at the top was only wide enough for an ancient handcart or a modern-day Fiat Cinquecento to squeeze through. 'Shall I get out and watch you through?' asked Gail, controlling her stress.

'You won't be able to – there isn't enough room to open the door. Can you get your head out of the window to check the clearance on those balconies? I'm not sure we can do it.' Not only were the rusty-iron balconies on each side close to each other, they were also close to our roof, and washing lines ran between them, potted plants and kid's bikes adorned them, and satellite dishes pointed hopefully to the thin, high-altitude slit of sky between the tops of the buildings (although how these worked in that cavern escaped me.) As we proceeded, the road took a dogleg turn to the right and narrowed again. If the first section had been a challenge, this was an Olympic qualifier. We emerged into a square fronted by a church, and set off into more of the unknown, the GPS being unable to get a reading because of the overhangs. Navigational tempers somewhat frayed, we found a brown sign with a motorhome on it pointing up another narrow and very steep street.

'Please don't go up there,' pleaded Gail.

'I don't think they mean up there – it's one of those signs that look like it points one way but means straight ahead on this Circumnavazione.' After a couple more U-turns and increasing stress, we finally turned into Parking San Giovanni – a tarmac area on the edge of Caltagirone with a park around it and views across a steep valley to a mountain ridge in the distance beyond. There was one other motorhome there which didn't look as though it was in use, a gridded dump, and a water tap. After a quick lunch we sought relief in our own ways – Gail walked into town, and now that it had stopped raining, I washed the filth off the van.

I was drying off the last bit as the rain predictably restarted, and Gail returned full of enthusiasm for the town.

'It's fantastic.' We had recovered. It had been our intention to go on to Villa Romana del Casale near Piazza Armerina, but we now had something else to look forward to visiting the next day – a discovery, as there was nothing in our guidebook. As we sat up in the evening congratulating ourselves on being economically independent of Jonio's fees, yet having water, waste facilities and pleasant views, two cars pulled into the park behind us and mounted a semi-circular area raised for seating at the end of the park. Young kids jumped out and it was hard to make out what they were doing, but there was a lot of shouting. A small white car pulled in opposite to us and parked. There was a flicker of flame from inside.

'They're doing drugs,' I said to Gail. 'Maybe this isn't such a good area – we'd better get ready to leave if we have to.' Another dark car parked immediately in front of us. I opened the blinds and it moved off. We packed everything away, turned the seats ready to drive, turned all the lights off, and peered out of the small rear bathroom window at the two cars still up on the mount.

'They're dancing!'

'It's just the boys in some sort of group dance making an exhibition of themselves in front of the girls.' After a bit more showing off and some fancy reversing, they finally left and we slept restlessly after a long and fraught day.

There were no further incidents in the night, and early the next morning (and despite the continuing rain), an orange day-glo cleaner man arrived in his little three-wheeler truck and set about sweeping up with his witches broom. Impressed by this civic pride, we realised that there had been a surprising accumulation of detritus overnight, that we eventually deduced came from the other cars that had parked for a while – not druggies, but lovers. Gail was keen to show me what she had discovered the day before, and by 11:30 a.m. I was bored with the rain. Walking up the street to the town centre we peered into the small shops, many just a doorway to a cavern behind. In one, a balding man in a white coat and pince-nez glasses perched on the end of his nose worked at close quarters on a piece of clay. Seeing us, he beckoned to us. He was sculpting a nativity scene, a vertical piece of intricate detail. The dusty workshop was full of other pieces – most were complete and in a modern style that we appreciated. This kindly man, speaking no English, showed us round, trying to explain each sculpture. Major works had been commissioned by the Hotel Nettuno in Catania, and he had done work for International Airports and major churches. I spotted a curled up card pinned on a board – *Professore Luigi Angelico.*

'*Un Professore*?'

'*Universita* for design.' The Professor clearly loved what he was doing, and was proud to be continuing a tradition based on four thousand years of local artistry. Caltagirone means 'Hill or Rock of Vases' and it had become the main centre for ceramics in Sicily. Continuing up the street, every third window was a shop or workshop selling ornate and colourful yellow and blue vases and figurines. If we'd had a bigger van a piece may have found its way to our lounge.

The Piazza Municipio was buzzing with teenagers and the obligatory contingent of old men. Local police stood around watching the goings-on. The Information Bureau housed in the Senatorial Palace has to be the one of the most impressive encountered. Once we had mounted the imposing steps (more teenagers squatting) and passed through one of the many modern glass doors, we entered a vast station-style auditorium. It had a café-bar with modern lounge style seating (more teenagers) and huge wall and ceiling murals. The rest was given over to exhibits of ceramic works and we were pleased to see our Professor well represented there. We were given such a huge volume of leaflets about Caltagirone by the girls at the small information desk you got the impression they had quotas to catch up on.

We entered a cave of a shop selling magazines and various other items. It was jammed full with five other shoppers. All conversation stopped for us and we were pressed to the counter so that everyone could see what we were going to buy. All I wanted was a new pocket notebook, although we couldn't see any amongst the stuff squashed onto the shelves. I produced the red, ringed-back one I had filled.

'*Lo mismo, per favore*?' The man behind the counter was keen to show his local customers that there was no challenge he couldn't overcome when dealing internationally. He found a child's exercise book and it had the little squares that I find so useful.

'*No. Troppo grande.*' A smaller one appeared from somewhere, but it was still too big.

'*No. Troppo grande.*' I took the existing red one and shoved it demonstrably into my trouser side pocket (I like to have a notebook with me for memory jogging later). The audience, silent up to now as they watched the proceedings, broke out into immediate discussion and pointing, and you could imagine what they were saying: 'See, that's what he wants – why try and give him those big ones!'

He burrowed away on a different and even untidier shelf and triumphantly produced a small pad of chequered paper stapled together with a simple cover. I could hardly refuse and disappoint him. But there was a ritual to adhere to.

'*Quanta costa*?'

'*Quaranta centimos.*' Not the time for negotiation then, at less than thirty pence, so I paid up and he smiled proudly.

'*Prego, prego.*' We turned to the others and made a great play of excusing ourselves for jumping the queue.

'*Prego, prego,*' they chorused, delighted at something out of the ordinary occurring.

'*Arrivederci.*'

'*Ciao. Ciao.*' We continued on Gail's tour of the town. The teenagers, I noted, were all in hoodies like me so I felt fashionable, but couldn't extend it to the low-slung, torn and underpants-exposing jeans. Haircuts were of the mullet variety with long and pointed sideburns. The uniformity was amazing, suggesting that one barber had the trend monopoly. The girls were in tight-fitting jeans, boots, and anoraks, but despite the cold always managed to show a bare midriff and their upper hips.

The ornamental gardens linked the old and new towns. A beggar approached us, hand outstretched. We encountered fewer beggars than we see begging in London, but they are more direct. They don't sit around – they make a direct approach, moving along the street or traffic at a junction, occasionally at the entrance to a church, with hand outstretched or hands together as though praying, asking for aid but without any form of aggression. Only in Siracusa did we see a sitting beggar with a dog (and he didn't look Italian). Being the ceramics capital we felt obliged to visit the Ceramics Museum, and it helped us get out of the rain. Frankly, I rarely get enthused about vast amounts of pottery bits, even when representing an extraordinary history. The information in English, although welcome, lacked logicality and the room plan was confusing, so by the time we got to the potter's wheel it provided an inordinate amount of interest as to its workings. Why did they sit sideways, and why no treadle? We decided they must have simply shoved the lower wheel round with their feet, the spindle rising to directly turn the working platform. It must have taken great skill to maintain a steady speed.

Caltagirone has many buildings worth viewing, but its major attraction is the one hundred and forty-two steps of Santa Maria del Monte, rising forty-five metres from the 'new town' to the highest part of the old town on the original hill, and clustered round the Arab-Hohenstaufen castle. Each step is decorated with different hand-painted ceramics. We climbed to the top of the town for a view over the many cupolas and the many grey or blue rooftop water tanks.

Mosaics and Enna

The following day started brightly and we decided on a day trip to visit Villa Romana near Piazza Armerina via San Michele di Ganzaria. As we hit the hilltop leaving Caltagirone, a wonderful panorama opened up, a Tuscan expanse of rolling, sparsely-populated hills of finely ploughed fields, fruit trees, and even, neat rows of prickly pear cactus plantations. Piazza Armerina appeared impressively on a hill to the right, crowned by a domed church that rose majestically above the surrounding, close-knit buildings. When we finally arrived in the car park, we were surprised at how few cars were there, as a report from a previous visitor said they had camped overnight to avoid the huge numbers of visitors arriving early by tourist coach. We relaxed and made coffee in the van, there being no facility open.

Villa Romana del Casale dates from the early fourth century BC (but built on the site of an earlier farm) and was used up until the twelfth century, when a mudslide kept it covered until excavated in the 1950s. It is on a scale and level of luxury without parallel in the Roman Empire, and ingeniously displayed with walkways and Perspex panels so that whilst the mosaics are protected, they are, for the most part, visible. The building, possibly a Roman hunting lodge but often described as a palace, was possibly owned by Maximinianus, co-emperor with Diocletian, and is impressive in its own right. It must have been sensational in its day. The mosaics are unbelievably good in their completeness, size, colours, and even humour. Every imposing room has a mosaic floor with rich hunting scenes, animals, personalities, children playing hunting, and girls in Roman 'bikinis' taking part in gymnastics. If I say that one hunting scene is sixty metres long and encompasses warriors, elephants, lions, tigers, ostriches, and a rhino, you may be able to envision the scale of this remarkable exhibit. The engineering of water collection and distribution is a wonder. It must have been a delight to live there, and little imagination is needed to picture the Romans in-situ.

Returning to Caltagirone, there was a battle between a weakening sun and dark rain clouds. The latter appeared to be winning. In the dark we heard a car drew up nearby. What were they doing – harmless visitors, or up to no good? Anxiety and feelings of insecurity often go together with wild or *sosta* camping. Unexplained noises mid-evening followed by a lot of male voices shouting and yelling in front of our van set me off. I desperately peered through our misted-up front window, struggling to see what was happening, but could make out no more than the red glow from a car's rear lights diffusing through the steamy screen. I was reluctant to do anything that drew attention to us like switching on the headlights. More yelling occurred and the car sped away. What had been happening? I made sure all our preventative measures were in place – it was so easy to become paranoid. Other cars drove in from time to time and parked quietly and discreetly, the occupants trying not to draw attention to themselves, but we knew what they were up to. There were no further events in the night, or rather, none that caused us to wake!

The following morning the heavy cloud had lifted and we had clear views across the valley to the distant ridge. Caltagirone is sixty kilometres from Enna. Duncan Fallowell told of the 'staggering' view from his Hotel Belvedere window: 'It is phantasmagorical, suggestive of a tale by the Brothers Grimm.' The Rough Guide described the approach to the thousand metre high ridge town as 'formidable as ever.' It was hard to ignore. As soon as we surmounted the hill leaving Caltagirone, the big-sky country views began. And, as we took the route to San Michele de Ganzaria, we were once again rewarded with a vista that demanded we stop and try and take it in. A small, stone three-arch bridge below us connected tracks to nowhere that could be seen, above an infinite patchwork of rolling hills of creamy-brown ploughed fields, or pale-green where crops had yet to be harvested or had not been subject to the plough. Beyond everything were diffuse, grey-purple, craggy mountains, and then, as you raised your eyes through the horizontal void to the huge blue sky, Etna, floating and aloof from it all, distinguishable only by the fresh snowfalls that covered its peak and slopes – a Christmas pudding of a mountain.

San Michele de Ganzaria provided nothing for the architectural memory but after taking a sharp right-hander into the main street we were struck by the number of men hanging about in groups, all clones of one another, dressed in thick coats and cloth caps to keep out the morning chill of a sunless street that substituted for a piazza. So engrossed were they in each other and their conversations that they would amble into the road, arms linked, oblivious to the traffic.

'This must be the jay-walking capital of Sicily,' I exclaimed, desperately trying to avoid another group who had stepped in front of the van. The main route was closed, so we were diverted down a dark narrow street about a hundred metres long, and flanked by grubby grey concrete buildings. There was only room for one vehicle so some bravura and gamesmanship was required to make the run along it before a car could start from the other end, otherwise there would be an impasse or collision in the middle. The people at the other end, like us, only came upon the street by rounding a sharp corner, and it was difficult to see from one end to the other, let alone offer any meaningful communication.

'If you observed UK manners, you could be here forever,' I commented, charging ahead with headlights blazing.

'I think you'd be horn-blasted into action,' said Gail.

In the region of San Cono there was field after field of orchards, not the silvery-green leaved olive, or dark-leaved orange and lemon groves we had become used to, but orderly ranks of prickly pear cacti. Many bore the erect, orange-pink fruit globes, but in others they had been picked bare. Soon after, the dome and cathedral buildings of Piazza Armerina rose above the town that spills down the hillside, but we flew past on the elevated by-pass to seek the continuation of the road to Pergusa.

The views towards Enna and Calascibetta atop their craggy cliff tops lightened a boring stretch of road through a closed Pergusa, where a modern motor race track circled the lake of the same name. We negotiated the base camp of lower Enna and a hideous display of new concrete blocks of flats, all festooned with washing lines full of colourful garments. (The occupants may have regarded them as luxurious, compared to what we were to see up the hill.) The climb up to Enna was steep and winding, and three-quarters of the way up we spotted a brown sign, 'Camper Services,' and quickly did a U-turn to investigate. A few cars were parked under the trees, the Council Services depot was at the end, a water tap and dump were adjacent to a derelict concrete block, a dusty road went through and disappeared down a hill, and there was rubbish dumped everywhere. We drove on, and along with most of the traffic, turned right onto Via Roma – an ancient street cobbled in places and jammed with parked cars on both sides and bumper to bumper vehicles queuing alongside people who found it difficult to balance on pavements the width of half a person, and reduced even further than that by the wing mirrors of parked cars. We slowly climbed the hill in the hope of finding parking, but ended up zooming down a cliffside hill and out of Enna towards Calascibetta, round the cliff and back up the original hill to park in the Camper Services, despite earlier misgivings.

The approach up the hill on foot was not encouraging. It had turned cold and that may have coloured our judgement. The road was bordered on each side and up the adjacent hillsides by concrete jungles of what appeared to be a mix of ancient and new housing that was indistinguishable in its awfulness. There was no order, it was a mish-mash, a hotchpotch of housing – a new roof here or ancient yellow-orange tiling that in a Provencal setting would be dreamy, but here was dispiriting. Impossibly steep stairways ascended between buildings, then disappeared. Much appeared abandoned or half-lived in. Buildings were perched impossibly on the edge of cliffs, a few grassy outcrops below. High up on the left-hand side, washing was strung between buildings on different sides of a gulch. There were TV aerials and satellites everywhere. It had a grey, slab-sided dreadfulness. What must it be for the poor souls that have to live there? When we reached Via Roma again, the traffic was still as bad, and we joined the pavement hoppers and tried to scrutinise the buildings we were being forced past. Piazza Vittorio Emanuele brought relief. There was room to walk on a paved area away from the traffic, watched by the many men all uniformly clad in blue quilted jackets, brown trousers, cloth caps, walking sticks in hand, and occupying every available bench under the low spreading trees in front of the San Francesco church.

Exiting the top left hand corner of the square, we passed an incongruous children's play area on the pavement to reach the belvedere, or viewpoint, Fallowell was so enamoured of. I won't repeat his lengthy and literary text, but will say that it would be hard not to be moved by such a panorama, particularly as we had the benefit of the sun striking onto the cliff-borne huddle of houses making up Calascibetta, snow-capped mountains to the far north, and a wondrous agricultural tapestry of rolling hills with the occasional pine wood on the mountain slopes. Clouds had formed and light was bleeding through to add to the patchwork that lay in front of us.

Coffee was badly needed but there was an unusual dearth of café-bars. Only when we had travelled further up Via Roma and reached Piazza Garibaldi did we find relief in the form of Caffé Italia with its purple awnings. We entered the pleasingly warm and steamy café behind a small group of men who were met by others inside. We waited patiently while the greetings proceeded with much hugging, embracing and reciprocal cheek pulling like I have only ever seen between grandparents and grandchildren before. I found to my delight that the café was a chocolate specialist, so I indulged with a chocolate filled *cornetto* that oozed and spread itself all round my mouth so that I looked like a clown and the pastry crumbled to pieces, creating a cat litter on the table.

A woman at the next table fascinated me. She was dressed in a leopard-skin, fur-peaked hat, knee-length, brown pleated shorts, brown high-heeled boots, and heavy, brown-patterned stockings. Her makeup was in the Julia Robert's *Pretty Woman* category, and with overdone lipstick she could have auditioned for the part, or that of any streetwalker. The huge sunglasses she wore would have been a distinct advantage, and she carried a man-size, large white leather handbag. As she got up to leave I could see her tabard was inscribed in large white letters: *Polizia Municipale*. Either she was on backhanders or police remuneration is better than I imagined – at 6.50 Euros it was certainly the most expensive coffees and a croissant we had ever bought!

We recommenced our tour, zipping up our anoraks as the temperature had dropped markedly in the sunless street. We stopped at a sign, '*Palazzo Policane*', and went in through the gate to have a look. There was a large courtyard, and to the right, a fine building in honey coloured stone with ornate balconies and grand steps leading up to the door. To the left, and cemented to the palace, is a horrid grey block of modern flats. What desecration. We passed other fine churches and buildings and reached Piazza Duomo, where the Duomo was end on to the square and therefore less impressive than it might have been. The grass growing out of the steps didn't help, and the lonesome Caffé Duomo seemed to have gathered a conspiratorial group of swarthy, shaded types in vehement discussion. Yet the bells were pealing melodically and there was a black-bereted man carefully renovating the gold on the locked iron gates. I moved closer, hoping for a photo opportunity, but the tin of gold paint he was holding didn't purvey that air of artistry I had hoped for.

Inside and out of the wind (which may have been an element of the appeal) the part 1307 but largely sixteenth century Duomo, although devoid of seating, was engaging. A cross-borne Jesus suspended by a thin wire flew above and to the front of the altar dome as though it was about to soar out over the congregation to smite any wrongdoer. The ceiling of the altar apse was richly adorned in three-dimensional carved cherubs, angels, and other biblical figures in creamy stone or alabaster, against an unlikely, mustard coloured backdrop. Supports radiating from the centre of this and the simpler dome to the left were like coral starfish arms, the whole spilling out to the front and sides of the apses. Stained-glass windows to the rear of the altars were brilliantly lit. The main body of the cathedral had a series of ornately carved, alabaster pillared arches running longitudinally, high above which were alternately splendid paintings and stained glass windows behind a walkway. On the walls of the arcade created by the arches was a sequence of smaller, but lavishly decorated altars, each with a huge masterpiece painting. Finally, the organ rose on the left front side, piercing the arches and rising to the walkway with pipes that had flamboyant covers, and below, a grand balcony for the maestro, outdoing anything available to the preacher.

We came to the thirteenth century stronghold, the Castello di Lombardia, and three hundred and sixty degree views across a countryside laid out below like a patterned carpet. A modern motorway on stilts snaked across it, a mere Scalextric track below a cloud-covered Etna in a blue, blue sky. The triangular post office building was depressing, but its workers had some of the best views in town, as did government officers in the Palazzo del Governo. We rather despondently headed down the Via Pergusa to our van and lunched there. Perhaps the continual cold was taking its toll on us.

'What did you think?' I asked Gail.

'I was disappointed.'

'You liked the views and the Duomo?'

'Yes, but without them it wouldn't be very attractive.' I agreed.

'Where would you like to go? We're about half way between south and north coasts – or we could go back to Caltagirone?'

'Let's go to Vittoria – there's a *sosta* in the book and if we miss that, we could go on to the campsite at Punta Braccetto.'

The road to Gela was downhill all the way. Scenically, it ran out after the junction with the S417, and deteriorated from the first oil derrick until you were amongst the pipe work, tanks, and chimneys of the coastal oil refineries. (Oil was discovered there in 1956 and the refinery and petrochemical plants created a major employment project). The scenery improved slightly as we approached Vittoria, and lifted immediately on entry, as we found a Lidl supermarket and had to stop to shop. The *Stade* in Vittoria never showed itself to us, despite some to-ing and fro-ing up and down the streets, and with a police car on our tail, we decided to go for the coastal option, arriving at Punto Braccetto in the dark as the guard was locking up to leave for the night.

Punta Braccetto

As I looked out of the window after breakfast, I saw Erich carrying his breakfast pots off to the sinks. Trailing behind was his tot of a daughter, Anna, chattering away in a pretty pink dress and carrying her own dolls-house pots and pans. Erich put down a wooden platform so she could reach the sink and they each set about the suds. He and his wife were of the 'open-toed sandal and cardigan' school of dress, and lovingly involved Anna in all their activities. Away from Austria, they were missing the mountains, and were atypical site visitors in their smaller than ours Transit-van conversion.

The majority of campers were over-winterers, mainly from the Germanic parts of Europe, in large vans and caravans with an overabundance of chairs, tables awnings and home comforts. Brits, Bob and Bridget, were spending their second year there. A medical scare and subsequent remission had made them re-evaluate their lives and they had bravely sold their business and house to travel. Friend's opinions had been at opposite extremes of 'you're crazy' to 'good on you!'

The site had a relaxed atmosphere, was next to an endless beach, idyllically planted, and 'pristine everything working perfect' – we even had our own private toilets. Angelo, the groundsman, walked around head held high, in a proud and deliberate, almost aristocratic fashion, whilst at the same time keeping on top of the work. Angela and her cousin, Conchetta, were theoretically his bosses. Apart from reading, writing, and beach walks, which we did, there was little else to do apart from chatting with and watching other camper's activities, that largely revolved around keeping their vans and pitches spick and span. A man from Austria has found that cleaning his Land Rover's engine to concourse condition was a good use of his time, as did the ants that colonised it a few days later. The weekly shopping required someone to drive their van or car to Santa Croce mob-handed with other campers because three had suffered robberies from unprotected vans. The blame was put on migrant workers from the extensive greenhouse conurbations.

Dave and his wife Joan were parked across from us – an East Londoner by accent and birth, he lived in the West Country. His van was huge, with a lounge and separate diner-kitchen. Dave had installed thirty-two lights, a TV, and sound system, but the TV didn't work. They planned to fly home for Christmas – the ninety Euro cab fare to Catania airport costing more than the flight.

Brian and Anne from Wales also had TV, and a Jodrell Bank-sized satellite dish outside, but had never had a picture. The German man from behind us, who had no problems with his own, spent an afternoon trying to fix it. During a gap in proceedings I offered Brian my advice that the Germans use different satellites, and that based on our experiences in the RV, he should change the settings on the Skybox. As I proceeded, the German returned with squawking meters and enough cable to run trans-Atlantically. With a 'how dare you interfere look' I was requested to change them back. Their endeavours continued until dark, and the next day Brian told me that they'd concluded that the Skybox was broken. I hadn't the heart to have another go.

We were taking it easy and it allowed time to reflect. We had covered 4,711 kilometres, averaging 9.87 litres per 100 km (28.8 mpg). The Sprinter van had been faultless, apart from that niggling fault with the gas supply, and we had grown to love its manoeuvrability and adaptability. We had often remarked that there was nothing in its arrangement we would change. Parked amongst the neighbouring leviathans it looked diminutive, but then most of those were simply 'get you there' vans, even to the extent of only being driven to and from the nearest ferry port, and few had explored as we had. I added up our overnight stopping places – thirty different ones, plus all the other places we had visited in between. Perhaps we had explored too intensively, and a Baroque church, more or less, wouldn't matter?

After a week of R&R, a day out seemed like another world. We set off early to explore the coast east of us first. It had fine views of a creamy-green sea rolling in, the surf producing a hazy mist as it spilled onto the sandy shore, with an unending backdrop of plastic greenhouses and tall, bamboo-like plants bordering the roads. Through Punta Secca and Cassuze few had stepped out to take the salty air so we drove on to Marina di Ragusa where life was apparent, but unfortunately not at the all-year campsite – it was closed. Further on at Donnalucata, the walking-stick men had taken up residence on the benches in the square, spaced one to a bench as though there had been a rift and no one was speaking after the night before. Donnalucata's campsite looked pleasant enough, although the supposed one and a half kilometres distance from town seemed to be stretching the imagination somewhat. We turned inland to Scicli, which looks small on the map, but turned out to be bigger than anticipated – probably because it's more concentrated, with narrow streets all laid out on a grid pattern. A victim of the 1693 earthquake, it looked worthy of investigation, but no parking place was apparent. As we climbed steeply away we were conscious of the landscape having changed. We now had limestone ridges and dry-stone walls bordering small rectangular fields, with a few cows and horses – it could have been the Peak District in Derbyshire.

Modica beckoned. We entered through the new town and descended to the old. Parking on a hill opposite a row of shops, we saw that the parking hours were 8:00 a.m. to 1:30 p.m. and then there was none until 4:00 p.m. I walked up and down the hill, but couldn't find a meter. A man parked next to us so I asked about tickets.

'*La*,' he said, pointing across the street to the shops. I went to the furniture shop he was indicating but not a soul answered my '*Buon Giorno*.' It did seem an odd place to be buying parking tickets. The man who'd directed me spotted me again and redirected me to the dry cleaners, where four thirty-minute parking tickets were finally purchased for 1.20 Euros. We walked down the hill and stopped for coffee.

'*Due cappuccino per favore*,' I asked.

'*Zwei cappuccino*.'

'No. Two,' we chorused.

'Why do they always assume we're Germans?' The tourist office provided a street map where the names were indecipherable, but forty-eight local attractions were clearly numbered. When the girl drew a route for us she only ringed twelve, so perhaps she had noted my involuntary groans every time she mentioned steps. Also devastated by the 1693 earthquake, Modica has been redesigned, and is full of impressive Baroque palaces and churches in a honey coloured stone. An historian counted one hundred churches. If it isn't a church it will probably be an ornate, balconied palace. The approach to the Cathedral of San Giorgo was up a flight of curved steps that would suit the entrance of a grand lobby, but in this case traversed four levels of roads.

Only the most determined got to commune with their religious patrons. The two hundred and fifty steps were bedecked with yellow, white and crimson flowers. At first you only saw the building's upper belfry, and then, as you mounted, the whole was slowly revealed – a giant wedding cake of a church, designed like so many others in the south-east of Sicily by the eighteenth century architect, Rosario Gagliardi. I wondered if he'd had a go at Stockport Town Hall. The interior didn't disappoint – a Wedgwood-style wonderland of raised blue carvings. Other buildings paled in comparison, and the castle, stoutly defensive as it might be on its rocky crag, looked weird with a white-faced, Big Ben style clock stuck on its concrete looking keep.

As we wandered we passed by a plaque announcing the birthplace of Quasimodo that intrigued us, only to realise that this was Salvatore Quasimodo, Sicily's Nobel prize-winning writer. Around the corner, under the restorer's yellow waste chute, was a series of cave houses built into the rocky base of the castle. An old man leaning on his walking stick was sitting on the bench outside and started to regale us, apparently assuming our destination to be the Chiesa di Santa Maria di Betlem below.

'*Mi dispiache, non parlo Italiano*,' I replied. Speaking Italian seemed to spur him on and the gesticulations and intensity increased.

'*Non, capisco*,' I offered, and he finally shrugged his shoulders. As we walked in the direction indicated he shouted after us,

'*Germania*?'

'*No, Inghilterra*.'

'*Ah, Inglese*.'

'Why do they always think we're German!'

Modica seemed to draw its fame from chocolate. All the cafés were festooned with displays of chocolate-this and chocolate-that. Discovering somewhere that might simply have a slice of pizza proved challenging, and the one selected opposite the tourist bureau, although providing the necessary, was a chocolatised patisserie, chocolate drinks, and liquors emporium.

The drive out of Modica to reach the E45 toward Ragusa and Comiso looked straightforward on the map: simply head towards the station. The size of the task became apparent when we started round the first two hairpin bends in the narrow streets of the old town and started to climb up the limestone cliff face the town is built on. Dramatically, and awe-inspiringly, up in the sky ahead was the road on a slender flyover, with dinky-toy trucks moving across it. At three hundred metres, it is one of the tallest in Europe.

'How on earth do we climb to that height through these streets?' I asked Gail, who stared intensely at the laptop, where she was running the GPS.

'I think we may be going underneath, there's no way to tell.' Idiots were overtaking aggressively on narrow streets before hairpins. The switchback was sometimes so sharp we couldn't make it and had to reverse and have two goes at it. Finally we emerged onto the plateau and into the open, where I grabbed a road to the left and miraculously ended up on the flyover where we wanted to be. It was one of those golden driving moments.

We headed to Vittoria for shopping. The road was good as we slipped by more limestone drywalls bounding neat little fields, a few limestone escarpments, and the modern industrial zone that sits south of Ragusa and then,

'Will you look at that,' I exclaimed, and we suddenly dropped, hair-pinning down the side of a cliff. The planet had abruptly, and without warning, opened up below us. A flat, misty plain stretched as far as the eye could see to finally merge with a distant sky.

'It's like we're flying and coming in to land,' said Gail. 'I've never seen anything like it. What a strange sensation.'

'That must be Comiso. It's like a model toy town, but I can make out the twin churches,' I said before negotiating the van round another hairpin. (I later learnt that the association with flying was apt. The US deployed their largest arsenal of cruise missiles there in June 1983. Comiso residents, famous for their resistance to the 1945 call-up, objected, along with one million petition-signing Sicilians. Comiso women and peace activists gathered in protest but were routed in a violent confrontation with the police. The last missile was removed in 1991.)

Shopping at Lidl was an anti-climax.

To Noto: The Golden City

Mid-morning of the 28th November, we heard a loud *CRACK* outside. I jumped to look out of the bathroom window and saw our German neighbour on his knees. Despite the wild winds and rain, he was nonetheless trying to get a perfect fit between his ground cover, awning wall, and interior carpet. He had been at it two days but was yet to achieve his wife's approval. Everything had to be perfect on their pitch – perfectly fitting, positioned, coordinated, and swept. But even he was distracted by the sound, and then sight, of the large main branch and leafy sub-branches of the tree next to us being rent asunder to fall and lodge against a support pole next to Bob and Bridget's van. If it had gone the other way it would have hit our van, or floored our friend just as he was finally butting up the carpet to the awning, and there would have been even more sweeping to do. A crowd gathered – a United Nations of investigators, all peering skywards, gesticulating, and voicing opinions. But like so many United Nation meetings, nothing happened until Angelo and a mate came and matter-of-factly dragged the branch away. The wind and rain persisted throughout the day and into that night, but we woke the next day to settled conditions.

We decided to leave before our arrangements obsessed us, or we became rooted and the highlight of the day became someone to talk to at the wash sink or on the way to empty the cassette in the *WC Chimique*.

'I feel we're being watched all the time,' I said to Gail.

'Why not draw the blinds if you're worried.'

'What? Think of the speculation that would produce at three in the afternoon.' The site had given us a break from travel, but we were ready for a move. It was time to turn back north-east and make for Noto.

I had been interested in Noto ever since an Internet search had thrown up Duncan Fallowell's 1989 book, *To Noto, or, London to Sicily in a Ford*, in which he drives to Noto and Sicily in a Ford Capri. It is a perceptive, eccentric, and compelling travelogue of personal experience that exudes a sexual rawness made to sound elegant through the use of sophisticated prose. Noto became Fallowell's focus and purpose, along with a search for an undiscovered, mystical black lake. We were on the verge of repeating his 'Big Moment', when he finally arrived in the 'Golden City'. I was excited, and hoped the travel insights gleaned from his book would not be dashed. I pulled the toilet cassette from the van, ready for emptying. Travel happiness to unknown destinations and facilities came with an empty cassette – and there was double pleasure if you were confined to quarters and it was raining outside. I was getting as obsessive as the neighbouring Germans.

'When will you leave?' asked the perfect German lady next door, unconscious of our imminent departure.

'Why?' I replied, taken aback by the directness of her question. She had probably been up all night practising the phrase, but was stumped by my response.

'I ask Brian.' Brian seemed to have endeared himself to them and may have had some of the German language (unless they had made a mistake with his strong Welsh accent).

'No need – we're going today,' I conceded.

'Oh, today. Now? *Wunderbar*.' Each day I had given them a cheery *Guten Tag*, so was fascinated as to why our departure was bringing such joy and happiness. 'We move to yours. We have care of the trees.' Aah. The falling tree had frightened them, and fear of one splitting and crashing onto their perfect pitch made her want to move to ours.

'Such a shame, he had finally got that piece of ground cover positioned,' I confided to Gail.

We used the minor coast road to travel east, which was fine apart from the water splashes left by the previous night's deluge, waves crashing over the wall ('Oooooh!'), and the boring, unfinished concrete blockitis of the coastal buildings. Yet, new building was underway and there were cranes-a-plenty. How, with so much beauty in their town and city buildings and fine architectural achievements post-1693 eruption can they be happy with this stuff? They've simply stopped caring. What caused the change? Once we had turned inland from Pozzalo to Ispica things improved, with open-air agriculture, dry-stone walled fields, and small farmhouses rather than plastic polytunnels.

'Can you see what's ahead?' Gail asked. A small lorry was carrying two ancient, gnarled-trunk olive trees that had been neatly cut from the earth, providing a large brown root ball for each. Stuck behind it on the narrow road (our right-hand drive not assisting overtaking), we were hypnotised by the swaying and shaking branches of silver leaves ahead, a biblical manifestation, and quite arresting. A man on his scooter came round the corner in the opposite direction, caught sight of the unusual load, and nearly wobbled off into the ditch.

'Do you think they're going to Noto? That would be a great title – *Two Olive Trees to Noto*,' I quipped. By then the traffic queue behind us had become embarrassingly long, so finding a clear spot, I sped past.

'I'm pulling in for LPG while we have the chance.' The Tamoil garage in Rosolini was doing brisk business in LPG and I waited my turn.

'Full?' said the smartly blue and white uniformed attendant with a big smile.

'Yes, please. I mean, *si per favore*.' (Why does what little we know evade us when questioned?) '*Como se dice in Italiano?*' I asked to recover.

'*Piano*.'

'Okay. *Piano. Va bene*.' It made sense: *piano* – level, level at the top, many plateau's seemed to be called '*Piano* this' or '*Piano* that' – and of course, it also meant floor, plan, and piano of the ivory keys. Why shouldn't it also mean 'full'? What an economic language Italian was turning out to be! The lorry with the olive trees pulled in and drove across the service station to park at the other end.

'*Olivo*,' announced the attendant.

'Yes.' *And there won't be any left the way those trees are shaking!* I thought, mistaking his *Olivo* (olive tree) for *Oliva* (olive).

'*Gran Bretagna è lontano*,' he said, continuing the conversation as he put the pump pistol away, with a wave of his other hand to somewhere in the far distance, but in the general direction of Tunisia.

'*Si*. A long way.' Before we could discuss our travels any further he was distracted by the arrival of a female customer for LPG and it was kisses all round. *Hard to imagine that down at the Canning Town Esso*, I thought.

'Get out here,' I joked with Gail, 'they're giving kisses away with LPG.' He set off for the office with our cash, paused for a moment before entering, and then walked slowly and deliberately back to me.

'*Pi-E-no! Non è piano*.'

As we closed on Noto, my excitement and anticipation grew. Our first view of the honey coloured stone buildings spread up the hillside lifted our hopes even further. Domes, towers, pillars, roofs, round, square, triangular, hexagonal, and octagonal all cohesively knitted together. Our Noto guide map showed a stadium with five coloured Olympic rings, and we had envisaged something on The Old Trafford scale, with appropriate parking. It turned out to be a single row of parking spaces along a road bordering a park. Huge, dark leaved ficus trees stretched across and were so dense they created a tunnel. We entered cautiously, and tried one of the few vacant diagonal slots, watched by a bench full of old men seeking shade under the trees. Gail, along with a chorus of hooters from passing cars, announced that our rear end was sticking out too much. Being a one-way street, we had no choice but to go on.

'The branches are very low,' Gail said, a slight tremble in her voice as she climbed back in.

'Should be okay,' I comforted.

'But they're getting lower. Can you get closer to the middle?'

'Not with all those cars parked on the left.'

'Can you reverse?'

'No, we're too far down. Anyway, it's one way and there's a line of cars behind. Oh no, the first one's a police car!' I do believe Gail shut her eyes at that point. We emerged unscathed, only to find a dark-uniformed policeman of the white diagonal, belt and holster type standing ahead of us and blocking the main entrance to Noto – the Porta Reale a sort of Arc de Triomphe, but in bright creamy stone. I seized a road to the right and climbed the cobbled back street to the next junction, where another choice for parking was inaccessible, and still followed by the blue and white police car, took the next turn right to complete a full circle and end up back in Piazzale Marconi, our starting point. After a U-turn, I returned to the previously inaccessible parking of the sort that National Car Parks used to adopt between site clearance and new construction.

'It is one of the most beautiful cities in Sicily and has an architectoric [sic] overview that is unique in the world for the unity and harmony of Baroque style that is truely [sic] splendid, emphasised by the natural beauty of the rosé colour of the stone used to build the town,' stated the brochure.

We walked to the Royal Gate, a triumphal arch surmounted by a castellated tower, a greyhound and a pelican in the honey coloured stone common to all Noto's buildings. The road of diamond shaped, lava-black stones stretched out in front and on each side were fine Baroque buildings. Noto was busy, but not crowded.

Our first call was to the post office before it closed to get stamps for Christmas cards. It's a modern building located behind the Santa Chiara Church and Benedictine Monastery, with a sensible ticketing system and differing numbers for the various sections. We took ticket '57' and proceeded to the point that had a big envelope sign on it. Only one window appeared to be open. The customer number being served was shown in a big, illuminated, digital '48' above. A straightforward procedure – simply wait for your number to come up with ropes to guide the queue. But this was Sicily. What is it about the Sicilians, or even Italians, that a perfectly orderly system like a red traffic light, no parking, one-way street, or 'no overtaking' sign is there to be beaten? The ropes were ignored and a small group hovered just ahead of them, ready to jump in should the correct number holder not appear instantly. They were in a conspiratorial debate. People detached themselves and came up, asking our number. One young man grasped Gail's ticket to compare his number with her '57' – his was '115'. He had taken a ticket for the wrong queue, and mortified, raced back across to the ticket dispenser, despairing that anyone should get in ahead of him. Behind the man serving at the window was a woman wandering about the office looking busy. If only they could catch her eye. Whoa! A young girl with no ticket at all managed it, and slid across her money for a stamp. The group surged forward, upset at the unexpected defeat, but ready to seize the new opportunity. Had she known the young girl? Had the girl called her name? How had she done it? Another man asked to see our ticket. What did he hope to gain by this? We were only one number away. An old man on my left surreptitiously leant on the edge of the window counter so I edged forward, letting him know I had my eye on him. '57' flashed. Bingo!

'*Trenta francobolli per Inghilterra per favore*.' Oh no, such a big order! There was an audible groan from the waiting group. The man serving shuffled away to get his books out – he had insufficient stamps of the required type, but slowly, oh so slowly, he cobbled together a mélange of stamps of various colours, designs and sizes to meet our needs. At last, we retired to the outdoor café opposite the cathedral and over coffee and a *piccolo crema cornetto* tried to stick our motley collection of stamps on without obliterating the addresses and then went back to post the cards. Two days later they had arrived in the UK.

In the warm sunlight we moved back across Piazza Municipio to the cathedral, or Church of San Nicolò, the most famous of Noto's many buildings, and its warm stone perfectly framed against a deep blue winter sky. After climbing the four flights of steps that span the whole width and more, we found the doors were firmly closed.

Fallowell was shown around by a local teacher, Professore Rosario Tiné. He mentions that after seeing the cathedral with his female companion, Von, the Professor took them to the corner of Via Salvatore La Rosa and Via Ducezio behind the Town Hall, the Noto Bassa region, and asked: 'Would you like ice-cream?' before taking them down another street and through the beaded-curtain doorway of an ordinary house that turned out to be 'a small emporium of ice-cream, biscuits, crackers, bottles, sweets, framed diplomas and silver cups.' There they were introduced to Signor Corrado Costanzo, *artigiano del dolce*, who offered 'rose ice-cream, jasmine ice-cream.' Fallowell had strawberry with tiny wild strawberries and juice on top, and Von had jasmine.

Fascinated by the thought of this, we decided to search for the location, even though Fallowell never mentioned the street. We searched up and down, until we came to the corner of via G. Aurispa and via Ruggero Settimo, where we found a smart *Pasticcheria, Gelateria and Café*, and round the corner, a string-beaded doorway – but it was the entrance to the bakery and preparation room, full of stainless steel counters, cupboards, and equipment. Returning to enter the shop, we found a huge display of delicious looking pastries and marzipan fruit delicacies, with the master standing proudly behind in whites, and a side-room café, but no sign of cups, certificates, or the famous ice cream as seen by Fallowell.

'We'll never know,' said Gail. 'Let's carry on.' In looking for cafés, I noted the interpretation of EU Health and Safety Regulations. Whilst in the UK great expense must be incurred building wheelchair-access ramps, in Noto at least, all that was required was a small, inconspicuous sign along the lines of 'If you need help getting in, ring the bell.' And, presumably, some five-foot-three waiter will come and carry you up the back stairs.

We walked the full length of Corso V. Emmanuele, the main street that crosses from one side of Noto to the other, marvelling at each of the Baroque palaces and churches (including the Nicolai Palace where carved stone figures of prancing lions, mermaids, gods and goddesses support the wrought iron balconies). We sat outside a cafe behind the *Municipio* eating the Italian equivalent of a Cornish pasty and looking towards the cathedral. It was quiet – siesta time.

'C'mon, drink up, the cathedral door is open,' I entreated Gail. We raced up the steps and inside. Fallowell found the interior to be 'sombre' but we were met by a blinding whiteness and the smell of fresh paint. The floor was made up of new, creamy stone tiles with small indentations. The walls and pillars were a pristine, unmarked, white Dulux matt. It had the feel of a new bathroom. We moved towards the main altar, passing one or two smartly dressed men all on their mobile phones, to a small group in discussion. A tall and imposing woman in a green-grey tailored suit and brown boots was addressing the group. A priest moved towards the central lectern, and with one hand on it, knelt on the raised box-like platform behind, stood up, and then knelt again on the other knee.

'He's trying it for size,' I whispered to Gail. 'We've invaded the handover for the new cathedral and probably shouldn't be here. That's why they've done it during the siesta, but had to leave the door open for the full effect.' The original cupola and roof of the cathedral collapsed in 1996 and had been under reconstruction ever since, so that most visitors were met with extensive scaffolding. We wandered round, taking professional photos with my pocket Olympus like we had every right to be there (and as best one can in T-shirt and hiking pants in my case, although Gail fitted in a treat). It was hard to know what to make of it. A brand new interior doesn't fit a three- hundred-year-old cathedral. The altars were attractive, the ceilings with their raised reliefs beautiful, but on the whole, sterile without solemnity. No worn flagstones, rough benches or dusty enclaves.

Our initial time in Noto had left us wanting more. It was different – light, spacious, and inviting. On our drive in we had seen a sign, 'Noto Parking,' with a picture of a motorhome on it, just below the city. We returned, hoping it would be a suitable place to stay the night so that we could explore Noto further the next day. The sign pointed down a road bordered on each side by lemon groves laden with the yellow fruit to a green, padlocked and barred gateway with Italian and German flags flying above. It was a country idyll, five minutes drive from a city. A track led round the back of the buildings, but there was no sign of life. A sign gave some telephone numbers in rain-smeared marker pen. Thinking it was closed, and with no one appearing, we did a U-turn and were about to set off when a dark-blue Fiat drew up beside us and the driver wound the window down. Michele was the owner. He unlocked the gate and after price negotiations he stripped two clementines from one of the trees, each retaining a single leaf, and presented them to Gail.

'Tomorrow you would like to go to Noto?'

'Yes,' she replied.

'At what time?'

'Nine-thirty?'

'I will take you, no need to go in the van.' We settled into the citrus grove, the only inhabitants. The trees were loaded with fruit, and a few flowers of the next crop were starting to open. Michele had constructed a new toilet block – only three cubicles, but sparkling, and a waste disposal. The showers were open-air, so we were pleased to have our own facilities.

At 9:30 a.m. sharp, and somewhat unexpectedly for Sicily, Michele was there to pick us up for the short ride into Noto. We passed a small car park for motorhomes provided by the council and I pointed to the motorhome parked there.

'Not good. *Zingaros*,' he said.

'*Zingaros?* Are they Gypsies?'

'No, *Zingaros Romana*. One thousand in the City of Noto.' I looked *Zingaros* up in my dictionary.

'We say Gypsies.'

'Yes, bad people. They have been in the south of the city for a long time.' Once more, we entered by the Royal Gate. A black and white dog lazing on the sunlit pavement adopted us. The first open area we came to was the Piazza Immacolata. Steep and numerous steps on the right led up to the church of the same name (San Francesco all'Immacolta Church and Convent). A magnificent example of eighteenth century architecture with a portal decorated in Baroque friezes, it was designed by Gagliardi and Sinatra. A small, slightly grubby man with a sweet face, sparkling eyes and welcoming smile greeted us at the door.

'*Prego.*' We started to look around and he stepped back with a small bow as though allowing us to take in the full atmosphere and aura of the empty church. As we approached a large painting in the first alcove, he stepped forward and started to tell us about it.

'*Mi dispiache. Non parlo Italiano*, I said. He was undaunted. I had just spoken Italian. He continued in his soft voice. We gathered the painting and others in the church had been brought from Noto Antica when it was devastated by the 1693 earthquake, and the present Noto was built to replace it. We continued. This one from this century and painted by Vizzini, this one that century and painted by Sozzi…

'Isn't he sweet,' whispered Gail. We nodded as kindly as we could and I responded where I could translate an odd word. Then we viewed a crucifix and he was desperate to get something across. Yes, from Noto Antica, the century established, the creator *anonimo*, but he strained – anxious to tell us something more. He gripped the bench seat in front of him and rubbed it. *His nails could do with a clean*, I thought.

'Ah. Wood!'

'*Si*. Wooouuld.' We found another one. He rubbed a bench again.

'Woooood!' we chorused.

'*Si. Wooouuld.*' A big smile creased his face, his eyes sparkling more than ever. When we got to the altar he disappeared round a curtain. Moments later a fluorescent blue light suddenly shone behind the Madonna (by Monachello) – the climax to his impeccably remembered and delivered talk. I reviewed my guidebook for the key points, in case we had missed anything because of the language problem.

'*Dov'é Bonasia*,' I asked, enquiring about a tombstone also brought from Noto Antica. He was crestfallen. He had already shown it to us. To compensate, I made to put an offering in the central collection box but his face sank further and he pointed to the little table at the entrance. The chink of coins on the open saucer on the white tablecloth seemed to relieve his distress.

Outside again, we gazed up at the pyramidal spire of the eighteenth century Basilica of S. Salvattore and monastery, an unusual building with a massive wall onto the central street, Corso V. Emmanuele, with windows that are richly decorated with friezes and wrought iron gratings, but open to the sky behind. We sauntered further along the Corso into the wonderfully open and welcoming, but slightly complex Piazza Municipio, past the steps up to the prominent cathedral to the right and the Town Hall to the left, this palace and that church all magnificent in their own way, but it was the cohesiveness and uniformity of the straw coloured stone that brought it all together. A pity then that the new cupola of the cathedral, rebuilt after its collapse, is almost hidden from view behind the façade and requires some angling by the iron bandstand to get a decent photo.

Many shops were inserted into ancient church and palace walls, a *Farmacia* and a *Tabacchi* amongst others. Beyond the Piazza Municipio the men were out in force, sitting outside cafés or on benches in the leafy Piazza XV1 Maggio in front of the gardens, the Fountain of Hercules rescued from Noto Antica, and two statues of notable locals. It was hot in the morning sun, but they sat with smart overcoats, caps and walking sticks, all reading and discussing what I assumed to be the same freebie newspaper. Piazzo XV1 Maggio had a different feel to the Piazza Municipio, probably due to the allowance of cars and parking, and unfortunately, construction works and hoarding on the left before the Town Theatre.

I was determined to follow up on the search for the Constanzo ice-cream emporium, so we proceeded to the *Pasticcheria, Gelateria and Café* we had found the previous day in case I had missed something. We had coffee in the three table coffee bar, taking five times longer than the men who came in for their shot of espresso and left two minutes later. The Carmine church relied heavily on gilt beautification with columns, cupids, and ciborium of the Madonna attributed to Monachello, the whole in the shape of a Greek cross. It was dark on entry, but lightened with time and had a big photo of a nun who must have been doing sterling work in some far-flung African country. Men were in the side office and laughing heartily. Returning from viewing the altar, I noticed a group of three at the back – an earnest, bearded, charcoal-grey suited young man, a teenage girl, and a male Down Syndrome youth who wore a lime-green jacket and carried a plastic shopping bag. The bearded young man appeared to be showing them round. The youth knelt in a pretend way at the red-curtained confessional box and then walked away, as though embarrassed. Encouraged by the others, he tried it again, looked momentarily serious, and then a big smile spread across his face and he burst out laughing, to which they all joined in. They moved over to the organ on the right and the bearded young man started to play. The church was filled with restrained and enchanting music, and then, unprompted, the pony-tailed girl started to sing a hymnal song. The Down Syndrome youth, Gail, and myself were at once enthralled and transfixed. I'm not religious – but for me, it was a spiritual moment.

It was 11:00 a.m. and as we made our way to the tourist office the streets had become a racetrack. Schools were out and scooter mayhem ensued. They fanned out at high speed in every direction and down every narrow alley, ridden by boys and girls all looking like movie extras in the latest cool glasses and outfits, and on their mobile phones. Some had no ride but soon bunked one from friends speeding by, swinging themselves on board with a practised art. The impressive tourist office was in the Villeta behind the statue of Hercules in the Piazza XV1 Maggio. The man at the desk was engaged, so I made for a smart, pale-green suited lady with tied-up auburn hair. She spoke some English.

'We are looking for Professor Constanzo's *gelateria*. Do you know where it is?'

'Oh, he's dead. His sons have a shop.' I showed her Fallowell's book, pointing to Constanzo's name.

'Fallowell visited in the 1980s and was guided by a local teacher, Professor Rosario Tiné,' I explained.

'I know Professore Tiné well.' We were speaking to Dottoressa Maria Amato, with the wonderful title of '*Assessore Turismo Promozione E Spettacolo*.' She is heavily involved in promoting Noto. 'We are not getting a fair picture in the guides,' she said. 'People think our buildings are surrounded by scaffolding and we have no hotels, but it has changed.' An interesting comment, and echoing that of Professore Tiné's to Fallowell. She was something important in the city – the closest UK equivalent would be a city councillor or Alderman. She wanted to know where she could get the book and we wanted to know where the *gelateria* was, so I used her very slow Internet connection to bring up Amazon and the book, and she marked the *gelateria* on our map and where the original *laboratorio* was. We were elated and set off to discover the *gelateria*, but now it was twelve noon and the second wave of lunchers were on the move. The streets were filled with jostling cars, and to alert everyone, all the bells rang out from the many churches in an un-coordinated, 'I'm better than you' sort of way.

'It's just behind the theatre,' said Gail, map in hand and jumping out of the way of an aggressive little Fiat Panda, relieved to get to a traffic-free, paved zone.

'Weren't we near there yesterday?'

'Look, there it is! There's a Constanzo sign engraved on the wall outside.'

'That's Caffé Noir,[6] the same place we had our lunch at yesterday! How did we miss it?' The boys behind the counter, presumably Constanzo's sons, knew about the book. One created two double-cornet ice-creams of stupefying proportions – Gail's a pistachio and ricotta, and mine a

---

[6] Although I have it recorded as Caffé Noir maps now show a Dolceria Costanzo on Via Silvio Spaventa owned by Luigi and Giuseppina Costanzo.

strawberry and chocolate chip extravaganza, and posed for photos. We followed the instructions to the original Constanzo house that Fallowell would have gone to and stood outside what we thought was the correct one, ices dripping. A lady stopped to help us and started to point us down a narrow alley but we couldn't be sure what she was saying and felt we had done enough: our little project was complete. (Later I mentioned it to Michele when he collected us. 'Father dead, very good ice cream. The sons, not good.')

We moved north, up the hill on which Noto is built, to Noto Alta, but because of the hour everywhere was quiet. At the Galiardi Church of the Sacred Crucifix, we rattled each of the fine doors within the portal to no avail – churches close for lunch as well. A couple of alleys later we rounded a corner expecting to find the Santa Thomas Monastery, only to be confronted by a man with a gun. We were taken aback to encounter, in the area of private palaces, a blue-bereted, black jacketed, heavily booted man carrying a Kalashnikov. The pill boxes we now saw at each end of the street should have given us a clue, but in a perfunctory conversation he gave us a better one as he crossed his wrists, emulating, charades-style, someone in handcuffs (or did he mean in chains?) The Santa Thomas Monastery had been converted to a penal institution, and the windows that would have given a five-star view of the remarkable city were covered with frosted glass. He directed us back to the centre of town and we departed south, took a right turn to explore the Impellizzeri Palace, and turned another corner to, embarrassingly, be eyeballed by our blue-bereted friend yet again.

We late-lunched at a café on Corso V. Emmanuele, which was deserted. After investigating a few more churches (all closed for lunch) we made our way to the bus station, where Michele picked us up.

'Noto?'

'*Bellissima*!' As we turned down the road to the campsite there was a man in red dressing-gown and pyjamas walking his dog.

No Kiss!

As I write this, I am not convinced that I have conveyed the overwhelming beauty of Noto. Personal diversions may have gotten in the way of a cohesive and logical introduction to this masterpiece of Baroque town planning and architecture, but then I don't want to come across as an alternative Rough Guide or Lonely Planet. That the 'new town' was built from scratch on the side of the Meti Hill following the devastation and total destruction of Noto Antica in 1693 and encompasses such exquisite magnificence is remarkable. The guide to the small centre lists nineteen churches, monasteries or convents, and eleven palaces, along with public gardens, markets, and other buildings. Each building is richly adorned externally and decorated internally through the efforts of local craftsmen working the soft white stone, and the whole exercise was controlled and coordinated by Gagliardi, Sinatra, and Labisi. Later districts of working-class housing were added, each with its own style, but not detracting from the whole. It is a credit to the present population that they have recognised their inheritance and have worked hard to preserve it, but not allowed it to become a Baroque

Disneyland – it is a functional, living place – indeed, a golden city.

At the lemon grove the six lemon pickers arrived each day at 7:00 a.m., provided it wasn't or hadn't rained, and had soon donned brown wellies and blue overalls and were hard at work up ladders. Lemons thumped into buckets that were then emptied into plastic crates on the little orange putt-putt, tractor-trailer combination. The little tractor then chugged back and forth, Michele at the wheel, to stack the crates in the barn. As a civil servant he had been given fourteen days to pick his lemon crop. At 10:30 a.m. they all returned to retrieve food bags from their cars for their mid-morning break before continuing picking through to 2:00 p.m., when they departed for lunch and siesta.

Noto arose following the total destruction of Noto Antica, along with most of South-Eastern Sicily, by the 1693 earthquake. We set off to discover what remained of the original city. On the road there, and just outside the main environs of Noto, we saw a sign to the left for the Hermitage of San Corrado di Fuori, and descended to a deserted but graffiti-covered car park. From the gate a long, walled garden path led to the hermitage, and as we passed through, the bells started ringing almost as though we had triggered an infrared sensor. The Baroque façade of the small hermitage came into view, nestled against the limestone cliff-face to the right. It was built in 1749 to commemorate San Corrado Confalonieri, who lived there in the fourteenth century. The inside was small, and dominated by a large painting of the Virgin with Child and the Saint Corrado. Off to the right was the Patron Saints cave with a marble statue by Pirrone. It appeared to be an altar, and Gail was reluctant to trespass, but with a little encouragement we did so and soon found the entrance to the information point and museum. From nowhere apparent, a small, blue-habited nun appeared, startling us.

'Would you like to look round the museum?' The ancient door unlocked, we proceeded upstairs to find a succession of weirdly fascinating votive exhibits. Football shirts, wedding dresses, hairpieces, skulls, jewellery, crutches, walking sticks, limb prostheses, and complete body casts, amongst others – all displayed in glass cases. Photos of youngsters dressed in brown, miniature monk's habits were hung on the walls. The nun met us as we descended the stairs.

'Would you like to go into the crypt?' We descended into the crypt, where a pleasing, large nativity scene had been constructed and we made suitably approving sounds. She told us that in the old days the figures used to move by bicycle, but the mechanism was broken and no one local with the required skills remained to repair it. The rear of the hermitage opened onto an impressive, verdant gorge. As we departed, the nun wished us 'Happy Travels' and our last view was of her sweeping up some of the rubbish strewn at the edge of the car park.

'Noto Antica,' read the sign, and we obeyed, anxious not to miss the way. We followed an orange lorry carrying a mini-digger down the narrowing road bordered by dry-stone walls and scrubby pasture in which grazed a few cows, their large bells donging.

'If he can get down, so can we!' At that moment, the lorry pulled off onto a farm track. Our road became a single car width, descended round a corner to a bridge over a gorge, then up the other side where the trees and bushes hanging over it were lower than our 3.1 metres. Gail got out and used the extending wash mop to try and push them out of the way. Fallowell reported that he was so pleased at being at Noto Antica that he became 'elemental' and took off all his clothes. I was therefore momentarily fascinated by an unrolled condom dangling from the branches on the left, and wondered if others had taken him at his word and gone one step further. Gail wasn't entirely successful in her efforts and branches rubbed along the roof, but I didn't snag the condom. We wondered if worse was to come, but we rounded the next corner to arrive, and park, in an open area in front of high, stone fortified walls and an entrance arch.

Noto Antica was the last stronghold of Muslim Sicily, a renowned cultural centre where there have been many archaeological finds, including a Sikel necropolis from around 800 BC, as well and Jewish and Christian remains. We walked along the stony road exploring some battlements to the right, and round some large olive trees to an oval tower and more walls and buildings overlooking a steep gorge. We deduced this to be the Royal Castle (eleventh to sixteenth century). Taking the path along the edge of the gorge we had pleasant views, but little in the way of buildings – just stone blocks being overtaken by the scrub – and it wasn't long before the thorny vegetation became so dense that progress was halted and we had to retrace our steps to the main route.

I'm not sure what I expected of an ancient city razed by an earthquake three hundred years previously. There was little to see other than piles of mould-speckled stones amongst scrubby plants, an occasional wall, a rounded pillar (an arch, possibly). The map pointed to exciting finds like the third century BC Gymnasium, Hellenistic Walls, Santa Maria Hospital, Bellaria Palace and various churches from the eleventh century, but nothing was marked and we found it hard to place any, even with the map to hand. Some imagination is required, some sense of previous beings living and working their crafts, tending their vines and other crops and animals, enjoying their culture and politicising their way through their days high above the gorge and keeping a watchful eye over the distant coast and travellers outside the walls. Beyond the commemorative monument the roads wound off in a way that led to map-reading confusion and we got to the end of one to enjoy excellent views down a valley to the sea, but nought else except an appreciation of the strategic location of the plateau occupied by Noto Antica. Back-tracking, we took another road, and after what seemed an age we got to the Hermitage of Santa Maria della

Providenza. I thought how sensible Fallowell had been to drive to it in his car despite the boulders. The L-shaped hermitage buildings are substantial and stand on a promontory looking seawards down the same lush valley, but on closer inspection they were in a ruinous state. Built after the earthquake to give thanks for I'm not sure what, the large buildings had gone the same way themselves – nature had once again intervened. The gate had a rusty chain and padlock, the windows were broken, vegetation had got a firm grip, and there was no hint as to how to gain access other than shouting in the hope that the 'ancient codger' described by Fallowell, (or his replacement), might turn up to show us round the chapel and small museum. (Our guide booklet from the Noto tourist office said the hermitage was open daily from sunrise to sunset and it was worth seeing for the original floors.) The Hermitage had gone the way of so many of the ecclesiastical buildings we were to see in Sicily – a fine edifice originally, but neglected and given over to birds and plants. Anywhere else, it would be a smart hotel advertising its history with wondrous views for get-away conferencing delegates. Perhaps it's better as it is, even if we didn't get to see round it.

We walked back along the rocky road, hoping something would 'crop up'. We had not met anyone else along the roads and tracks, and the views over the adjacent hills and remote farms were bucolic, so as a place to get away from it all and perhaps become 'elemental', it had merit. We took a side track through thorny bushes and came to a field where a flock of sheep were grazing on the edge of the gorge, their bells tinkling away, the new lambs bleating for their mothers and the mothers calling back – a pastoral scene. Then we found a better way back to Noto, thereby averting the condom adorned branches.

The next day we had arranged to go to Syracuse, and under Michele's instruction, had bought tickets at the travel agents in Noto. His sister waved from the gate – she would run us up to the station in her car as the lemon pickers had already been working for nearly two hours and no one could afford a break. The timing had been discussed at length. The train, we were assured by the agent, left at 9:15 a.m. Michele, who normally travelled by train to his work in Siracusa when he wasn't picking his lemons, insisted we were to be ready at 8:45 a.m. for the five-minute car ride. Gail sat in the back, I in the front. Michele's sister was chatty.

'Siracusa?'

'*Si*.' I hoped there wasn't confusion and she intended to drive us there. I asked her name:

'*Como ti chiama*?'

'*Corrada. E tu*?'

'*E impossibile in Italiano*,' I replied.

'*Impossibile*?'

'*Si. Mi nome e* Keith.'

'*Kiss*?'

'No. Keith,' I said, emphasising the 'th'.

'*Kiiiiiissssssss*,' she tried again, but leaning over this time, her jaw jutting into my face as though she was about to, well, kiss me!

'No kiss! Keith,' I insisted, withdrawing as far as the side window allowed. She tried again, oblivious to the road and traffic, with an even more pronounced exaggeration of her jaw – a set of prominent front teeth heading towards my face, a pink tongue jiggling between them, and fine spray of spittle launching into the air.

'Chitttttttttthhhh!' We were doubled up with laughter.

The station was deserted, all the faded facilities locked some years before, and none of the eight or so platforms had a number on them. It was a World War Two film scene – the escaped prisoner hoping no one would come along before he got on the train. The track came in on a curve from the left and went out on a sharp curve to the right (or vice versa), almost completing a circle around the edge of the hillside. There was graffiti in English, 'Welcome to Noto,' on one of the decaying buildings across the tracks. We checked a timetable in a dusty window; reassuringly, the 9:15 a.m. was there. At 9:05 a.m. a man arrived dressed smartly in a blue Barbour and corduroys, brown boat shoes, and the obligatory leather shoulder bag. Was he an academic, or just dressing in the preppy mode? Gail needed reassurance about the platforms.

'*Va bene qui per Siracusa*?'

'*Si, si.*' A small family group arrived around 9:10 a.m. dressed for winter with heavy, quilted coats and boots. At 9:20 a.m. we were still there, and the sun shining on us required the family to discard their extra clothing. At 9:28 a.m. bells finally started ringing over my head. I turned to see they were labelled 'Modica'. If that meant the train had just left Modica, we still had some time to wait! Then we saw it coming round the headland, and by 9:30 a.m. the underwhelming, two carriage, blue-grey time scarred diesel train pulled in. It was presentable inside, with uniform blue-plastic seating, brown headrests, and sun-screening curtains. The diesel engine beneath us throbbed, a gear was engaged, and the little train moved off as a smart, green-uniformed ticket inspector came along to view our tickets (fortunately we had validated them on the platform after seeing our Barboured-acquaintance do the same). However, it was still necessary to write profusely all over them. The train picked up speed and we ran through lemon grove after lemon grove, rank after rank of dark green leaved trees. Foliage fused together into a continual dark green mass, with the lemons twinkling like yellow jewels in the morning sun. Inland, a range of calcareous rock rose up to form a mountainous sentinel ridge. Our only stop was Avola – a seaside resort but also famous for its excellent quality almonds called *pizzuta*, and Nero d'Avola red wine. Here, deciduous trees (presumably almond) intervened between the lemon groves and there would be an occasional orange grove. We passed crop pickers in fields bent low to pull vegetables from neat furrowed rows of dark brown rich earth, but as we moved away from the sea in our approach to Syracuse, the earth became rockier and was given over to olive groves.

We thoroughly enjoyed our day in Syracuse and wanted to spend more time there, so it was fortuitous that as we walked down Corso Gelone we saw a large blue sign for motorhome parking in the city. As the same little train took us back, tooting urgently at each of the many level-crossings, we decided to return in the van and try for the parking. Corrada met us at the station with her mother, who was equally delightful, and we exchanged simplistic banter from front to back of the car in the way that one does when a paucity of language prevails.

The next day we waved farewell to Michele and the lemon pickers and retraced the train route by road. Passage into Syracuse was busy, but without incident, and following the blue signs we arrived at 'Sosta Parking' on Von Platen. It was alongside a huge, open-storage building for around sixty motorhomes and a park for tour buses. The guys had done a great job grassing it over, providing lighting, and convenient electrics and water. (Strangely, in two corners, high on iron supports, were two glassed-in watchtowers as though it had previously been a penitentiary!)

On arrival, one of the men at the gate led us the twenty yards on his bike and waited patiently whilst we set up. When we were ready he went through a precise presentation with photocopied maps of the city – explaining where we were situated, the distances to major attractions ('One kilometre here and one kilometre there') and essential information on the electric, water, toilets, showers and waste disposal. He was wonderfully helpful. I tried to ask him how many amperes the electric provided.

'*Quanti amperes*?' He looked puzzled.

'*Inclusivo.*'

'No. No. *Quanta electtricità?*'

'*No. No. Inclusivo.*' I looked at the fuses in the box, but was none the wiser, so we left it there, neither of us satisfied. (I tried to ask this question many times in Sicily but never got an answer other than that, or, '*basta*', meaning 'enough'!)

When there was no-one to escort in (and there were only three vans on site that could accommodate I would guess sixty), he was the main gardener, rubbish clearer, grass cutter, concrete pourer and general factotum, watched at all times by his boss who, unnervingly, stood less than two yards away, supervising and commenting on how to do each task.

Syracuse: It's Hard to Leave

We liked Syracuse so much we left it twice, only to return. It was founded around 734 BC on the small (now downtown) island of Ortygia, and built with stone from the limestone quarries, or *latomia*. It was only a short walk from where we were parked.

Below the man-made limestone cliffs in the Parco Archeologico della Neapolis we found exotic and luxuriant sunken gardens, befitting the name Latomia del Paradiso. Orange, lemon, fig and palm trees protruded from the lush vegetation and completely hid the floor, plants scrambled over and engulfed huge boulders and pinnacles of limestone that had been cut, or had fallen, from the quarry face centuries ago. Nature had reclaimed the destruction brought about by man's sweat and toil and had produced a tranquil, verdant spot where the casual observer might linger, unaware of its dark history.

In 415 BC around two hundred ships and thousands of men set sail from Athens to quell Syracuse, where they felt their Greek cousins were getting too important for their own good. The war of attrition lasted until 413 BC (with winter breaks for the Athenians in Catania). The advantage swung back and forth. Then, despite reinforcements being sent from Athens, the Athenians became trapped in Ortygia harbour and 40,000 were forced to attempt an escape overland, with little in the way of provisions or water. They didn't succeed, and all but seven thousand died or were massacred. The survivors were taken prisoner and thrown into the hellhole of the sun-blinding, bare limestone *latomia* to perish.

John L. Stoddard tells us that 'those who were able to recite to their aesthetic conquerors passages from the plays of Euripides, were drawn up out of this appalling charnel house, and set at liberty.'[7]

We entered a cave at the base of the cliffs. I expected dankness, but the floor and walls were dry. They arched above and curved away from us to disappear into darkness. As we penetrated further, we found that we couldn't see, and instinctively stretched our hands out in front of us like a game of *Blind Man's Bluff*, our calls echoing round the walls. Not knowing where we were, and amazed the authorities hadn't provided lighting, I relieved our momentary desperation by taking a flash photo. It produced a picture of the solid rock wall that we were about to collide with (and now know was sixty-five metres from the entrance). With no-one else in the cave there was a cool, uncertain, tomb-like atmosphere – a sensation of a depressing mass twenty-three metres above, and it gave an inkling of how deeply disheartening it must have been for those political prisoners incarcerated there by Dionysius I in later years. Because of its shape and acoustic properties, it became known as Dionysius's Ear.

---

[7] John L Stoddards's Lectures.

I am indebted to Wikipedia for the following story: Once, Dionysius had Philoxenus arrested and sent to the quarries for voicing a bad opinion about his poetry. A few days later, he released Philoxenus because of his friends' requests and brought the poet before him for another poetry reading. Dionysius read from his own work and the audience applauded. When he asked Philoxenus how he liked it, the poet replied only, 'Take me back to the quarries.'

In addition to the *latomia*, the park contains the fifth century Greek Theatre, cut directly from the limestone, and 'the largest remaining theatre of its kind,' seating 16,000. The backdrop is of a distant Ortygia port, the sea, and the closer, and hideous, new concrete cathedral. Alerted by the guidebook, we searched and found the carvings on the rocks to demarcate the high-level seats reserved for the 'Royal Family'. We walked around the curves of the seating and then down to the base, and looking up, we took an actor's point of view from the stage to the auditorium, the caves above, and 'the greatest monument of theatre architecture which we have today'.

We walked up a hill from the Greek Theatre past an enormous slab of stone known as the Altar of Hyrone II, where four hundred and fifty oxen were sacrificed to Zeus and Eleuterio each year by the third century BC Syracusans. Further up the hill, we arrived at a café where business was slow to non-existent and a man outside had to shout to the owner to come and serve us. He was so pleased to see us that along with the coffees we ordered, he warmed up two *cornetti* – one filled with pistachio and the other with ricotta, and presented them to us '*gratuito*.'

Four conspiratorial guys sat on chairs under a porch at the entrance to the Roman Amphitheatre and eyed us as we approached – or were we simply getting suspicious of the national dress of black leather jacket, jeans, and aversity to shaving?

'*Prego, prego*,' said the youngest, standing to wave us in. Once again we had the site to ourselves. Whereas the

Greek Theatre was impressive, we warmed more to the third century Roman Amphitheatre – perhaps the coffee had had a restorative effect. We wandered in and out and sat on the stone seating, our imaginations fired. With tunnels for the animals and gladiators to enter the elliptical arena, we felt it could have happened, we could *see* it happening – but maybe that was as a result of watching Russell Crowe and *Spartacus* movies!

We drove out to Belvedere, a village, not a viewpoint (although there is a good view so that's probably how it got its name). Shortly before the village there is an ancient, but ruined massive Greek fort, the Euryalus Castle, built in 402 BC by Dionysius I to defend Syracuse from land invasion, but remodelled by many thereafter. At the entrance kiosk, being the only visitors, we had the full attention of the young girl and a diminutive old man. Gail prolonged their enjoyment of our company by counting out the admission fees in centimos. We walked along the rock-strewn route, most of the walls having collapsed, to the far end and views down to Syracuse. However, over to the left, and belying the name 'Belvedere,' lay the aesthetically less attractive, but nonetheless mesmerising, industrial complex of coastal refineries at Augusta. Toy-like tankers waited on a deep blue sea for their time to be called in. Returning along another path, and almost by chance, we saw a small sign: 'Allé *Galleria*'. What a surprise. Tunnels and passageways below the rock walls ran the length and breadth of the castle. Exploring one passageway, it became deeply puddled, but undaunted, we traced the route over ground to start again from the far end, and enthusiastically crouched down to enter into a dark and low tunnel.

'Ooooer, what's that? We've disturbed something!'

'Can you see what it is?'

'No, it's dark. It's flapping around – oh God, it's coming at me! – There's not enough room – duck!'

'No, let's get out.' We scrambled for the entrance, falling into each other, and were followed by a pigeon. If we hadn't seen the obscure sign, we would have missed an incredible series of tunnels and stairs built for the swift movement of troops and entrapment of enemies.

The next morning, we woke to the bells of the New Cathedral – a laboured and indecipherable tune devoid of melody that sounded like a child's first attempt on a Rolf Harris stylophone. The Catacombs of San Giovanni were our morning's target – we hoped the necropolis would provide something a little racy, uncertain, on the edge, but not too scary. An English guide was to be available an hour later at 10:30 a.m. to show us round. At the appointed hour, our guide appeared. A small, fair-haired lady in her mid-thirties, she wore a black anorak, blue sports pants, and silver trainers. The impressive torch she carried rekindled our excitement. A young American couple and two academic-type Italian men dressed smartly in sweaters and corduroy trousers joined us. Our first stop was the Church of San Giovanni Evangelista – the first cathedral of Syracuse and last resting place of the city's first bishop, San Marciano. The Arabs devastated it, the Normans rebuilt it, and finally, the 1693 earthquake brought the roof down, so now it is a ruin with an external door and some end walls (Norman façade and a rose window) remaining. One of the Italians knew something more about it than the guide and began to explain it to the Americans. The other Italian's mobile phone rang, so he missed everything until we descended into the crypt of San Marciano. It dates back to the fourth century and the highlight was the little altar and pillars, but primarily the knowledge that Paul the Apostle had dropped in for a three-day sojourn 'preaching the faith.'

Our guide had excellent English and an extensive knowledge of the church and the catacombs, but we did have to decipher some words. Having watched '*Allo, Allo*' in the past was helpful, as the '*Nomans*' had apparently built part of the church and the '*mandibles*' (skull) of old bishop San Marciano had been removed. We couldn't wait to descend from the crypt into the Christian catacombs, 'an underground city of the dead'. It augured much: 'Second only to those in Rome.' We were soon in dark tunnels, created partially by enlarging the original Greek aqueducts that off to the side had graves for early Christian families. Each open grave was cut into the limestone, then as the need arose, another was cut behind it in a series of troughs, or when subsequently viewed on the plan, horizontal ladders radiating out from long passages. Up to twenty bodies could be in a row, large, small and baby-sized ones – 20,000 tombs arranged over a disorienting maze of tunnels, rooms, galleries, and caves. We proceeded in reverential silence in the knowledge that we would be lost in the darkness without the guide. The sensations, heightened by the silence and the darkness, were only alleviated by the lighting being switched on at strategic points, the guide's torch accenting some feature, or occasionally, daylight streaming in from an opening above.

The highlight historically was the discovery in 1872 of 'a fine Roman fourth century sarcophagus that held the body of Adelphia, wife of the consul Valerio,' and much decorated in bas-relief with figures from Old and New Testaments. Unfortunately, it had been removed to the archaeological museum. Of more social interest was the information that on the anniversary of the death and the rising of the spirit to eternal life, the relatives had a picnic party by the grave and poured wine, milk, honey and other delicacies for the deceased through three holes in the covering slab.

'But where are all the skeletons and bones?' I enquired at the end of the tour.

'They were removed and placed in mass graves.'

'Why?

'There are bad people everywhere.'

'How did people find their way to their family's grave – was there a caretaker or plan to show you the way?' asked the American guy.

'There was no problem.' Questioning curtailed, we walked in silence to exit the empty city of the dead.

There were only a few French and Italian vans on site, but the groundsmen were working hard to make us feel at home. To the left of the entrance, on a triangle of grass, they had already created a huge cross of red-bracted poinsettia plants for Christmas to go along with the fairy lights round their reception hut. The man diligently watered the flowers each morning. Poinsettias appeared to be indispensable for Christmas decoration – they were being sold on corners everywhere – roadside stalls stacked high, backs of Fiat Pandas and little Piaggio three-wheelers trucks ablaze with their red colour.

'*Buongiorno. Dové* Laundromat?' I asked the man in the reception hut two days after we'd arrived.

'Lavanderia?'

'*Si.*'

'*Corso Umberto, Ortygia.*'

Blimey, I thought, *that's a long trek!* We didn't want to take the van down there, as parking was tricky, and irrationally, my next thought was to drive four kilometres to a campsite reportedly with a laundry at Rinauro. We were soon packed and underway, south from Syracuse and crossing the River Ciane (where papyrus still grows) to turn off before the Q8 station and down a country lane, slowly crossing the level crossing (an oxymoron where those in Sicily are concerned – nowhere else have we found such violent crossings – in Noto we saw a car take one at speed and nearly flip over). The green-barred gate to the campsite was closed and locked.

'Give the buzzer a go,' I yelled to Gail from the cab. A tall dark girl in her twenties eventually arrived and Gail established that they were open.

'Do you have a *lavanderia*?'

'No.'

'Oh, we must have a *lavanderia* to do our washing, that's why we came.'

'I will do in my house.'

Agriturismo Rinauro was an agricultural idyll – a broad meadow of long grasses and swathes of yellow and white flowers flourishing below ancient gnarled olive trees and a cloudless blue sky. Butterflies danced through the stems alighting on the flowers. Flowering cacti and red-poker flowers surrounded the little wooden reception hut. Bird song overwhelmed the distant hum of traffic bound to and from Syracuse and the occasional train on the same errand. It was perfect for those wishing to commune with nature, 'sixties-flower-power' style. And we weren't disappointed. Off to the right was an older campervan and at a table sat the only other site occupants, threading beads. She was in thin, blue-patterned splayed trousers and sweater; he in a taupe cardigan and faded brown sweat pants. A couple we later came to know as Evelyn and Roland.

The owner's complex of house and tumbledown outhouses lay way off to our left, darkly shaded and almost hidden by huge olive trees. An older (than me) white-haired lady emerged and walked over to us. Despite the heat of the morning she was dressed in a dark blue baseball cap, a thick, cream-coloured fleece with blue patterns on the sleeves, a pink cardigan over her shoulders, walking boots, black trousers rolled up to just above her ankles, and was carrying a large satchel.

'*Passaporte. Documentario*?' We handed over the necessary and she disappeared into the reception hut. I sat outside, swatting the few flies that had decided to investigate the newcomers. Later, Gail took our two weeks washing over to the house, stimulating the many dogs into such a barking frenzy that she was reluctant to proceed beyond the protective iron gate. She was relieved when the girl collected it from her.

Bored by the idyll, I wandered over to introduce myself to our fellow campers and Tequila, their half-Rottweiler dog. Their toolboxes were full of semi-precious stones bought from Asia, precious beads and every colour and length of thread. Their end products were attractive necklaces and bracelets. They are Austrian and spend the winters working up their collection, ready to sell them when they camp at a popular Austrian lake for the summer. I asked about the dog and was told they acquired him from a dog's home after they had a night-time attack on their motorhome when parked by the harbour in Catania. Roland's telling of the story came quickly and in detail, as though told many times, and as the days went by I wondered whether it had grown because of the trauma, as many acute observations had been made despite the night-time darkness. In the afternoon we heard singing and guitar playing – Evelyn was performing for Roland on a concrete patch below an olive tree. A little dog we knew to be shut in one of the outhouses near us started howling. Later Roland played his saxophone as he wandered through the olive grove, and set the dog off again. As the sun set, magically reddening the flowers round the reception hut even more, we retired to the van.

The next morning and after rain in the night, the warming sun rose from behind us, streaking across the olive grove. The girl arrived with the washing and Gail pegged it out as Roland, Evelyn and Tequila paid us a return visit. I liked them. Evelyn had written a book and Roland wanted to write one, an autobiography, as he had 'many things to tell.'

'Something in particular?' I asked

'Oh, the incident in Catania.' The incident clearly weighed heavy on his mind and he went over it again, with me asking questions of detail to show continuing interest.

'You tried to ram them?'

'I drove round and came back to ram the car in front.'

'But you were sandwiched in?'

'The front car moved forward when I started the engine, leaving enough room to get out.'

'Oh.'

'The man trying to get in the door was a big, big man. When I escaped and drove off he got in the car behind and chased us for miles.'

'And the car in front?

'They left after I tried to ram them.'

'Where were you going when the other car was following? Couldn't you drive to a police station, a garage that was open, or a place with a lot of people?'

'No. I only wanted to escape the big man.' I had no doubt there had been an attempted robbery, but the time sequence of events started to elude me, and I eventually concluded that they had been robbed the previous year and had gone home and rescued the dog that summer. Later I saw them industriously working at their table threading beads. They seemed to have set themselves a rigorous work schedule, and had their lives well sorted. I was also surprised by the value of the goods they produced, and wondered whether that had been a possible cause of *the robbery*.

The old lady crossed from the house to the reception hut, muffled up in her winter clothes, whereas I was sat out in shorts. Roland told me she was the girl's mother and the girl, the youngest daughter, was a vet. 'She goes out when phoned.' We hadn't seen her go out – they had ten dogs, so maybe there was plenty to do on site. Later, the elder sister arrived and started to ladle out olive oil, presumably home produced, from a steel milk churn into plastic bottles. A man arrived in a car and parked a short distance away. He put on a white, plastic abattoir boiler suit, a heavy leather apron, plastic-visored helmet, and Wellington boots, and then took out a strimmer and proceeded to destroy the swathes of lovely white and yellow flowers and meadow grasses around us.

The next day we returned to Syracuse with clean and fresh smelling clothes. After a rain-soaked morning we sauntered down the road into a café for a coffee, but then the heavens opened and the rain descended again.

'Let's try their fancies and hope the rain stops.' I made a selection of the mouth-watering cakes in the form of a strawberry, lemon, banana, walnut, and others forgotten, all beautifully made in marzipan. The rain stopped as I stepped up to pay a whopping twenty euros for the cakes. Fireworks sounded outside as the bill was rung up.

Café-bars are the lifeblood of Syracuse. By the market in Ortygia and across the road from the remaining Doric columns of the Temple of Apollo, old men sat outside in the morning sun, apparently not buying anything. Inside, glass-encased counters displayed vast arrays of *cornetti* and delicate cakes, in another, pizzas, trays of hot pastas, and other enticing fast-food, and in the glass cases along the walls, chocolates. There was a bar with shelves stacked with liquor bottles, and steaming coffee machines below tended by a tall skinny man. Trays of fresh food continued to arrive from the kitchens behind to be served by a young girl and boy in baseball caps. Watching all this by the open door was a man in a wheelchair, we presumed he was the boss. Although it was busy, everyone entering embraced and bid him '*Buongiorno*.'

Ortygia is the original Syracuse, a city strategically overlooking the sea where three thousand years of Mediterranean civilisations followed each other and overlaid their influences. This little island is stuffed with history and palaces and church buildings being used as either galleries, municipal or retail buildings, workshops, hotels, restaurants, and private accommodation – and yet each time we visited, it was surprisingly quiet and empty. Small as it is, there are different quarters with different characteristics. Looking at a street map and having walked for a couple of hours, you feel you know it intimately and there is little left to see, then suddenly a narrow street leads you to discover another area of faded architectural stonework. The buildings up to Piazza Archimede (their most famous resident) and round the cathedral square have all been renovated, but you don't have to wander far to find that many suffer the Sicilian disease of being 'Under Restoration' and are simply shells with a bit of corrugated iron blocking a door or window. Near the Vigliena fort we came across a delightful terrace of seaward-facing houses being pleasingly restored that produced one of those 'if only I had the money' moments. However, a few streets into the island, in the Old Jewish district, many houses are seemingly beyond repair, held up and forced apart by giant wooden braces criss-crossing the narrowest of alleys.

We set off inland for Pantalica via Sortino. The town had a very regular grid system of roads that ended with a sheer drop into a gorge. An unexpectedly poor coffee in a bar was only lifted by the arrival of a granddad who showed off his pretty granddaughter in a pink bonnet to all his mates. Judging by the affection she was shown by these tough characters, the idea that Italian children are the centre of the universe was certainly upheld here.

We drove out of Sortino to cross the gorge with only a scrubby sign to assist us. We were on a narrow road in a wilderness without people, habitation, or signs of agriculture, and didn't appear to be getting anywhere. After some time worrying, we finally came to a gate across the road. There had been no signs and there was no turnaround – just the width of the road. We were literally at a dead end: the Necropoli di Pantalica, us, and supposedly, five thousand tombs. The style-gate entrance gave us no clues to where we were – an earth path led into the limestone gorge. As we walked further and looked across at the face of the gorge opposite, we could see that the many limestone outcrops amongst the green and low bush scrubland were potmarked with a honeycomb of holes. On our side, worn steps in the rocks started to appear, and then some caves. We peered into one – it was empty apart from a rocky shelf (I'm not sure what we expected). Pantalica is described by guidebooks as the 'largest rock necropolis in Europe'. Human activity dates from the thirteenth century BC, after the population of eastern Sicily ran away from the Siculi, abandoning their coastal homes and agricultural holdings to seek protection inland. Pantalica became the most important of these settlements. 'Today, Pantalica is an archaeological and natural oasis of lush Mediterranean vegetation and was inserted in UNESCO's World Heritage List on the 17th July 2005 along with Siracusa.' As we walked on, newer, polished wood signboards appeared, but without information. Red spray-painted arrows led over the cliff edge to a large cave about halfway down, but it seemed impossible to reach it. After a couple of miles we found a path down to the bottom of the gorge. Below a large complex of caves ran a crystal-clear, fast running river. Apart from the rushing water it was eerily quiet, and there was a feeling that we were trespassing on centuries of history – inhabitants had lived there since the Bronze Age and it was they who had carved out these tombs in the rocks. The skies started to cloud over, so we retreated back to the van as rain started to fall.

'Shall we park up here for the night?' I asked Gail over lunch. 'There's no one around.'

'Exactly! No thanks.' Disoriented on the small back roads, we ended up returning via Mellili, with panoramic views of the conglomeration of Augusta oil refineries shooting flames into the blackness of the sky, before joining the Autostrada.

Over the next few days a United Nations of motorhomes arrived, including a thirty year old converted Dutch Mercedes fire engine – in red of course. George and Maryanne told me they had been overwintering for ten years. They travelled the six winter months, as we did, then his wife did supply teaching in the summer and he earned a little from publishing his overwintering guide – *So Much More Than A List Of Campsites*. He bought the fire engine on a whim and took it to Greece where, with the help of his brother, they converted it to a motorhome. He told me in thrilling and intricate detail about getting his caravan stolen from his front drive in Holland as he was loading it up to go away. He chased it down this road, and then that one, through Holland, and even across the Belgian border. Calling the police on his phone during the chase, they quoted border restrictions and wouldn't help! He, having been a university lecturer in law, cited European law back at them, but to no avail. I responded with an account of the experience of Roland at Rinaura.

'Being a lawyer, I don't believe any of these stories without evidence. Many grow in people's imaginations...' Right, George.

Lars and his wife from Finland were to be interviewed by the local radio station on the unassailable premise that they, like Sicilians, also lived on an island off the mainland. We, double qualifying (Great Britain and Isle of Dogs islanders) weren't approached. A couple from New Zealand parked up. Harries and Jean with Lordy, their lovely Collie-cross dog, parked their Arto motorhome next to us. Jean was Irish born and bred; Harries a German who spoke English with a strong Irish accent. They were non-stop talkers and amused us with many Sicilian travel stories and information, mostly related to restaurant eating. On the basis of our visit to Noto, Jean was insistent they went back so she could have an evening there. They would stay at Michele's site.

On the 13th December, Santa Lucia day, Lars was walking his white Westie dog across the site when the first celebratory fireworks of the day went off. They sounded like bombs and we felt the tremor in the van. The poor Westie, with an amazing turn of speed, ran like a scared rabbit, going past our van in a blur. Lars, somewhat stunned himself, started the chase and we were pleased to see them finally re-united. More bangs erupted and we continued to feel the vibrations despite our fine Mercedes suspension. Santa Lucia is the Patron Saint of Syracuse and is often depicted with a dagger through her neck, and her two eyes on a plate she holds in front of her. Born in Syracuse around AD 283, her father died when she was young and her mother betrothed her to a pagan bridegroom even though she was a Christian. However, Lucia's prayers to Saint Agatha of Catania cured her mother's long-standing haemorrhagic illness, so together they agreed that she should dedicate her life to God. The usurped bridegroom reported her to the Roman Governor of

Sicily as a Christian and she was banished to a brothel for a life of prostitution, but the guards who came to take her found her immoveable 'even by a team of oxen,' so they tortured her and tore her eyes out, and then sentenced her to death by burning. When the fire couldn't be lit, they stabbed her through the neck. Miraculously, she could see even without her eyes.

We watched the statue of a silver Lucia being carried out of the cathedral and down the steps, escorted by men in green hats to a jostling crowd in the square, all hoping to touch the cortege. Many were barefoot. The Cardinal addressed the multitude from his balcony in an overlong speech. Then the procession, led by a golden coach drawn by two white horses and guided by an old boy in a lop-sided white wig, green tail-coat, green satin britches and black tri-corn hat, set off round the island. As Lucy is Patron Saint to and for the blind, cutlers, dysentery, eye disease, eye problems, fire, glaziers, haemorrhages, labourers, martyrs, notaries, peasants, peddlers, Perugia, Italy, saddlers, salesmen, servant girls, stained glass workers, scribes, Syracuse, Sicily, tailors, throat infections, virgins, weavers, and writers, no one had an excuse not to be there.

Pete and Di were in a small Knaus motorhome – we recommended they go to Noto (we were firm Noto enthusiasts), so they did, and George and Maryanne went off to Catania in the fire engine. We decided on a trip out. Our route was via Canicattini Bagni on the SS287 – a good road with nice country scenes taking around forty-five minutes. Palazzolo Acreide welcomed motorhomes and provided a modern area of dedicated, open-air parking paved with black lava blocks and some concrete, swirly ramps and walls that had already been graffited. Unfortunately it was some distance away, at the bottom of the town. Climbing up, we came to Piazza del Popolo, dominated by the majestic façade of *San Sebastiano* raised up a flight of steps, and the galleried Town Hall. However, coffee called and we partook of this in a modern café where papers were available so we could look up the weather forecast (that turned out to be very mixed). A small, interesting museum was indicated in the guidebook so we set off to find it up Caso Alberto, lined with Baroque palaces, and then a back street, Via Machiavelli. The huge, stable-like outer doors were open, but the inner, folding, green wood and glass doors were locked. We gave the bell a try and a small, black-haired lady of middle age came down and opened up a side door for us to lead us into a stone atrium. She presented us with a comprehensive room-by room guide in English, and we were ready to wander off when she made it clear we were not to be trusted and she would accompany us. The *Casa-Museo dell'etologo Antonio Uccello* was said to be a palace once owned by Baron Ferla and later turned into a house-museum by another owner, the ethnologist Antonio Uccello. It is one man's dedication to local history – each room is set out as he has researched and imagined it would have been, with artefacts, remains, and working tools from the peasant civilisation of Sicily. We loved the museum. It is arranged in a way that gives the impression the occupants are still in residence but have momentarily left the premises. In the farmer's family room everything for their daily needs is shown: a small oven for bread making, milk and ricotta cheese preparation tools, spinning and weaving looms, and wine casks. In a smaller room there are many religious and family pictures on the walls, their clothes (including the bridal dress), the great bed with a 'night vase' under, and above, a cradle for the baby suspended by wires from the corners of the room. Most of the pottery items come from Caltagirone. On the ground floor is a working room containing a large, stone-wheeled oil press and a giant, wooden, corkscrew honey-press. Stepping down from the mill room there is a large, cave-like storage house where the animals could deliver and collect loads of wheat and the grain that had been winnowed through a large sieve.

There were many Baroque churches throughout Palazzo Acreide and if I listed them all here you would be as bored as I was when seeing them all. Even the most glorious Chiesa di S. Paolo dedicated to their Patron Saint Paul was locked, and its magnificent towered façade and wonderful statues running the full length of the roof were covered in pigeon excrement. Across the road, scaffolding surrounded Chiesa Madre.

We lunched close to Piazza del Popolo on Vittoria Emanulele III in a café-*pasticcheria* watched by a young boy who was so fascinated by us that he stood silently by our table, his head just coming over the top, eyeing up every fork and mouthful we tasted. It was almost as though he was willing some of the food into his own mouth. His mother, who was wandering round the café, didn't seem to think this unusual. After they had gone, I perused the stunning display of delicacies.

'*Ossa re Muorti*?' I enquired.

'*Si.*' 'Bones of the Dead' are available all over Italy, and given to children on 2nd November as gifts from the dead. They are usually shaped as limb bones, vertebrae or skulls. The shop had piles of the leg bone variety – Palazzolo Acreide is a specialist, and visitors are apparently attracted from all parts of Sicily. There were other delicacies – *facciuna, ciascuna, and giggiulenna,* respectively filled with almonds, dried figs, or sesame seeds with almonds, and cooked with sugar and honey. The bones filled with walnuts and honey were dry, crumbly, and a big disappointment. Perhaps they'd been hanging around for the last month and a half.

One of the main reasons to visit Palazzolo Acreide was to visit Akrai – probably the first colony founded by Syracuse in 664 BC, and part of the Roman Empire. We walked back down the hill towards the car park, and came to a town plan that we stared at for some time without revelation. The usual gaggle of old boys sitting on stone benches watched us. Then one came over and stood behind us, watching our fingers trace over the map but offering no help. Fed up of him scrutinising us, I asked him where it was.

'*Dové Akrai*?' He stared at the map and shrugged. '*Teatro Romano*?' I tried again. He pointed to a street five minutes away in an easterly direction. '*Si*?' I asked questioningly.

'*Si*,' he said, turning to point down the road.

'*Grazie*.'

'*Prego*.'

'He's wrong. We should be going west,' I said to Gail.

'He seemed confident.'

'I think he simply couldn't lose face in front of his mates and admit he couldn't answer the question,' I grumbled.

'Surely not!' Five minutes later we came to an open square and the entrance to a park.

'See, it's not it.'

'I'll ask the girls sitting on that step.' From their faces and words of 'long way' and 'up,' we were clearly way off track. We walked the narrow back streets down a hill, but as we started to climb another I'd had enough, and we went and got the van and retraced our steps, driving out of town up the hill and following brown signs to '*Parco Archeologico*'. It was high above Palazzolo Acreide, on a flat headland, and had an impressive theatre and a town of crumbled walls spread over thirty-five hectares. There were low limestone cliffs with caves that acted as Arab rock dwellings like those we'd seen at Panatalica.

We drove back to Noto on a small and lovely road through Vetrano, Rigolizia, Mezzo Gregorio, and Villa Oliva. When we arrived, Pete and Di were there and we spent the evening in their van going over maps. Brrrr! It was cold when we woke, so I turned up the heating a lot and then Gail got the kettle going, or rather, she attempted to get the kettle going, but there was no gas to light. At that moment the little red heating warning light came on and it shut down. I went out into the cold and hammered the regulator, then switched from one bottle to another, but nothing worked. I was in a foul mood. I went to see Michele, who was buried in the forest of lemon trees in the grove next door. He phoned people, but none could help. I decided we should return to Syracuse, where there would be more chance of help. We arrived at the *sosta* in Syracuse and I explained the situation – the boss man and others gathered round and said they would phone. But did they? I had another go with the rubber hammer – the gas came on!

It rained hard for the next day and poured all through the night, continuing into the morning. We were the only ones left on site, but the site workers were nonetheless busy digging a ditch round the front and far side of the plot of land behind us, trying to convert it to accommodate more motorhomes. Their efforts were closely supervised by the big boss in a black anorak who stood over them constantly issuing instructions about how and where to dig, but did nothing himself. In turn, his efforts were supervised by the big, big boss who had a cream-coloured anorak and came by at regular intervals with his Alsatian dog to get long reports from the big boss about how the digging was going. Late into the afternoon the digging crew had finished and were racing to pour concrete into the ditch – the dark overhead clouds forewarning the possibility of more rain and a ditch full of water. It certainly worked. No water was trapped in their ditch – all the water that might have resided there ran smoothly along the concrete to flood the area round our van. We were marooned in the middle of a small lake. With continuing rain, the small lake rapidly became a large deep lake, and of necessity I had to wade through it to empty the cassette. But their new plot was dry. We decided to leave the next day if we could extricate ourselves.

South then West by Agrigento

As we woke, something had changed – the cathedral Stylophone was playing a *Guess That Tune* medley of Christmas tunes.

'I've got it – Oh Come All Ye Faithful.'

'No, that one's got me foxed.'

With the sun breaking through after the rains we decided to leave for the south-east coast. We had been trying to explore it for a while to compare it with Fallowell's experience.

We drove along flooded roads to the coast and Lido di Noto, deserted but for a few workmen digging up the impressive *lungomare*. An interesting feature of the *lungomare* was the cladding of the railings in blue Perspex panels, thereby giving the filthy and tempestuous sea an effective turquoise, Caribbean Sea makeover. As we left, the sky became blue-black, the heavens opened, and what wasn't flooded before became a raging torrent.

We struggled to find our way to Eloro and the eighth century remains of the town of Helorus by the river Tellaro, but we were already in a river of muddy water and although

I could see the chimney, I could also see that the tiny road descended and the waters were picking up debris from the fields, so I ducked out (if that's the correct expression…)

On still more deserted back roads we found our way to Pachino, passing the aptly-named marshlands of Vendicari that the guidebook informed us was a nature reserve with a 'Mediterranean sea climate,' and 'amongst the driest and hottest in the whole island, with very low rainfall and African winds.' At the precise time of reading it, we were coursing through a road awash with water; muddy, Zambesi-style rivers were issuing from every opening and gateway; the skies were black and the rain was thundering onto our roof.

Paschino appeared and disappeared through a blur of rain and deeply cratered puddles, and we finally reached Portopalo di Capo Passero and parked in its port. The sun broke out, but even in the harbour the sea was tempestuous as we watched the small blue and white boats and larger, gaudily-painted Arab dhows with Arabic script on their bows and rust dribbling over their sides rise and fall in the swell. We lunched in the van, watching fish vans coming and going and fishermen mending their nets on the harbour side. We were as near as it made no difference to the most southerly point of Sicily and below the parallel of Tunis. It was an evocative scene as the sun finally found its way through the thunderclouds.

Portopalo earned a place in history as the landing point for Anglo-American troops on 10th July 1943, but the area also reportedly hid a dark secret. On 26th December 1996, in the sea off Portopalo, two hundred and eighty-three of three hundred South Asian migrants drowned when the eighteen-metre fishing vessel they were being transferred to collided with the freighter, *Yohan* that had brought them. 'Harbor (sic) officials and fishermen from the port of Portopalo kept silent and the Italian government denied the tragedy ever took place, and refused to accept the testimonies of survivors.'[8] Only in 2001 did a local fisherman finally talk to a journalist about it.

We continued along the coast and returned to Punto Braccetto – it appeared to be a haven. Bob and Bridget were still there and Pete and Di had arrived from Noto.

The next day we set about restoration, but not relaxation, with me washing the van with Angelo's agreement and use of his ladder and Gail doing washing and ironing ready for our next journey. More and more vans were arriving on site for Christmas and there was much manoeuvring onto pitches. It made us question whether we should stay and be amongst fellow campers, many of whom we had got to know well, but only for a moment: there was so much more to discover.

We left early the next day with a van sparkling in the sun, but from the first corner were mistakenly taken through the centre of San Croce by the GPS. It redeemed itself in Vittoria, taking us straight to Lidl for shopping, where I waited outside to watch the van. A scruffily dressed candidate for the breaking and entering game slid past the back of the van without seeing me. Then he did, and broke into a smile.

'I know what you're up to,' my look said.

'It's a fair cop,' he grinned back at me, and sidled away across the car park to some rough buildings on the other side of the road.

The sun was shining as we drove into Gela, the ugly petrol-refining and chemical town, for the second time on our journey. It provided little reason to stop and a lot of reasons not to, the worst of Sicily concentrated in one place. It desperately needs a new by-pass, because the one we were on also performed the function of a never-ending high street.

The countryside beyond varied from precision-rowed newly-planted vineyards and meadows with prickly pear cactus and palms to ugly polytunnels with a backdrop of

---

[8] http://en.wikipedia.org/wiki/Portopalo_di_Capo_Passero

distant hills. The fourteenth century Castello di Falconara looked mightily impressive as a sea defence, standing on a rocky promontory surrounded by a luxurious palm garden.

'The ancient tower was used to breed falcons, hence the name. It is privately owned by the Chairamonte Bordonaro family who make it available for exclusive hire, as an apartment with service staff included or, receptions,' Gail read out from the guidebook.

'Maybe next time.'

We by-passed Licata on a decent road and it was a strange phenomena – the sky was black over the town but bright blue to our right, the sharp dividing line exactly reproducing the curve of the road. We stopped for fuel at an AGIP station. I had always found Italian attendants very protective of their pumps, however, the sign said 'Self Service'. I could see the grey-uniformed attendant in the glass-fronted office and unsure what to do for the best, I waited until he came over.

'Self Service,' he pronounced.

'*Si. Va bene.*'

I got to work pumping the diesel and he stood, embarrassingly, no more than a couple of feet away and watched me fill the tank. I made faces at Gail through the passenger window and she tried not to laugh. Credit card in hand she went to the office to pay. As she got back in the van our friend was busy checking the oil on a newly-arrived car. Gail and I looked at each other.

'Self service?'

As we dipped in and out of the black cloud it rained on and off. Palma di Montechiaro looked a concrete abomination, as did so many others when viewed from the back. We arrived at Agrigento via the seaside at San Leone, and eschewing the Nettuno and Olivia sites, settled for the deserted Valle dei Templi.

We discovered the site had a number of quirks – including many water taps that had *Non Potabile* signs.

'What would you use it for?' I wondered to Gail.

'*Dové aqua potabile?*' I asked the young girl in the office, thinking she might welcome some conversation.

'*Supermercado.*'

'*Nessuno qui?*'

'*No.*'

Yet the brochure said to fill with water for three Euros and the dump was outside the camp in an entrance area and cost a further two Euros. Once again, we would have to manage.

We dined across the road at a Trattoria that you might find anywhere in South Kensington in London and then walked it off by heading for the archaeological site, the Vallei di Templi. Having the same name as the campsite, we expected it to be in reasonable proximity. After one-and-a-half kilometres we could see that we were less than half way and that crossing the arterial road junction to get there was a 'life in your own hands' risk we weren't prepared to take.

On return to the van a thunderstorm broke and persisted into the evening and through the night. The Gods were angry about something. We would make our peace with them the next day.

As we approached the site of the Greek temples looking for parking, I spotted a cratered sandy patch on the left almost submerged in water. There were wooden tourist information kiosks, but only two were open and a prominent sign: 'No Motorhomes'. I drove straight in, avoiding the worst of the lakes. Gail is always nervous on such occasions with dire warnings of clamping, towing-away, or fines but nobody approached us, so we bought tickets from the information centre and started our tour.

The Temple of Concordia is a well-preserved example of a 430 BC temple. Beautifully placed on a ridge between the shimmering sea on one side and a valley on the other, it is an uplifting sight for those approaching from below. On the hill above was the more modern medieval town of Agrigento. The temple's preservation was due to it being converted to a church in the sixth century. Its sandstone colour resonated in the few shafts of early morning sunlight that had managed to find their way between the columns.

At the top of the hill we found the Templo di Giunone – a half-ruin with patches of red on the stonework attributed to fire damage in 406 BC when the city was sacked by the Carthaginians. As we left, it was about to be sacked by a crocodile of camera-clicking Japanese tourists clambering up the path from their coach, the only other visitors.

The more modern temple of coffee, or café, half way along the ridge was our sanctuary. The toilets round the back were a surprise, as on entry there was a male attendant sitting there with a side table and a radio playing softly. Toileting whilst someone sits outside the booth unavoidably listening to the ministrations is unsettling – he should turn his radio up louder! Being the only visitors to the café, we should have had the full attention of the young server, but she took our order; made the coffees; got the one *cornetto* out for me; delivered it all to the table; took our money; and finally, cleared the table with a mobile phone at her ear the entire time. Quite a feat.

Back down to the entrance we skirted the closed necropolis to visit the sixth century BC Tempio di Ercole and carefully counted the nine columns that had been re-erected. The pieces of the remaining thirty-eight lay scattered around on the ground like a stonemason's yard. How do they know they were ever put up?

Across the road, in the rain, is what is known as the 'western zone'. There were more piles of rocks, masonry, and rubble strewn about, some big walls and the Tempio di Giove – the largest Doric temple ever known – but never completed. The most fascinating item was an eight-metre high figure of a male lying on his back with arms raised, supposedly to act as a supporting column. It would be a perfect reproduction if someone wanted a statue of a man sunbathing.

Looking back on the temples and the ruins of Pindar's 'most beautiful city of mortals' and our guidebook's 'the most captivating of Sicilian Greek remains and a grouping unique outside Greece,' I didn't get the same elation as I had at Paestum. But then ruins are like skeletons – all life, all personality has gone, and a vivid imagination is required to put it back. With less rubble perhaps it was easier to do it at Paestum.

The car park had filled up, the wooden souvenir shops opened, and a man approached us for a fee. After some jocular badinage we agreed that he was not an official, wouldn't be able to give us a receipt, and needed the money because he had no work – so we willingly handed some over. He'd earned it – and he hadn't reported us for parking in the 'No Motorhomes' parking area.

We drove up the hill to a busy, pre-Christmas-shopping Agrigento but after two circuits couldn't find anywhere to park so set off along the SS115 with the skies becoming increasingly blacker and rain falling more heavily. Further along the coast we took a small road out from Montallegro to the remote Eraclea Minoa founded by the Greeks in the sixth century BC, with most of the remains dating from the fourth century BC. The car park had many cars in it, but only one other couple was sightseeing. The rest must have belonged to the gang of leather-jacketed men hanging around the office eyeing us up in what felt like an intimidatory fashion – what were they all doing there so far from anywhere else?

Eraclea Minoa was a disappointment. The sandstone theatre said to be the centrepiece was covered in a steep and sharply-pointed galvanised roof with a water collecting system that obscured the whole spectrum of the theatre. Many of the houses, initially impressive, had on closer inspection been over-enthusiastically restored with pointing and rendering crudely applied. The saving grace was the sea view along the white cliffs to the east and the rolling coastal views to the west, particularly from the World War Two pill-box at the top.

Our thoughts turned to where to stay for the night. The Caravan Club Guide listed two campsites in the area: one under Montallegro, the other Siculiana. We returned towards Montallegro and took another small road across country and back to the coast, arriving at a farm on a hilltop. Parked in the yard was a van I recognised – it belonged to Erich, who we'd met at Punta Braccetto. He was surprised to see us and told us it was a good site and they were the only ones camping there. When Maria, the guardian, told us there was a minimum stay of three nights, we were dumbfounded. Even after explaining we wouldn't be using their showers, toilets or electricity, she was resolute.

'I can't believe that happened. She's turning away money and she doesn't have to do anything. Crazy!' I grumbled all the way back to Montallegro, heading for Secca Grande and Camping Kameni (described on some Internet notes I had as 'the worst campground ever.') But it wasn't a time for being fussy, and the man came out to greet us with an energetic welcome and a good fourteen Euros inclusive deal for the night.

It was hard to believe that in five days it would be Christmas.

Christmas

Dogs barked through the night and owners of the two German vans near us stepped out in the morning to walk their Alsatian and West Highland White dogs. As we breakfasted I glanced at the Kameni Campsite brochure. 'No dogs allowed.' I looked through the morning drizzle towards the entrance, where a black Jeep Cherokee leant dispiritingly on its punctured tyre. A moss-covered caravan had also dropped over with a flat tyre, and another had an open window crudely sealed with blue plastic tape. Along the once impressive central building there was a detritus of broken washing machines, blue piping, a rusty trailer, and a scrapyard of other stuff. At the entrance to the building there were signs that someone was running a tyre-fitting business, with stacks of old tyres and an air-line snaking out into the road. Behind us were wooden cottages in permanent occupation. I found the dump point after wandering in and out of more cottages and realised that the site was huge and aimed at holiday cottage owners. Most had junked theirs up with a variety of tarpaulins, awnings, sunshades, tables and chairs, fridges, barbecue sets, abandoned kids tricycles and toys, planters with dead plants, washing lines and other paraphernalia. For those who came for their summer break it was probably an idyll for them, a much needed break, a time to meet up with old friends, let the kids run riot and participate in communal games with camp leaders, or run safely down to the beach. As I emptied the cassette down the drain it was a Marie Celeste of a wooden-bungalow-holiday village that I had no desire to see brought back to life. But, we were on the nicely gravelled touring van area and it had been our salvation.

The farewells were as warm as the welcome had been and we set off in the drizzle for Sciacca (pronounced Shaka). The morning traffic was chaotic and parking ridiculous. People had parked centrally in the road so Gail had to get out and push back wing mirrors so we could get through Fiat Panda-sized gaps. Frustrated, I parked on a wide, tree-lined road leading down the Grand Hotel delle Terme and the Roman hot springs (Sciacca Terme) under a sign that said something about no motorhomes. As I passed the car parked in front to feed the meter I saw it was being slept in by a suspicious-looking man with three days of beard growth. But then, didn't all Sicilian men look like this?

I won't bore you with the misdirections of the townsfolk, our failure to find a tourist office and having to use a map from Gulliver Car Hire, or the climb up the steep narrow streets to the ruined Spanish castle that simply formed part of the town's walls and was inaccessible. However, the central squares were good, and in front there was a small park with sea views. We retreated to a coffee bar that was narrow with wooden-booth seating, a strong smell of coffee and a hissing, burbling, coffee machine. Two policemen came in, soaking wet from the rain that was pouring down outside, and had their espressos. Then, reluctant to go out again, they settled for two more. As we drank ours four schoolgirls came in and sat in the next booth eating steaming pizza slices. My salivary glands, olfactory senses and rumbling stomach went into overtime and minutes later there was a *'ping'* on the microwave and two delicious slices came our way over the glass countertop.

We made a puddle-hopping dash for it, and back in the van drove down the hill to the coast and on through pleasant countryside of orange and olive groves, neat vines, ploughed fields, mountains and no more rain to Selinunte, the westernmost Greek colony.

The archaeological site has been cleverly obscured by large grassed earth mounds, forcing payment of the six Euros entrance fee to the indifferent, but conversationally busy ladies in the modern entrance building. Our sole intrusion into their day produced no more than a grunt and a ticket, but to where we weren't sure.

We found our way through some gigantic doors to the eastern end of the site, where two impressive temples and one complete ruin were set off by the afternoon sun. It was an evocative and uplifting scene. We were free to roam around unhindered through the fifth century remains and clamber onto toppled column pieces. The two temples designated 'E' and 'F' were as impressive as those at Agrigento, with a large number of the columns present along with portions of the architraves and friezes. Metopes had been removed to museums. The site is more natural than Agrigento, as rather than being on a rocky outcrop, the temples are surrounded by grass and yellow flowers of the celery plants that gave the place its name. Temple 'G' was 'the fourth largest Greek temple ever built,' except that it was never apparently completed and looked as though it had been knocked over as easily as a clay model. The massive fluted column pieces and capitals were scattered randomly on top of each other and propped up at crazy angles. This group of three temples was built away from the town of Selinunte.

The acropolis and site of five other temples could be seen far away across a valley – it looked a long walk. A round hut had information on golf trolley hire for up to fifteen Euros for the longest trip, but it was closed. At that point thunderous clouds swept up over the hills the rain started again. We ran back down a road that took us to the car park, where I caught sight of a uniformed guard going into a security post.

'*Scusi. Possiamo andare in camper?*'

'*Si. Nessun problema.*'

'*Fantastico. Grazie mille.*'

'*Prego.*'

We could drive down to the other site in the van – why hadn't those lazy girls in the office told us?

The ancient town site was enormous and looked out to sea. With the remains of five temples, city streets and huge overpowering walls it should have withstood any attack, but it was not the case and in 409 BC, 100,000 Carthaginians arrived with ladders tall enough to scale the walls and a ghastly bloodbath of rape, pillage and the murder of 16,000 townsfolk ensued. The destruction meant the end of Selinunte, and the Carthaginians finally destroyed it in 290 BC so the Romans couldn't have it. With rain pouring down we now sought shelter there by clambering up to an opening in the walls by one of the gates.

We felt thwarted – we would have liked to have spent more time there, particularly as we had the vast site to ourselves, but the rain drove us back to the van, from where I saw another motorhome parked in the road outside the perimeter fence. We drove round to find a young Swiss couple in a parking bay clearly marked 'No Motorhomes', but they told us they had already spent one night there without trouble. We decided to do the same.

The *Carabinieri* drove past in their blue and white car at 7:30 a.m. We were awake to see them as we'd had a poor night's sleep – Gail waking at 3:50 a.m. convinced that with the dashboard air vents closed, we would suffocate.

Troubled sleep seems to accompany our attempts at wild or unsupervised camping. The *Carabinieri* didn't stop or get out, probably because they would get their hats or smart uniforms wet.

Our Swiss neighbours asked us about wild camping in the UK and I nearly said 'no, because you're going to get robbed by some toe rags,' but checked myself and said the police would probably move them on so it would be better to use an official site.

We drove into Marinella, the little fishing village next to Selinunte. The café was already crowded with the men hanging round. The waves were crashing onto the shore and churning up the sand but the little fishing boats were bobbing in the water, protected by the harbour wall. It was unlikely anyone would be going out that day. We left down a back road and were surprised by how many quality houses there were. For the most part they were shuttered. The road was flooded from overnight rain and whilst I steered a course around the worst of it, the Italian drivers seemed to regard it as a challenge and overtook at full speed – their filthy bow waves splashing all over our screen.

We took the deserted motorway west to Mazara del Vallo where, conscious that Christmas was in three days, we thought it would be nice to find a campsite close to a town. However, the 'Sporting Club' with grounds full of palm trees was under attack by yellow JCB diggers and we had no appetite for it. We parked on the seafront opposite some Roman-Byzantine remains and public toilets that would require you to run the gauntlet of a seedy-looking group of men to gain entry.

Mazara was a pleasing surprise, with elegant sandstone buildings, open squares and gardens, re-worked pebbled pavements and roads, and many pedestrian areas. The information centre was closed but a helpful lady in a bookshop prevented us buying an expensive map and gave us a small tourist one instead.

We had coffees and one ricotta *cornetto* for me in a café in the main square. It started to rain again and when we checked the weather in the local paper we saw it was the same all over Europe, which didn't make us feel any better. Being only two hundred kilometres from Tunisia we felt we deserved better!

When it had abated a little we did a tour of the town, admiring the many modern shops before diving into the narrow backstreets of the Arab quarter, where open windows and doors showed plain, cave-like rooms with no more than a table and chairs and groups of men playing cards or chatting.

We made our way, not entirely successfully, through the maze of streets to the western fishing port – Sicily's most important – and a hive of activity as nets were arranged and repaired; boats of all sizes attended to; plastic bins of fish wheeled into warehouses; and decks, pavements and forecourts been hosed down by men. Marzara is famous for a two-metre high, fourth century BC bronze satyr hauled out of the sea by fisherman in 1998 and showing a male figure in an 'orgiastic' dance. We found it at the Museo del Satiro and it looked just like the thousands of postcards and posters all over town. Exiting into rain, we became weary of trudging round and as much as we liked Marzara, decided to try and find somewhere to stay.

Camping Biscione (on the coast, beyond the town of Petrosino) came to our rescue. It was out in the sticks and the access road was sandy, deeply potholed and puddled. We prayed that having driven that far out of our way, it would be open. The entrance was impressive, with a large rectangular gateway, the ceiling of which had lost its light fittings and been scored by those who hadn't realised the road surface ramped up there. The young guy in the office opened up a side gate for us – once again the only campers.

'*Quanta costa?*' I asked before we got too settled, although I think we would have paid any amount!

'*Diciotto.*'

'I see. Eighteen.' We looked depressed. ' *É inclusivo?*'

'*Si. Inclusivo.*'

'*Quindici?*'

'*Va bene.*'

'*Come ti chiami?*'

'*Federico.*'

'*É voi.*'

'Gail and Keith.'

'Gail and Kiss?' I sighed.

'No. Well, sure, that's fine.'

We were on for fifteen Euros in a pleasant, grassy area between fruit and palm trees. Federico explained that the men's toilet was 'work in progress.'

Like the whole of Sicily, I thought.

'Could you use the women's? I have to go to the airport to meet friends for Christmas.'

We settled in, the winds blew, heavy rains started and once more we were alone and confined to the small van. With Christmas three days away, our resolve was under test. (Christmas in the big van had been a joy as we could walk around, watch television, read books, have visitors, and not feel claustrophobic!)

By the next morning the weather had not improved, but by the afternoon we were determined to get out, and seeing a break in the clouds we donned anoraks and walked the short distance to the shore. The houses we passed were concrete complexes, the shutters closed and gates padlocked. One or two had a patch of land given over to vines – it hardly seemed worth it. Three mongrel dogs left in a yard barked frantically and leapt about, straining on their chains as we broke their monotony. Silver-lined clouds raced across the sky in front of motionless dark clouds. Waves were determined but not aggressive as they broke onto the shore. An occasional car cruised slowly along the beachfront road, but otherwise the little village seemed deserted. The low-rise buildings facing the sea were rendered, but on most it had fallen off to reveal patches of breeze block and weeds had taken over stone-flagged yards. In the midst of these would be one that was neat and brightly painted, as though it had been planted to put a smile back on your face. Then we rounded the corner and a beam of sunlight broke through onto the curve of the coastline, leading our eyes round to Marsala and the three offshore Egadi Islands to the northwest. A sign for a bar raised our hopes, but it was shuttered and padlocked like the rest of the village.

As we threaded our way back to the seaside we came across another bar-restaurant. On the outside it had posted menus for Christmas and New Year celebration meals for thirty-two Euros and surprisingly it was open, but also empty. We went in to find a small room with long tables for groups of ten. Through a beaded curtain I could see a man preparing food on the stainless steel worktop. I coughed loudly and he came out.

'*É possibile per due persone per Natale?*'

'*É completa.*'

'Oh. That's a shame,' I said to Gail, looking as crestfallen as possible, but not moving.

'*Faccio un piccolo tavolo per voi.*'

'A *piccolo* table for us? *Fantastico. A che ora?*'

'*A uno*,' he said, writing *Inglese* at 1:00 p.m. in the reservations book.

The sun shining from clear blue skies with a light wind made Christmas Eve a perfect drying day for Gail (and for wasps doing flying practice). When Federico arrived to unlock the gates we were able to get the washing machine underway and I was able to use the Internet to check our emails in Federico's office while he wrapped the book he had bought his sister for a Christmas present. Later he handed the keys over and said the campsite was ours, although his uncle could be reached if we wanted anything.

Christmas day arrived and the weather was hot and sunny. We phoned family and friends and I felt a small wave of nostalgia for the gatherings we used to have back at home.

But, we were going to a restaurant for a Sicilian Christmas lunch. At this point I do have to confess that we went with some trepidation, as when we first looked at the menu there was a long list of dishes, most of which were unfamiliar to us. We had tried to find something in what we assumed to be the starter, mains and dessert sections we recognised (and secreted a language dictionary in my pocket).

The restaurant was beautifully set up. At the end furthest from us, the restaurant opened onto a raised patio that overlooked the road and then the sea, where they had started to set up glasses and champagne bottles in ice-buckets on a table. The young white-shirted waiter brought out the umbrella-sunshade for a final touch. It was more of an umbrella than a sunshade and stood about four-feet high, just poking above the table. With some help from those assembled we managed to get it perched on the adjacent wall.

By 2:00 p.m. all of the forty-eight smartly-dressed diners had arrived, but I couldn't say it was buzzing. On the large table on the left were, I guess, three generations of a family – and they were deferential to the oldest man, who looked as though he worked on the land but was dressed smartly and had been scalped at the barbers the day before. Everyone came to pay their respects and he had a jolly twinkle in his eye for all of them. The seating arrangements on the long table were such that all the men had to clamber round to sit with their backs to the wall and the women sat with their backs to the room. This was probably engineered by the women so that between courses they could go off in groups and socialize. Meanwhile, the men who were pinned against the wall were strangely quiet, and at one point when all the women had gone, stared blankly ahead, silent. The other tables with smaller family groups were chattier. The relatively subdued atmosphere was a surprise to us – we hoped our presence wasn't the cause. There were only three children and a baby. The plump young girl on the table next to us was dressed in a knitted top and skirt with Christmas scenes and frost edgings. She was fascinated by Gail and stood at our table watching her. Grandma took over the crying baby and had soon lulled it back to sleep, showing her granddaughter off to Gail. The other child on the long table made up for the quiet of the rest of them by being mardy and cantankerous. The choral music being played from the speakers was a blessing.

It was a non-smoking restaurant and little wine was consumed, although Gail thought was very acceptable. Many of the women drank Coca-Cola (I thought this might be because they had been designated as driver for the day, but on reflection, I don't think it works like that – do Italian men allow themselves to be driven by women?)

There was only a young lad waiting, and what a fantastic job he did – after the first course the women wandered from the table but he always seemed to be able to judge their return so they were served their food just after they sat down again. As to our concerns over the menu – as soon as we arrived we asked if we could see a copy and surreptitiously consulted the Rough Guide and a dictionary, but we needn't have worried – the meal was course after course of interesting, colourful and delicious seafood with wonderful sounding names such as *capriccio mare* (a variety plate of smoked raw fish with potato salad); *orecchiette* (little ears of pasta with scampi; artichoke and strips of radicchio); and *involtini di spada* (swordfish rolls with asparagus, stuffed grouper and prawn kebabs); and to follow, gelato *affogato* drowned in chicory coffee; a plate of many fruits; and other delicious items.

On Boxing Day we cleaned the van, and with great satisfaction saw it gleaming in the brilliant sunshine. With the upturn in the weather and the enjoyable Christmas meal any previous despondency had quickly ebbed away. And we had some company – an Italian van arrived in the early evening as the sun faded. As the temperature dropped, I turned the gas heating on but it didn't fire and the red warning light came on. It had to be that regulator. I went round the back to the gas locker and hammered at it with the rubber hammer again, turning valves on and off, but to no effect – it was finally knackered, and during the Christmas holiday too.

Neither of us slept well that night. In the morning each member of the Italian family greeted us with a merry '*Buon giorno*,' and I replied as cheerfully as I could, but my inner mood was subdued. Then something crossed my mind, and the more I thought about it, the more convinced I was.

'I'm sure I saw motorhomes for sale as we drove through Strasatti on the main road just before we turned off.' Gail was surprised.

'I don't remember anything. We haven't seen any motorhome places since Catania – are you sure?'

'I can visualise it on the left as we drove past. There were a couple of motorhomes on display and flags flying.'

Unsure whether it would be open on the day after Christmas, we were excited to find a yard jammed with motorhomes of Montalto Caravan. The young girl behind the reception counter looked bored to be working, but was good enough to come out so I could show her the problem.

'*Non funziona*,' I said, pointing to the regulator. '*Bombola di propano è piena*' (remembering my friend's advice in the garage about the word for full).

'*Aspettare! Venti minuti.*'

So we had to wait twenty minutes, but not sure what for. There was no one else in the showroom and the workshop was in darkness. I paced up and down the street outside, relieved we had found somewhere open but not sure a solution was forthcoming. Would I have to send to England for a replacement?

An hour passed and I spent the time cursing the passing trucks and cars for splashing the flooded street water all over my newly cleaned van. I began to think we were on Sicilian time and that nothing might happen when a young guy pulled up in his car and motioned that I should drive round the back to the workshop. He had come from home especially for us. Less than ten minutes later he had replaced the regulator with a higher throughput one. Then the jovial boss arrived to check everything was going according to plan and thirty Euros cash later (no receipt required, wink, wink – don't mention the 'M' word), we were on our way.

We were buoyed up by the guys fixing our problem and even found a gas supplier across the road from the motorhome place. Things were going our way. I could always clean the van another day.

To Purgatory and Beyond

Marsala, known for its sweet dessert wine, is probably the westernmost point of Sicily (excluding the islands), and takes its name from Marsah-el-Allah – the port of Allah again reflecting the Arabic influence over this region. We cruised along the *lungomare* and parked in front of an old-fashioned fairground carousel with the carved and elaborately painted horses galloping round in time with the organ music. It was a short walk through the pedestrianised area and town gates to the main square Piazza della Republica, where in front of the Baroque cathedral and Palazzo Senatorio, stood a conical Christmas tree of dark green leaves decorated simply but stylishly with bunches of grapes. There were elegant streets with high-quality shops and an Arab quarter, but our main reason for visiting Marsala was the museum's Punic warship. It was recovered in 1971 at the request of the Sicilian Authorities by nautical archaeologist Honor Frost, under the patronage of Sir Mortimer Wheeler (British Academy), and Dr Richard Barnett (British Museum), amongst others.

The story of the recovery of this thirty-five metre long, four-point-eight metre wide, one-hundred-and-twenty tonne ship, by the British team is remarkable[9]. With an almost complete stern and the bow of a sister ship, Frost's team calculated the dimensions and determined that it was probably rowed by sixty-eight oarsmen. Bones demonstrated that someone and his dog had gone down with the ship, and it was well supplied with animals, wine and cannabis. Carbon dating put it around 235 BC.

Knowing the story better prepares you for the exhibit that at first glance is less complete than might be expected, but on reflection is better that way rather than being restored to a mere model. That anything at all was brought up out of the water is remarkable.

We walked back into the city centre as Gail wanted to see the town's castle, but after much fruitless searching and her relentlessly urging us on, I was all for giving up. When we found a yellow sign, *Castillo*, lying on the grass with nothing behind it I felt vindicated, but all was forgiven over lunch in the Antica Pasticcheria.

We drove out of the city along the small coastal road in sight of the sea and in the bright sunshine. The land was flat, the sea calm with an occasional boat and a wide expanse of salt pans and windmills. On a bend in the road was a low building with signs for tickets for a little ferry boat tied up below that ran out to the island of Mozia. We were tired and ready to stop, and noticed a chained and empty car park opposite.

'I'll go over and see if there's anyone there and if they'll let us stop overnight,' I said stifling a yawn. A man dressed in a thick, dark blue sweater spotted me through the window and came out.

'*Prego.*'

'*Scusi. É possibile parcheggiare per la notte?*'

'*Si, si.*'

---

9 http://www.saudiaramcoworld.com/issue/198606/the.punic.warship.htm

'*Quanto costa?*'

'*Cinque Euros.*'

Fifteen? For a dusty car park and no facilities? I thought, registering dismay. He looked puzzled.

'*Cinque é buono, no?*'

'*Oh, cinque* – yes, five! *Mi dispiace! Penso quindici*, fifteen.' I stumbled through an apology, touching him on his forearm. '*Grazie mille.*' I *was* tired. Fortunately, he was in a good mood and laughed, holding up five fingers to emphasise the point. I put a five Euros note into them.

We parked the van, he chained us in, indicated we would have a good sleep by putting two hands to the side of his tilted head, '*Molto tranquillo qui*,' got in his car, and went. We were alone.

I sat outside for a while and watched the sunlight deepen in colour across the red-topped windmills with spider web sails, the gently-rippling water of the lagoons and sandy salt pans, the swaying palm fronds, and then the islands of Mozia and Stagnone become hazy and grey on the horizon. What an idyllic spot – it was a privilege to enjoy a scene that was a land apart from the Sicily we had seen so far. Closer to Africa than mainland Italy, it had remained unchanged since the Phoenicians created the salt pans and extracted the white gold that preserved olives and stopped fish putrefying.

A smart blue tractor was driven along the road towing a trailer with an older tractor with tracks on it. Once in the field and unloaded I could see it was one of those mini-tractors in faded red with '*Agritalia*' or similar on the side, and had a plough attached. The driver started it up with a pall of diesel smoke issuing from the smokestack and proceeded into the field, turning the sodden soil. (The Italians were the first to put a diesel engine into a tractor in 1927 and to build one with four-wheel-drive in 1952). It had to work very hard and the tracks bit deep into the earth, throwing up sods into the air. For such a small vehicle and its slow speed it made a lot of noise! The sun finally set over the islands, the tractor driver went home, and we spent a peaceful night as the guardian had told us we would.

The next morning the boss and tractor driver were back, manually broadcasting seeds from buckets into the furrows cut by the plough. The boss man took a handful of seed and distributed it all into the furrow. The older tractor driver also took a handful but managed five distributions and hence covered the ground five times faster. They covered the seeds by kicking over the furrow and tramping the soil, but later, with legs tiring, resorted to hoes.

We drove around the chain supposedly guarding us and set off north hugging the coast, salt flats and windmills; a mystical view in the early morning light. We passed another embarkation point for Mozia and came to a photogenic spot. Initially, I had tried to exclude the piles of rustic tiles that lay about on the sides of the salt pans from photos, but eventually realised they were an integral part of the salt drying process: they were used to cover the piles of extracted salt, simultaneously allowing the wind's drying action. The position of the salt in the pile apparently determines its quality.

Our destination for the day was Trapani and its port, thereby avoiding the maze of streets comprising the old town. The port lies on a thin slip of land (historically referred to as a 'sickle' or 'scimitar') with blue sea on three sides and served Erice (ancient Eryx), which sits atop the mountain behind and was founded by the Elymians (possibly from Asia Minor and occupied western Sicily around 1200 BC). The guidebook suggested that Trapani had 'little to keep you long.' We parked in a street alongside the port with nothing to suggest any restrictions, and were approached by the usual grubby guy asking for a fee. With Trapani often quoted as 'Mafia ridden' and he being unusually large, it conjured up thoughts of punctured tyres or broken headlights and I meekly paid.

The docks were packed full of ships – serious ferries towering above the pavement, modern squillionaire yachts, and cargo ships being loaded. A café provided the usual coffees and one *crema cornetto*. The tourist office was housed in an unusual 1927 building with a palm tree growing through it. We followed the waterside past the statue commemorating Garibaldi, the Chiesa del Purgatorio, and scene of one of the most visited and deeply felt Good Friday parades, to visit the green-domed Church of Francis of Assisi that dominates the harbour. On Via Ranuncoli there were a few market stalls, but trade looked sparse.

'*Prego, prego,*' shouted a stallholder, pushing pieces of bread with something on them towards us. '*Ummm. Deliziosi, no?*'

'*Si, si.Che cos'è?*'

'*Sorrd-a-fish, smokee.*'

'Aah, smoked swordfish. *Molto buono*.' And it was good.

'You like buy? *Quattordici Euros*.'

'Fourteen? *Non grazie*,' said Gail, trying to explain we were in a '*piccolo*' camper and had no storage.

'*Piccolo. No problema.*'

'*Più tardi*.Later.'

The sheltered harbour was triple parked with blue and white trawlers bristling with radio and radar aerials, flags and pennants. On the boat decks and along the harbour side were groups of four or five men sat on stools in yellow waterproof trousers with crossed braces, each working on a mound of unfathomably meshed brown fishing net. Across the road was a fish market – not the main one, but a more impromptu one on Via Colombo where traders were trying to sell off the last of the day's catch – a giant octopus here, a squid there, or a box of prawns or plump fish. Outside, a small crowd gathered round a stall of large eels. One shopper demonstrated to us that they were very fresh by poking them and inducing a wriggle before the stallholder scooped one up and started slicing into it.

We turned back into town along the northern seaside, defensive towered walls in an unrestored area to Via

Carolina and Via Santa Anna. We wanted to penetrate the walls to view the sea, but could find no way through. Two men stood chatting and beckoned us over to a gate.

'*Prego. Prego.*'

At the gate we read that some notable had constructed an extension to the wall then chopped off his wife's head and hung it in the gateway as a warning to unfaithful women. (Which notable I am unsure as my notes fail me and I have been unable to research anything subsequently so I can only assume there was a plaque at either Porta S. Anna or Porta Botteghelle.) The remainder of Via Liberta provided a succession of interesting churches, palaces and decent shops before getting to the official fish market. From here we could see the rest of the town curving away along the seashore. Via Corso Emanuele was equally attractive, and ended with the crowning scene of the elaborate pink clock towers of James II and the Palazzo Senatorio, except that it is upstaged by a hideous block of taller modern flats behind, albeit also edged in pink. What corruption allowed that?

We drove out of Trapani along the motorway through pleasant green scenery to Segesta, another archaeological site with a Greek temple and amphitheatre and a rough and tourist-busy car park. The next bus to the temple wasn't due for thirty minutes. I asked the attendant if we could park overnight and, if I interpreted him correctly, it was a, 'no way, not in a million years,' response. We could see the temple poking over the top of a hill, bathed in the afternoon sun. Being much like those at Agrigento and Selinunte (except that it was unfinished) and with time against us, we left, taking a long-winded route to San Vito lo Capo and looking for campsites on the way.

We travelled east then north to Castellamarre del Golfo and the sea, then inland again, climbing through small remote mountain villages to Custonaci. Beyond, the landscape was strange with barren hills and the isolated, towering, tooth-shaped peak of Monte Cofano. Soon afterwards we entered Purgatory (Purgatorio), a small village of about four streets and bland, sandstone-block houses where no-one ventured out. (I have been unable to find any information about Purgatory apart from someone's photos of puppets outside doorways for a festival, and its listing on an Italian News website entitled *Sex And The Many Animals On The Streets Of Italy* about strange Italian town and street names!)

Leaving Purgatory, the lush green fields alongside the road were swathed in violet flowers. The land beyond was wild and mountainous and reminiscent of the Scottish Highlands and with only a couple of small hamlets, there was a distinct feeling of entering a new geographical area. San Vito lo Capo jolted us back to reality though, as the modern entrance road is a grand, palm-fringed concrete dual carriageway with an occasional car, a sporadic house or business yard, and in all probability the result of Euro money. A short way along it we found a *sosta* and drove down their long tree-lined drive to a single-storey, sizeable white house with many outbuildings that doubtless originally belonged to a farm. Behind the house was the majestic grey cliff of Monte Monaco. The lady in the house was indifferent to our arrival and more interested in getting her washing hung out. A couple of other motorhomes were already there so we politely parked away from them.

The wind and rain was so great in the night that the van rocked and set off the intruder alarm. By morning the rain had stopped but the wind persisted, it was cold, and clouds had obscured the upper reaches of Monte Monaco. We walked the three hundred metres down the carriageway into San Vito, stopping off in a square in front of the thirteenth century church and Saracen fortress attributed to the martyr Vitus and Saint Crescenza. Gazebos were being erected for art, music and cycling events.

The organisers of the bicycle race must have said their prayers as the next day was brilliantly sunny and San Vito seduced us into staying three more nights. It is an unspoilt gem of a place at the end of a mountainous peninsula with a gently curving white-sand beach lapped by a crystal-clear turquoise sea. The little village is home to around 3,750 souls and their blocks of white houses huddled under the watchful gaze of the rugged cliffs of Monte Monaco. It is sandwiched between the Zingaro National Park to the east and Monte Cofano National Park to the west. A fishing port guarded by a lighthouse and expanded to provide a yacht basin, its Arabic flavour is endorsed by its September couscous festival. Council men in luminescent orange boiler suits swept up palm fronds brought down by the winds – San Vito was a clean and sparkling place that even out of the tourist season retained a spirited atmosphere. Sitting on the white calcareous rocks by the harbour and gazing round the arc of sandy coast line, the thin sliver of white of the village and its palm trees were almost lost against the grandeur of the cloud-topped mountain range behind and the contrasting luminosity of sea in front. We just wanted to drink it in, absorb the colours, and relish the peace and harmony. But the bicycle race was calling, or more correctly, an organiser was shouting, through a megaphone.

The triathlon had turned into a biathlon. A small man with a megaphone and a jacket announcing 'Trapani Sport' addressed the small crowd behind the crash barriers in the main street. One by one he introduced the Lycra-clad men and women competitors and one by one they applauded themselves. A long broadcast followed in which he described the course and then put the megaphone down momentarily, only to be tapped on the shoulder by a competitor who wanted him to go over the instructions of down the street, turn right, to the end and come back. Two local personalities were introduced and the younger one in a green tracksuit was handed the starter horn only to have it snatched back by the announcer who proceeded to start the race himself. We watched as the race proceeded until the bicycle changeover, then nipped in the bar for *ricotta cornetto* for Gail and *arancino* (filled with rice, peas and meat) for me.

The thirteenth century or fourteenth century church (depending on which brochure you read) is housed inside the impressive solid, sand-coloured, square fortress-tower and dedicated to St Vitus – the young Patron Saint (born in Marzara del Vallo) who, on turning to Christianity, was forced to flee with his nurse, Crescenza. Tragedy struck in the form of an avalanche, and he died whilst Crescenza was turned to stone on the spot where the church is now built. Subsequent miracles attributed to the pair brought many pilgrims and visitors, and this seems to be the way that previous tourist boards have stimulated custom and commerce: a weeping Madonna here, a miracle there. The structure was fortified to provide further protection, and in the eighteenth century houses were built around it. The interior was unexpected – it was simple and in the shape of a Greek cross. On entering, we were immediately faced with a central set of steps descending to the crypt. On the wall on the right was a modern painting showing workmen lowering Christ from the cross. Most have their heads in their hands and one at the top of the ladder is using his hammer to hit an attendant on the head. The meaning was obscure!

One afternoon we took a walk to the port past fields of wild irises in full bloom, then up a steep hill to the Strada Panoramica that runs along the western edge and above the town. As its name implies, it has stunning panoramic views of the town below and sea views in three directions. At the point, a magnificent modern house had been constructed and we wondered how planning permission had been obtained when the rest of the area gave the impression of a conservation area. As we descended the hill at its southern end, goats leapt up on the rocks to check us out and we came to houses with their garden walls a mass of yellow flowers.

San Vito had everything going for it – history, beauty, recreation, supermarket and artisan shopping, bars, cafés and restaurants. It was a pity then that our stay was spoilt by some strange behaviour on the *sosta.* When we originally pulled in I parked well away from the two motorhomes that were already there as we tended to do to give people privacy (I subsequently discovered they were unoccupied). On our first day another van arrived and parked one space from us. Later, another arrived – obviously friends – and parked on the other side, only to be followed by another, that parked between us. Around a hundred other spaces and they wanted to cuddle up to us – I have never understood such behaviour (or maybe having been on our own for so long I am people averse!). They hooked up fairy lights and spotlights and sat outside the van next to us chat, chat, chatting until late. The owner of the neighbouring van was a giant Neanderthal of a man with a thickset, acromegalic jaw who I somewhat cruelly nicknamed 'Slob the Slav'. Rather than ask them to be quieter, I simply moved our van half-a-dozen spaces away, but when we returned from our afternoon walk the following day they had set up tables and chairs directly in front of our van and spent the rest of the afternoon drinking and playing cards. The following afternoon I was woken from a nap when they started a football match in front of us, despite enough space on the far side for a full football pitch. The numbers eventually declined and only a young boy and Slob were playing so all five-foot-three of Gail went out and gave all six-foot-six of him a look, and he left. (Later, being New Year's Eve, they retaliated with a round of cannons and rockets!)

It was New Year's Day, dark clouds hugged Monte Monaco, rebuffing soft and fluffy attacks from seaborne white ones, and rain was in the air. Slob and his friends had left and we decided to make a fresh start. We drove through San Vito to follow the peninsula east round the foot of Monte Monaco and the huge tooth of a rock at the end where traces of ancient cavemen and fourth century BC civilisations had been found in its many caves. Shortly after, we could see on the headland the disused factory-like buildings of the Tonnara del Secco. Here, a series of special nets is dropped into the sea a few metres from shore in an orgy of ancient ritual killing (*la mattanza*) of the trapped springtime migration schools of bluefin tuna. After only eight miles of climbing round the wild coastal area, we arrived in front of the log cabin marking the entrance to the Riserva Naturale Orientata dello Zingaro. The small parking area clung to the cliff edge below the sombre, scrub-covered mountains above.

The view round the eight kilometres of protected Tyrrhenian coastline was spectacular, with beams of light streaming through gaps in the moody clouds onto a series of precipitous promontories and rocky ravines plunging into the sea. It was reminiscent of the Cinque Terre but outwardly devoid of man's intervention. The park was formed after local residents protested about a road being built there. The 'Zingaro' was intended to refer to the roaming population of shepherds and transitory fishermen. There were few towns as farming was done from 'bagli' (rural houses) that hosted workers whilst harvesting wheat and olives. Ruins of one of the largest Bagli Cusenza can be found in the park.

After coffee we paid our three Euro entrance fee and armed with a guide map and picnic, set off on the marked trail round the coves to discover that in parts it was like a tropical garden with dwarf palms and olive trees, and in others wild and unruly. The Grotta dell'Uzzo was barriered off, along with the continuation of the main path, giving sense to the cross the warden had marked on our map. We dropped down the little track to an idyllic cove with a white sand beach and aquamarine sea spuming over the calcareous rocks at Cala dell'Uzzo. There we ate lunch in a heavenly setting. As we returned to the main path an Italian couple were coming along the barriered section: 'It is forbidden, but we do it.'

We took the chance and climbed up the path to the Grotta dell'Uzzo, which had provided the first evidence of human habitation from ten thousand years ago. When we saw the massive and spectacular rock falls where the path wound round the base and left no room for escape, we decided not to linger but clambered round them. The path continued between fallen boulders with creviced plants, round rocky coves with palm trees, past wild flowering gentian irises and yellow bushes, cacti, grassy fronds waving in the breeze, almond trees, riots of autumnal hues, craggy limestone cliffs, above the crystal-clear sea where gulls skimmed the waves, and past abandoned habitations. It was an inspiring time. From Cala della Disa, the mule trail (for that is the only way materials are brought in), we climbed steeply to another barrier: ‘It is forbidden because of falling rocks.’ We returned back through the ‘paradise of nature’ to the entrance, and were so captivated that we decided to stay the night. Where could be more perfect?

The Zingaro was a wild place and hid many ghosts from the past. In 1862, following the abolition of the serfdom that existed in the area, peasants and shepherds burnt down homes and killed many noblemen. Brigands roamed and hid in the hills, including the notorious Pasquale Turriciano. In the twentieth century Salvatore Giuliano made it his home, as well as American gangster Frank Mannino, who took refuge in the Grotta dell’Uzzo.

The few remaining cars left along with the warden, so we were alone. Dark clouds rolled down the mountains above us whilst the sun continued to shine over the sea. Towards evening the coastlines changed from red to a purple-grey and into an inky blackness save for lights twinkling on distant shores and the stars in the sky – never have I seen stars so clearly. I pondered our utter solitude in an isolated wilderness perched on a thin slip of a cliff, the sea below, and the rocky mountains high above.

I hope none of those rocks fall down and sweep us into the sea, I thought, but didn’t think it wise to voice my concern.

Erice: Dog Bites Man

It looked like an atomic explosion as the sun rose above the horizon and forced its rays through the clouds. Skimming across the water, first the plants below were painted with a glistening light and then the headlands and coves began to be lifted, one by one, from darkness to purple-grey shadows. Finally, the cliff face behind us was suffused with the full luminosity of the sun's glow. It all happened in a few minutes – from a scene of pitch blackness and isolation to one of warmth and energy and a feeling of amazement.

After breakfast we drove back to San Vito, through Purgatorio, where the sky darkened, to Custonaci, and then along the coast road before turning inland to climb six hundred and fifty metres through the six miles of hairpins to Erice. Motorhomes were side-lined off to their own parking area that required another hundred metre walk up to the medieval fortified village perched on an outcrop of rock.

Amazing views opened below us – a flat coast, and then like a great tooth emerging out of land and sea, Monte Cofano and the range of mountains of the Zingaro. Erice is a self-contained town of narrow, wind-protecting cobbled streets, stone buildings, little lanes, and courtyards with occasional discrete rows of souvenir and delicatessen shops. Not following any set route through the maze of streets, we burst into the main square, Piazza Umberto, lined with Baroque palaces and outdoor cafés, and took advantage of a helpful tourist office and morning coffees. Even with a town map it was confusing, but we found our way to the Saracen Pepoli Castle below the walls on such a sharp pinnacle of rock it seemed impossible that anyone could gain access to it. Further on was the more substantial square block of the Norman castle, built on top of the Ancient Temple of Venus, Goddess of Love. It was here, shrouded in the mists that normally cover Erice, that sailors paid homage by visiting the 'beautiful prostitutes who were sacred to her,' but not before they had washed 'in purificatory waters, to remove the saltiness and the smell of fish' and changed into 'clean hygienically correct garments, in view of the function they were about to perform.' This is said to be mimicked by the sprinkling of holy water in modern day services.

The aerial landscape view from the balustrades at the Norman Castle of the salts flats of Trapani, Mothia and the Egadi Islands was remarkable – like a Google Earth map, and we were blessed with none of the mist that normally surrounds Erice. We passed through the gardens, down more lanes, under arches, down steps, past many churches and palaces to the cathedral and its separate bell tower by the Trapani gate. There we discovered that entry required payment. I bemoaned doing so to enter God's house, and more so when seeing the ample parking in front that would have saved the steep climb we'd had up the hill! Descending the steps to another viewpoint, I whispered,

'Good dog,' to a large furry thing lying in the sun. As we walked away, it ran up behind me and launched itself.

Sinking its teeth into my leg, it proceeded to shake it vigorously.

'Bloody Hell,' I cried out, wrestling my leg free and aiming a kick at it. It stood its ground, lips curled and lower teeth exposed, snarling.

'What did you say to it?' asked Gail.

'Good dog. In English.'

'Well, it must have been the way you said it or looked at it. Did you look it in the eyes?'

'Only momentarily! It looked up at me when I spoke.'

'Perhaps God sent divine retribution because you wouldn't pay to go in the cathedral.'

My leg had teeth marks but the skin was unbroken.

'What are you doing?'

'I'm getting a couple of stones. We have to go back the same way.'

And there it was – standing implacably on our route. I launched a stone and it ran off. What had happened? I've quieted even the angriest canines in the past!

I limped my way to lunch, garnering sympathy all the way, and then we drove back down the mountain and along the coast past Comino and the beach under a bare rugged Monte Cofano, where we decided to wild camp for the night.

By the gently lapping water we were treated to another sunset and a bay of twinkling lights, but the biggest fascination was Erice's lights, which looked as if they were floating on top of the black mass of mountain that rose from the sea. As the skies blackened and all shape and form of the mountain disappeared and became indistinguishable from the night, that thin strip of ethereal orange light remained, flickering occasionally, suspended between earth and sky. No wonder sailors of old thought Erice a magical place and couldn't wait to get washed and changed to ascend that stairway to Venusian's heaven.

We woke to a calm sea gently lapping against the rocky foreshore of lava cooked and solidified in lumpy sets. Erice wore a dark cloud like a top hat dropped onto the peak, but as the light increased the cloud changed to grey and then almost white, and slid away to fuse into the general cloud bank. When I looked again it had been replaced by a beret shaped cloud which bumped into the top of the mountain then slid over it like a snail crawling over an impediment, then down the far side to continue on its way at the original altitude.

We took a tour along the coast and through countryside with olive groves, fruit orchards and fortified farmhouses, to Bonagia and its tuna factory. This small fishing port is dominated by a square castellated, cream, seventeenth century fort with protruding battlements and arrow slits. Around its base are the extensive buildings of the tuna factory, an activity that has been there since at least AD 1299. The greater part is now a four-star hotel and there is a tuna-fishing museum and congress centre, but it is still a small harbour in an isolated backwater and no one was offering coffee – so if getting away from it all is what you want then I imagine it's a great spot, otherwise don't bother. Onshore, five black-hulled rotten wooden tuna boats resembling Norse boats were beached with row upon row of rusty anchors. In the picturesque harbour lay a few small fishing boats – fisherman sitting on board, on the harbour wall, or outside small garages, mending nets – an idyllic, tranquil setting compared to the frantic tuna catching '*la mattanza*' actively pursued there in May and June.

The sun shone as we drove the rest of the coast to Trapani, then back inland to the original *sosta* at San Vito, where as the only visitors we took time to sit out and enjoy the sun.

Scopello is a small village perched on the eastern side of the peninsula at the southern entrance to the Zingaro. With square Saracen watchtowers and an ancient and evocative Tonnara the whole scene is preposterously picturesque and formed the backdrop for the Hollywood crime film *Ocean's Twelve*. We departed for Castellammare del Golfo to rejoin the SS187 road, where earlier we had seen marble being cut away from the hillsides in huge blocks scarring the landscape. (Although we love it in our bathrooms, once it has been cut the landscape is damaged forever so full marks to the people of San Vito and Scopello for preserving the Zingaro).

The road runs high above Castellammare del Golfo. We stopped to look down at the inviting scene of the castle at the end of a harbour promontory. I tried to work out whether it was possible to drive down and then thought, *What the hell; let's go for it*.

The road swept down the cliff and disappeared into the old town's labyrinthine, cobbled one-way streets and off the GPS. Rustic balconies hung out, cars parked awkwardly jutted out and as we progressed further I got the impression the buildings were closing in on us. Gail was looking out and up to check the roof, I was ready to peel in the wing mirrors, and impatient drivers behind were honking their horns. At a crossroads I tried to escape but cars were parked in such disarray I couldn't make the turn so was forced into another series of impossibly complex back streets. Then road works necessitated us to go through a tiny piazza as though we were in someone's yard, until I saw an alley that put us in a larger square in front of the bus garage. The relief was tangible.

The castle doubled as an information centre. We pleaded as to how to drive out again and after much deliberation by the attendant and then his boss, a route was marked in pen on a map. Taking the steep steps down to the harbour provided a picture-postcard scene of lots of old seafarers mending their nets, but the wind was blowing a gale so we (okay, I!) struggled back up the steps to the van. We set off on the marked escape route, only to find it took us down one-way streets the wrong way. No-one appeared to mind.

The pleasant coastal road alongside the vineyards, interspersed with holiday developments and the Autostrada, got us to Sferracavallo and Camping Degi Ulivi to be greeted by Pete and Di. We sat in their van comparing itineraries and found theirs was remarkably similar to ours, and probably thousands of others before us. They had taken the train to Palermo and being warned of pickpockets Pete had stuffed his wallet and passport down his trousers. There was acute embarrassment when asked for identification to use the Internet.

Sferracavallo is a small seaside town and we took advantage of the many empty trattorias, spaghettarias and pizzerias competing for our business in the evening for us to enjoy the pizza 'Viagra' that was firm, crisp and delicious. Pete had pizza 'something else' that was flaccid and lifeless and hated it – it wasn't his day. We had coffee back in our van and they were amazed four could sit in it.

Gail and I took a walk round the town the next morning whilst Pete and Di took the train into Palermo. We selected Bar de Golfo because of its inspired display of brightly coloured delicacies in the glass counter on the left, sandwiches, hot dishes of aubergine, beans, potatoes, pizzetas, and beyond, a gelateria with a rainbow of ice-creams, uniformed waiters and servers. To the right were shelves and glass cases of beautifully presented wines and chocolates and the smiling lady on the cash till. The glass gleamed, the brass shone and the coffee machine gurgled, hissed and growled. It was hard to avoid buying a *cornetto* – the only problem being the choice, but chocolate it was.

The little town had multiples of everything: fish shops, butchers, greengrocers, *ferramentas*, and general stores. We entered one to have a browse. I was taking some notebooks from a shelf when an assistant came up and stood close by, uncomfortably in my space, in my face. I gave her the notebook to take to the cash till, but she didn't move. We moved, and she followed. She hadn't got change for the ten Euro note I offered and had to go off so she called the other girl, who came over to adjust things on a shelf near to us that clearly didn't need adjusting.

'She thinks we're going to pinch stuff!' I whispered to Gail. 'Do we look that disreputable after three-and-a-half months travelling?'

'Perhaps we do.'

Sferracavallo has a small concrete harbour with a few fishing boats hauled up onto the roadside. Men sat in, and stood around, them playing cards. I peeked over but didn't recognise the cards – they looked like picture cards for Snap. Two young boys were fishing with rod and line off the harbour wall and showing their Mum how they did it. They had caught one fish and popped it into water in a plastic sandwich box. It was still alive – its body in the water, but its head sticking out.

Beyond the harbour things deteriorated with overflowing waste bins, plastic bags and bottles on the rocks. Black bags of household waste spilt out onto the pavement and there was dog crap around the base of the trees. All of this lead to a beach area and fishermen with long rods casting into the sea.

We met Pete and Di in the evening, swapped some books and listened to their tales of Palermo with its chaotic traffic, extremes of art and architecture, and scary markets and backstreets cheek by jowl with fashionable shops. Above all (and our guidebook confirmed the sentiment), 'Don't drive in Palermo.'

I love a challenge. Our book of *sostas* gave two potential sites close to the centre of Palermo. It was five years out of date but Jean at Syracuse had also suggested there was a place to park in the centre of Palermo. We set off the next morning, the GPS all programmed, and being a Sunday hoped for lighter traffic. We went wrong at the first turn out of the campsite, then having rectified that, missed the entrance to the Autostrada and had to wait until we could turn back.

'Where did we go wrong?' I queried.

'I don't know – the map's not right.'

'It looked fine when I programmed the GPS.'

'Oh, so it's my fault they've changed the road?'

'I wasn't saying that.'

'Don't get in a mood.'

'I'm not in a mood.'

'Yes you are – your lips curled down.'

We redoubled our efforts. It was very busy with cars and people as we finally got into the centre of Palermo. Turning off down a side road, we did a couple more turns and then realised we were lost in a backstreet so I had to turn and retrace our steps. An old man dumping his rubbish in a green wheelie bin came over.

'*Dové parcheggio per camping cars?*' I tried, shouting across Gail as his head appeared at her window.

He looked around inside the van and then smiled, pointing vigorously over the high brick wall behind us.

We got the message but how did we get there?

'*Come?*'

He clung onto Gail's half-wound-down window so I couldn't drive off and told us the way three times in Italian. We got the '*semaforo*' for traffic lights, the crossed arms against his chest for crossroads, the arm outstretched for left and right turns. After lots of head nodding, '*buonos*, *eccellentes*, *grazies*' and '*grazie milles*' he finally decided we had understood and let go of the window. We had discovered a star player for a charades evening. And, it worked.

We pulled into 'Green Car Parking' off Via Quarto Dei Mille. It was a large tarmac car park surrounded by blocks of washing-line adorned blocks of flats, but against the back wall were three motorhomes and we could stay for eighteen Euros a night inclusive of electricity, dump, water, sink and a solitary shower and toilet – it was great, and it was only 9:30 a.m.

We took the short walk into town stopping for coffees and one ricotta *cornetto* – the most expensive yet. Being Epiphany, the cathedral was packed and the sermon sounded uplifting. Light streamed in from the upper windows, highlighting the statues on the ledges halfway up the pillars. The architecture was simple and bright. Exiting from a side door onto Piazza Settangeli, we spotted a three-wheeler Piaggio Ape truck brightly painted with a knight on the front and princess on the door, the rest in flowers like a hippie had got hold of it.

We entered into a cornucopia of festival paraphernalia: painted hand carts, puppets, old photos, newspaper cuttings, paintings of festival processions, Lambretta scooters richly adorned with painted scenes and more decorated handcarts. Gail was allowed to sit on a scooter for photo taking. The man showing us around was unusually tall for an Italian, with an angular, drawn face and a few missing teeth, yet in the photos was a tall, handsome film-star of a man. Gail asked if it was him.

'*No, piccolo.*'

He was the baby in his father's arms. The privilege of producing the carts and other processionals was handed down from father to son – the older photos were of his grandfather. Everything was magnificent in a gaudy way. I sat in the Ape outside for my photo – '*fantastico.*'

Where Via Vittorio Emmanuele crossed Via Maqueda we eagerly anticipated 'The Heart of the old city' Quattro Canti, or four corners, 'a newly restored and gleaming Baroque crossroads that divides old Palermo into its quadrants.' Expecting an Oxford or Piccadilly Circus, we found a less impressive, carbon-coated crossroads. But Palermo was shopping. Via Maqueda was pedestrianised for the day and crowded with smartly dressed families enjoying their sunny Sunday and the inspiring and stylish window displays of the fashion shops. The theatre was impressive, with pots of red poinsettias all the way up the long entrance steps. Horse-drawn carriages touted for business outside.

We diverted towards the docks, to a crowded and bustling market where steam issued from large pans of fish being cooked by barking stallholders. Palermo had captured our interest and we decided to stay a week.

Palermo

I was the first to see a body. Dressed in a faded greatcoat and cravat, it hung from the wall above us. The head and shoulders were slumped forward, the arms crossed in front, the jaw had fallen open to reveal a full set of yellowed teeth, and the skin was stretched tight over the facial bones and hands. I felt it was staring down at us. Suspended next to it was a gaunt female in a long brown frock, shawl, and dainty, buckled shoes. She was turned to look endearingly at the male corpse, her husband. It was not for the faint-hearted or weak-stomached. Some of the contorted facial expressions were reminiscent of *The Scream*.

We were in the Catacombs of the Capuchin Monks of Palermo, a human library of more than eight thousand cadavers preserved since the sixteenth century and displayed in their finery in cases on the walls, standing alone or together in little scenes. They were categorised into: Men,

Women, Virgins, Priests, Monks, Professionals (including doctors, lawyers, military and painters such as Velasquez), Adults, and Children (including the most recent – the perfectly embalmed body of baby, Rosalio Lombardo, who died in 1920). We toured in near silence, whispering to each other, any unexpected noise having the potential to make us jump. Although originally intended for friars, it eventually became a status symbol to be entombed here. Families would pay for the pleasure of preserving loved ones and it is said they would visit to hold their hands and join in prayer.

We exited the gloomy cellars into bright sunlight thankfully, bidding farewell to the friar at the door who seemed incongruously dressed in brown habit, jeans with rolled up bottoms, brown sandals, and blue socks. (I shall remember him for the fifty cents change he didn't return to us on entry.) The Catacombs said it all: Palermo was like no other city in the world.

Almost opposite, at the end of Via Quarto Dei Mille and off Corso Calatafimi, was La Cuba. As we entered the arched gateway a group of four girls clustered round a doorway momentarily stopped their chatter. All were dressed in thigh-high black boots, tight jeans, and anoraks, and were overly made up with red lipstick and black eyeliner. They could easily have been mistaken for a certain profession, however, one dispensed two tickets for us to visit the interior and they resumed their chatter. La Cuba was built in the twelfth century as a Royal Pavilion in a Royal Park, but had seen better days. Battered during many attacks and suffering the indignity of being used as a barracks, after much procrastination and planning blight it was a miracle that anything had survived at all. It was still a wreck, with a tree growing in the middle, pigeons roosting, and no roof. Sloping plastic screens protected some intricate carvings and gave more support for the pigeons, as did the jagged pieces of masonry around the carvings. The exterior gave a small clue as to the previous glory, but the interior had been messed about with, and the outbuildings (presumably used as the barracks) were dilapidated. Overlooked by a ubiquitous, washing-strewn concrete blocks of flats and a couple of factory chimneys, a vivid imagination was required to picture a Royal palace in its heyday.

As we left, we saw a crowd had gathered on the pavement down a side street in front of some scaffolding. A grey Mercedes hearse was double parked in the road alongside and a group of men were shouldering a dark-wood coffin out of it. They placed it on a trolley under the scaffolding and the crowd gathered round. Old and young folks, all casually dressed, started wailing and crying and comforting each other. Shopkeepers and householders emerged to watch. Behind the hearse, twenty or more cars waited, their engines running. Five minutes later, the coffin was returned to the hearse and the procession had gone. Within minutes, it was as though nothing had happened. Then, walking from the railway station (where there were no British newspapers but the WC's were excellent and MacDonald's had a conventional Italian Gaggia-type coffee maker) along Via Macqueda, we saw another (or perhaps the same) grey Mercedes hearse parked in the middle of a side street. Behind it, a truck had raised a conveyor up to one of the iron fire-escape landings of a tall brick building and a coffin was being lowered down. Our initial reaction was that they couldn't get it down the internal stairway, but then we realised that the building was the Hotel Orientale – 'Housed in the royal apartments of the Fliangieri Palace - a rare example of seventh century Sicilian architecture,' and carrying a coffin out through the front lobby would simply not have been good for business (unless you were running *Fawlty Towers*). Monday was obviously a busy day for funeral directors, and with our visit to the Catacombs, death was omnipresent. Later, down a back street that good sense told us we shouldn't be, I came across what looked suspiciously like a bullet casing wedged in a crack in the cobbles – or was my mind running overtime?

'Don't pick it up,' whispered Gail.

'Why not?'

'You don't want to put your DNA on it.'

'Now whose imagination's on overdrive?'

Palermo we found to be a city of contrasts: look down a side alley and it would be narrow, dark, and rubbish strewn – a scene of despair and a no-go area, and yet down another only a short step away would be a beautiful, porticoed entrance to a fine building. This was a scene that was often repeated: a small door in an elegant building led to a beautifully planted and decorated courtyard, another to piles of rubbish, derelict cars, and scooters. There were elegant, palace-bounded squares and tranquil gardens. Noisy outdoor markets in dark, narrow backstreets had been there since the tenth century and were more reminiscent of an Arab souk in Tunis or Cairo (they even had a different language) and yet were only a few steps away from theatres, opera houses, museums and fashion stores with window displays that only Italian flair can produce.

One street had a continuum of metalworkers rolling, pressing, cutting, filing, hammering and grinding in deep, dark, cave-like workshops. Their wares were displayed on the pavement – those shiny, whizzy, chimney tops that keep birds out, baskets, bins, and other unknown metal objects glittering in the sun – whatever was needed could be made. Near the huge and lively Ballarò market, the caves were stacked with crates of fruit and vegetables or carcasses of animals, others were cafés or shebeens. Often a shady exterior hid an ultra-modern café with uniformed staff, yet two doors away there were worn tables and unshaven men. Men gathered everywhere in conspiratorial groups, eyeing you up as you passed. Intriguingly, at intervals there were rooms opening onto the street that were bare and empty except for a simple table with one chair behind it and two in front. The floors were covered in linoleum or tiled and there were no cupboards, drawers, or posters on the wall. There was always a man in a black leather jacket and dark glasses sitting on the single chair behind the table with a few sheets of paper in front of him. What was his business?

Off Corso Vittorio Emanuele we ventured into a cobbled courtyard, where at the rear we found a workshop containing a huge table surrounded by busy men and women carving and painting figurines. Nearby, cars disappeared into a black hole of a garage but another had pristine marble floors, tiled walls and immaculate stacked drawers of tools like an operating theatre. There was scaffolding everywhere – tiny, narrow alleys between tall, leaning buildings were bridged by a complex arrangement of poles and planks. But they were rusty, with no evidence of '*Lavori in Corso*' (work in progress), and being used to prevent the buildings from imploding. Above the ground floor caves and activity the upper floors were often derelict with peeling stucco, open windows sprouting grassy mounds, and the whole missing a roof. Towards the sea and to the east of Porta Felice are elegant palaces, but at the back, on one side of Via Butera, the rear entrances are in a poor state, and on the other side of the road, buildings are still shot from WW2 bombing. The marionette museum was somewhere in the wreckage. Further east, the open spaces created by the bombing were being used for organised football but the surroundings were dereliction propped up by scaffolding. If you looked hard enough there were signs of habitation at ground level. Some streets were daunting, even in daylight, and we went down too many of those. It was a discomforting area – yet a stone's throw from the charming Piazza Marina.

The huge Ballarò street market at Piazza Ballarò running to Piazza del Carmine continually drew us back into its maze – it was a scene of unrelieved activity and fascination, with fine displays of fruit, vegetables, fish and meat. We stopped for coffee at a family-run café-bar. Baby was sleeping in the pram in the corner so Mamma and Grandmamma could keep an eye on him from behind the counter and every café entrant could go up and make appropriate goo-goo sounds to the proud relatives before ordering an espresso. Unfortunately my laughter (caused by one of my own jokes) woke him and he started to cry, so everyone rushed round to try and get him interested in the Father Christmas mobile dangling above his pram and I was subject to a sea of scornful faces. Mamma scooped him up and started to bounce him around to lessen the cacophony of wailing, the crowd made clucking noises, and with only a young lad left to serve us, we paid and quickly slipped away. We asked a man standing in the doorway of a subterranean garage if he could direct us to a restaurant recommended in the Rough Guide described as 'difficult to find.' He directed us down the road to what turned out to be a university building. (On another day's reconnoitring we found what we thought was the restaurant, or more precisely, a long-time-closed corrugated-iron shack, just across the road from where we had spoken to him, and appropriately called '*Il Garage*.')

On each of our days in Palermo we walked around fifteen kilometres, viewing most of the churches and palaces and other places of interest highlighted in the Rough Guide and local literature. There was much to see, and on the first day we were disorganised and wasted too much time looking for the restaurant, but there was pleasure in our wanderings. On day two we set off determined to see San Giovanni degli Eremiti (Saint John of the Hermits), built in 1142 and the most Arabic of the city's Norman relics, with five terracotta domes, cloisters, a luxuriant garden, and a postcard favourite. But the dreaded '*Lavori in Corso*' was underway and the whole shrouded in scaffolding and plastic. Undaunted, we were once again drawn towards the Ballarò street market down Via Antonino Mongitore. We passed under a newish block of concrete flats to the church of San Nicolò, and despairing that we would find anything open, climbed the steps and pushed on the heavy wooden door. It creaked open and an old lady in head-to-toe black emerged from the vicinity of the altar, where a quick glance suggested there was more '*Lavori in Corso*,' or a general disarray of stacked chairs and covers.

'*E 'aperto?*'

'*Si. Si. Prego. Vieni con me.*' She grabbed me by the elbow with a bony hand and shepherded us down the left hand side of the church, calling to someone with me protesting that we only wanted to look around. A small man appeared from the gloom of the side aisle and took over my elbow, and before we knew it we were through a door and out of the church into a small paved area. Here we were handed over to a smartly dressed man in yellow-brown corduroy trousers and an olive Barbour jacket, who took us up some steps and into the vestibule of a tower to be greeted by a worrying sign: '*Molto Pericoloso*' (Very Dangerous). He indicated we should ascend the circular stone stairs. '*Prego. Prego.*' I pointed to the sign and he shrugged his shoulders with an '*essere prudenti*' that I took to mean, take care! As Gail led us up we came to a series of small rooms with wooden sloping floors and a few tables containing nativity scenes made by local schoolchildren, as well as photos of old Palermo. At the top of the stairs the steps narrowed and were lit only by an observer's slit in an iron door. A wriggle of the ancient, giant key, and we were out onto the open, tiled bell-tower with two to the right and one on the left, and a three hundred and sixty degree panorama over the rooftops of Palermo, inland to the mountains and east to the sea. There were cranes, shiny green cupolas, the cathedral towers, the Palazzo dei Normanii, palms, and below us, the higgledy-piggledy buildings of the market quarter with rustic terracotta-tiled roofs, many covered in rubbish or sliding to oblivion. Scaffolding held up walls where the roofs had collapsed. Even the height of our viewpoint couldn't sanitise the hustle and bustle in the dirty streets. We moved from one side to the other, stooping under the bells on their cradles to pose for photos and laughing uncontrollably as the bells struck the hour just as Gail's photo was being taken.

Even more determined to continue our sightseeing as a result of our success, we wended our way through the market to the first Jesuit Church in Sicily (where, surprise surprise, there was '*Lavori in Corso*'), and past the university to Piazza Bellini, a short distance from the Quattro Canti. The square in front of the Town Hall, or Place of the Eagles, is home to a huge, elaborate white marble fountain, the Fontana Pretoria. It is surrounded by enormous naked figures (the males with detailed testicular appendages that stimulate personal comparison). Whilst it had become *de rigueur* to enter churches and then become jaded by the interiors (even though individually each might have much to offer), the three churches arranged on the other two sides of the square were remarkable for the differences between them.

On the southern side, steps go up to the raised, palm-fringed mound that houses the small gem of a twelfth century cubic Norman church of San Cataldo topped by three red, but slightly blackened domes. The walls are simple, and pierced by only three high arched windows. Inside, the same simple stone walls and a series of arches produced a tranquil mood and wonderful views up to the inside of the unadorned stone domes, the bases modestly decorated with small windows and alcoves. Owned by the Knights of the Holy Sepulchre, the graceful and simple solidity produced an enduring ambiance more powerful than many richly-adorned churches.

Passing out of San Cataldo and along the terrace, we came to the twelfth century graceful campanile and entrance to La Matorana. The contrast between the two interiors was startling. La Matorana (also of Norman origin) had been Baroqued and become a floor-to-ceiling, ornate, glittering, gold-encrusted, columned, mosaicked and domed church with the 'shock-amazement-wow' factor. Not an inch of space was left unadorned with gold leaf mosaic, a painting, or marble figurine. There were beautiful paintings on the ceiling. The dome housed a blue-robed Christ surrounded by angels, with a glittering gold background. Below, a blue and gold wedding cake of an altar bounded by a panoply of intricate figure carvings was surmounted by a painting of a heavenly Christ and earthly Madonna and apostles. To the rear of the church, inside and across from the entrance, hung magnificent oil paintings surrounded by ornate relief work. This church made a powerful attention-grabbing statement, but for me, Santa Cataldo had achieved the same by its simplicity.

Santa Caterina sat at the rear of the square, a slab-sided rectangle of a building and its '*Lavori in Corso*' fortunately completed. If we thought La Matorana was ornate, nothing could have prepared us for the outrageous, exuberance-gone-mad reliefs of Santa Caterina. I have never been physically conscious of my jaw dropping before, but it certainly did here, and as I sat to the side of the entrance it was amusing to watch others have the same involuntary, wide-eyed, jaw-dropping, and whispered, 'Oh my God' sensation. But that was the point of seventeenth century Baroque – communicating religious themes in an impressive, dramatic, visceral-involving, powerful way – and in Santa Caterina it worked. Although there was only a hint of gold, the profusion of exuberant Baroque reliefs was simply overwhelming, as though each artist working on a panel had been trying to competitively squeeze a more turbulent and exaggerated composition than the artist working on the next one. The eruption of stucco work was only broken by a few interspersed plain panels in brown, and the altar would have been lost to us if not in the accustomed place and marked by a gold chandelier. Only on the ceilings was the relief work spared to allow for delicate and colourful biblical scenes.

There are an endless number of churches in Palermo and we just had to cross Via Maqueda to enter San Giuseppe dei Teatini – a dark, sombre, seventeenth century edifice with twenty-two pillars, a precious wooden crucifix, an ornate painted ceiling, and beggars at the doors. The Piazza San Dominico was an unusually plain church – builders had '*Lavori in Corso*' on both sides of the altar and there were many tombs of local notables. Our church-going appetites finally sated, we were positively relieved to find that entrance to the Oratorio del Rosano needed a ticket only obtainable from the Oratorio Santa Zita (which was about to close) and we had a good excuse to seek out a place for lunch.

Skirting past the Palazzo delle Poste (a massive fortress of a post office along the lines of the Bank of England) and the elegant theatre area and Sant'Agostino to the Capo market area, we were sucked into and captivated by the labyrinth of stall-filled streets, until it dawned on us that we were lost. Our exploratory pleasure diminished at the same rate as our perception of the seediness of the streets intensified. We zigzagged our way along this alley and that, until we caught sight of an armed guard in dark blue uniform patrolling behind a defensive fence – 'Is it a prison?' It was the Palace of Justice, from where Palermo prosecutors Giovanni Falcone and Paolo Borsellino fought their battle against Cosa Nostra, convicting hundreds in 'maxi-trials' in an underground bunker only to be killed by them. We turned south along Via Papireto towards the cathedral, and relieved, ate comforting bowls of expensive pasta across the road although we should have followed the students pouring out of school to their value eateries. We stopped at a local supermarket just off Corso Vittorio Emanuele called Sima. They seemed very keen to see us. Gail asked for muesli, pointing helpfully to Kellogg's Corn Flakes. The owner took her by the arm and led her to the bread counter, where he insisted, unsuccessfully, that she take a country loaf. The man behind the delicatessen counter thrust tasty pieces of Gorgonzola under our noses, followed by pork slices, picante provolone, and yet more cheeses and meats until it became unnecessary to buy any food at all, as we had eaten quite well!

On Corso Vittorio Emmanuele Gail drew money from the Bancomat hole in the wall overseen by a flak-jacketed armed guard smoking a cigarette and leaning on his motorcycle. We had seen them all over Sicily, in the bigger towns and the smallest villages, all looking the same – blue uniform, black boots, flack-jacket, a pistol holstered at a jaunty angle, and sometimes a more offensive weapon such as an automatic rifle. There was a message there somewhere.

Many cities are described as 'walkable', and we found Palermo to be so, with all the tourist sites accessible on foot, but the statement does need qualification. The pavements are blocked with cars, trucks, and scooters parked chaotically (in our opinion, but clearly normal for the Palermitans). Cars are parked so tightly against each other that it is often impossible to reach the road from the pavement.

Some Palermitans have tried to keep the pavements clear of the piles of dog shit in the sand surrounding the bases of trees planted in the pavements, but the roving packs of dogs and irresponsible citizens have not, and it pays to be watchful at all times and be ready for a hop, skip and jump.

Pedestrian crossings are an oxymoron. All are unsafe. Drivers simply don't see you. They have important things to do: speak on their phones, discuss things with passengers, clean their sunglasses, smoke their cigarettes, play with their babies on mothers' laps in the passenger seats, remonstrate with their rear-seat children who are misbehaving, or to hoot to friends driving past or walking on the pavement. Many of these activities occur at the same time, and pedestrian crossings simply provide an excellent place to pull over quickly and park when you see a friend and want to chat. All scooter riders (including families of Mum, Dad and a child on one scooter) ignore everything related to traffic law and race down back alleys and along pavements, buzzing in and out of cars and buses and swarming across road junctions as they ignore traffic lights. It is also necessary to run the gauntlet of old men who hang around street corners, bars, cafés, newspaper kiosks, and entrances to public buildings. All manner of goods are sold from stalls on the pavements or from three-wheeler Piaggio Apes parked on corners and piled high with giant cabbages, oranges, or lemons. A clear piece of pavement is a selling opportunity. Rubbish skips are always in threes, and full, so behind each group is a mound of rotting rubbish, household goods, fridges, and mattresses spreading back across the pavement.

Wednesday 9th January was a lovely-weather day and in accord with our thirty-seventh year of marriage. We chose to go to Monreale by bus and followed the guidebook instructions to board either AST bus 309 or 389 in Piazza dell'Independenza. Buses were flying around the square in all directions but AST helpfully had a little caravan to one side with smartly-uniformed officials outside. Unfortunately, none seemed willing to talk to us until a passer-by intervened. After much discussion and deliberation worthy of planning a world tour, they redirected us across the square to a little blue kiosk in front of the *Farmacia* on Corso Vittorio Emmanuele. Emerging with four tickets, I spotted a 309 pulling in to the side of the road where a large group of passengers was surging forward, so we ran for it. On board, the ticket endorsement machine didn't work and everyone tried to help us, but to no avail, so a man went to the front to tell the driver, who stopped the bus mid-traffic on one of the busiest streets in Palermo and came to see for himself. It worked perfectly for him.

'*Va bene per Monreale?*' I asked the young girl next to us.

'*No, no, no! Tre, otto, nove!*' all around us chorused, making us feel as though we had committed some great sin by taking their 309 instead of the 389. '*Scendere l'autobus!*' said everyone, reaching for the 'STOP' bell. We tumbled out of the bus at the next stop, which happened to be at the entrance to the street where our van was parked, and from which we had set off from what seemed an aeon ago. 'Full Circle,' as Michael Palin would say.

'You don't think this is some sort of omen, do you?' I asked Gail, reflecting on the anniversary achievement. Twenty minutes later we were on a 389 bus and chugging up the mountain to the square in Monreale.

The Norman King William II's Duomo was the main attraction in Monreale, and the rectangular exterior belies the highly decorated interior. The gold mosaics cover all surfaces and it is recorded as 'the most impressive and extensive area of Christian medieval mosaic work in the world, the apex of Sicilian-Norman art.' The interior was overwhelming – a massive twenty metre high, head and shoulders blue-robed Christ looks down from the apse, and biblical scenes are all around. They display great workmanship: the beams holding up the roof are gold-encrusted, the figures delightfully coloured, the rear wall a showpiece of eight easily identifiable stories from the bible, and more scenes run along the top of the side arches lit by light from the windows opposite, but, for me, the decorations appeared to be big for bigness sake. Almost hidden in one corner, we found a staircase that took us onto the roof, where we had outstanding views across the leaded dome, the monastery cloisters below, tall, slender, African palms stretching to the hazy blue mountains beyond, and looking east, the bay of Palermo. We rounded off our visit looking in on the cloisters and then the town of Monreale (it was larger than anticipated, and apart from the square, gave no sense of being a tourist town) before settling into a restaurant for a lingering lunch prior to our bus journey back.

The following day we visited the renowned archaeological museum and were particularly interested to see the famous metopes retrieved from Selinunte showing the detailed sixth century carvings of three-dimensional animals and mythological stories like Perseus beheading Medusa. Upstairs, many armour pieces and Roman mosaics caught our eye. There is another, roped off floor which housed a variety of complete vases and mosaics, and then bits of vases and mosaics, making us wonder how far restoration had gone. Are the coloured bits what they started with, or added?

On another good-weather day we set off for the Palazzo dei Normanni, or Royal Palace, an outwardly confusing

Norman building that houses the Regional Parliament. The tourist entrance was to the rear, on Piazza Independenza, whose gardens and cafeteria support many men playing cards. At the entry kiosk an attendant tried to list what we were able to see and what we couldn't, the latter being much longer than the first due to '*Lavori in Corso*.' Nevertheless, we paid our six Euros each and went ahead. At the top of the ramp another official directed us to the second floor of an impressive stairway, where there were no signs, so we plumped for some double-glassed doors where a group of smartly uniformed ladies sat chatting. One detached herself and we gathered she was a guide.

'*Siete Tedesco?*' We looked at her blankly – we weren't German.

'*Vous êtes Français?*'

'*Non. Inglese.*'

'I don't speak English,' she explained. '*Parla Italiano?*' (I wonder if this is getting as tedious and frustrating for you as it was for us?) We settled on French, as she didn't seem motivated to ask any of her chattering colleagues whether they would be willing to speak English that day. Then we were off, on some type of timed tour round rooms damaged by the 2002 earthquake, along with torn tapestries, and many '*lavori in corso*.' Her French was excellent and each mini-speech given at great speed, thereby far exceeding our own translating ability. We went upstairs, downstairs, through the council chamber (with lots of '*très beau*' from us), into the ballroom furnished with a long table and microphones for delegates, and next, the cosy President's suite with its high-backed, brown leather sofa and chairs, working desk, and flat-screen TV. We flashed past pictures of past presidents and were out through another set of glass doors with an '*Au revoir, arrivederci*,' and '*ciao*.' Although she didn't say, 'Good riddance' (and we wouldn't have understood if she had), we felt she might just as well have. I don't think we had met the dress-code standards of the normal visiting Italian delegates.

'Didn't the man at the gate say something about a crypt?' I asked Gail.

'Yes, I'm sure he did, and didn't the guide mention it as well?' We descended to the bookshop to ask and were pointed down more stairs to find some beautifully presented Punic walls under glass, and from there to corridors where a woman had been bricked up, and then finally to a crypt and a door to the outside (the way we should have entered in the first place).

We walked the full length of the Barato market in bright sunshine to the station (the only place in Palermo you could buy an English newspaper – except they hadn't any less than five days old). From there we walked down Via Lincoln, past the Botanical Gardens, to the gardens of Villa Giulia and sat for a while to take in the peace and tranquillity before making our way to the seafront. We skirted the Marina to the Castle (a huge disappointment as it is diminutive and set amongst the warehouses and detritus of a working port) before walking through an elegant Bloomsbury-like area to Via Roma. We lunched at little expense somewhere in a back street in the backroom of a workman's café and enjoyed it greatly. Then we once more braved the myriad streets of the Capo district and confidently found our way back to the cathedral.

By Saturday we were alone save for one other van parked next to us and occupied by a man, his wife, and a small brown dog. The man exhibited a curious behaviour pattern that fascinated me. He would go off on his own, then come back and go off with his wife, before coming back again and audibly banging things in his van or fiddling with things outside. He always had a cloth bag over his shoulder.

'That guy next to us is nicking stuff.'

'No, surely not,' said Gail.

'He's just nicked a hub cap from a car on the far side of the car park, tried it for size on his own wheel, found it didn't fit, and is trying to get it back to the car he stole it off.'

'He probably found it lying there and thought he'd try it on his wheel,' rationalised Gail.

'The car park guy swept there this morning, so he didn't see it, and why did he hide it up his back when he returned it? He definitely nicked it to see if it fitted, and if it had he would have got the rest!'

'No, he couldn't have. And what about the car park attendant? He's always walking round with his brush and pan, and they're here twenty-four hours, as well as his Alsatian guard dog.

'That's what he's sweeping up – the dog's shit. Anyway, you're so trusting of people. One day I saw him checking a shiny exhaust tailpipe he got from somewhere against that motorhome that's permanently parked up. Backwards and forwards he went from his van to the other one. Then suddenly he looked through the van's windows and tried the door. Then, yesterday, he went over to bash the door on that little blue Ligier car that's parked here every day by a young girl. The door had a dent in it and at first I thought he was seeing if it was plastic and it would spring out, but now I'm convinced he thought that with a damaged door the lock wouldn't hold and a couple of good thumps would open it. And, where does he go each day with a knapsack on his back? I'm telling you Gail, he's on the blag,' I insisted.

'I can't believe it; he's here with his wife and dog!' A queer fish indeed. We locked our doors and decided to leave the next day. With our limited Italian there was no way to confront him, and we didn't want to anyway. During the course of the day we heard a mullah-like call to arms from a loudspeaker in and around the flats that surrounded the parking site. Then there was shouting between an old lady leaning over her top floor balcony and someone hidden behind the high wall that separated us. She lowered a small, round wicker basket down on a rope, and two minutes later the basket was precariously being hauled back up again, swinging dangerously close to the lower balconies. Another delivery success – Tesco could learn something here.

Later that evening I reflected on our visit. It had been an intensive week. We had passed through streets, dark alleys, lively souk-like markets, churches with exquisite, Byzantine-style mosaics that have no equal, Arab-Norman palaces, a treasure trove of museums, restaurants, cafés, and elegant shops. We had photographed, written notes, and read endless brochures and guides. Below the surface, but never witnessed, lay the allegedly dark underbelly of '*pizzo*' – Sicily's Cosa Nostra, extorting protection money, colluding in the development of the atrocious housing and public works that had destroyed historic buildings and blighted great swathes of the city, and trafficking drugs and people. It was panache and poverty, beauty and ugliness, a place to love or loathe, taking your camera but never losing sight of it. We were hooked.

Corleone

Don Vito Corleone was the main character in the film *The Godfather* about a Sicilian Mafia family in New York City. The name Corleone was not a mythical creation by author Mario Puzo, or a fabricated Hollywood notion. The village of Corleone sits buried in green hills surrounded by farmland and vineyards fifty-eight kilometres from, and five hundred and forty-two metres above, Palermo. It is the birthplace of several Mafia bosses and the local Mafia clan known as the Corleonesi – 'the most violent and ruthless Mafia clan ever.' It is alleged that the Mafia committed one hundred and fifty-three murders in Corleone between 1944 and 1948.[10] In 2006, Bernard Provenzo, 'Boss of Bosses,' was arrested there – he had been in hiding for forty years.

How does a place with such a history function? As tourists, we will never know. As transients, we observe and photograph the physicality and discuss and read guides produced for us. We have small exchanges in restaurants, bars, cafés, or *tabacchi*. Occasionally we are surprised by a touch of humankind or a helpful direction, but without the

[10] Norman Lewis: *The Honoured Society.*

language, the confidence of the people, or the communication, our information is limited, distorted, and we cast it to fit our preordained picture. We will never really know these people – the intricate workings of their daily lives. We would certainly like to.

After early morning sunshine, a '*Buono viaggio*' from the car park attendant and payment of one hundred and twenty-six Euros for the week, I steered the van through Piazza Independza, past the Royal Palace, and up the hill out of Palermo into darkening and forbidding skies. Turning off into the small village of Altofonte to gain the SP5, we faced a three metre height restriction and had to turn down a narrow back road to regain the SS624. The rear-view mirrors showed a sunlit Palermo nestled compactly in the bay by the blue Mediterranean waters, hemmed in by mountains. We climbed steeply on a good road into rain, yet the hills held their beauty – so close to Palermo, yet already a moody remoteness prevailed. We crested the Porta di Paglia to pass into the luxuriously verdant Jato valley. A sign, 'Corleone' and '*Roccamena*', took us onto a small, rotten road that deteriorated badly. A country lane more for tractors and 4x4's, the surface was covered in water and mud and had subsided in many places to produce van-tipping furrows. A glance at a map will show you a complexity of faint, tiny, twisting, interconnecting roads, none appearing to be a direct route to Corleone, and it would be easy to end up where you started. It was close to here, at the Portella della Ginestra some 2,500 feet above sea level, that the 1947 May Day massacre took place. People from the villages of San Cipirello, San Giuseppe Jato, and Piana degli Albanesi, were celebrating the passing of a land reform act that took land away from the Mafia and others when *mafiosi* (led by Giuliano's men dressed in white raincoats so they couldn't be distinguished from each other), machine gunned and threw grenades into the 1,500 people below. Eleven died and sixty-five were wounded.[11]

I pulled over to allow the only car we had seen, pass us. It deliberately slowed alongside, the passengers turning to stare up at us. Were we so unusual? Were they from Corleone? There was nowhere else to go to. From time to time there was a farmer inspecting his waterlogged crops or pruning his vines, a scarf wrapped round his head Bedouin fashion, to keep out the wind. The vines here were grown to head height, higher than in other parts of Sicily. In the midst of this moody magnificence we came across an isolated vinery with shiny silver tanks, like rockets awaiting launch at a remote space station. Up a final wriggle of hairpin bends and we had passed the sign for the outer limit of Corleone. What did we expect? Men in dark glasses with black overcoats and violin cases clandestinely standing around, an enigmatic small village, a brush with unannounced danger, a thrill, an adventure, an encounter to provide a tale to tell? Momentarily, I wasn't sure why we were doing it. We would stand out unnervingly. The outskirts had a few farm buildings, then we passed the ubiquitous blocks of flats and a heavily palmed park to the main square, Piazza Vittorio Emanuele, a junction of four roads with a statue-bearing, triangular paved area in front of the park.

'Look at all those men standing around. What can they all be doing?' Men were ever-present standing in squares – it was the Sicilian way. But this was different. A crowd of men (in dark glasses despite the damp and gloomy conditions) stood in groups outside the bar-café to the right, another large group stood to the centre by the statue, there were more ahead in front of another bar-café, and over on the left in the bus shelter sat another group. The women appeared to have left town. Self-consciously, we parked at the edge of the square. As I checked the parking position I saw three smartly-dressed old men pointing at us from across the

[11] *Midnight in Sicily*, Peter Robb, The Harvill Press

street, discussing us, pointing again with their walking sticks, stopping for more discussion, and then walking on. Somewhat ill at ease, we donned anoraks (a bright orange anorak did nothing for blending in) and stepped out to tour the back streets, looking for the small museum about the Mafia – a brave step for the town. Unsurprisingly, it was closed. Above us loomed a sheer rock topped by a dark lookout tower. We followed signs to a bridge with a view of a concrete-sluice of a riverbed running down the mountain and carrying the recent rains.

Back on the main street and into the main square, we squeezed through the unmoving men to enter the bar-café. The guy on the till looked rough and tough. Normally, we ordered at the counter then paid at the till on the way out, not knowing what we might buy. In many places people pay first, but it's a system we have never mastered. Conscious of our environment, I decided to check. The man at the till became child-like and shrugged his shoulders, but I paid nevertheless. It was a good strong *cappuccino* and a fine *cornetto crema*. Men stood around in the bar and they kissed newcomers, they kissed Mr 'Rough and Tough' the till man, they kissed the coffee maker, and they kissed the provider and wrapper of delicacies. There were no women other than Gail. A father brought in his beautifully dressed son. The young child stared wide-eyed at the displays of cakes and sweetmeats and had trouble choosing. His choice finally made, it was attractively wrapped for him and he gripped his parcel tightly whilst Dad kissed the assemblage goodbye. Was the extra parcel for Mama?

We stepped out into the rain to view the town guide at the front of the park. It is a fine park, with abundant large palms planted close together, ornamental gardens, and many statues, but because of the continuing bad weather we decided to leave. We had discovered little of Corleone – it was like many ancient Sicilian hilltop towns: a maze of narrow, often steep, back streets, some Baroque churches, a modern school, and on the way out the main SS121 was bordered, surprisingly, by modern shops, apartment blocks, and a hospital (In 1948 the chief doctor was a local Mafia boss.[12]) Home to 11,000 souls getting on with their lives despite a dark and bloody past, a past attracting curious tourists hoping that something different would happen to them – but safely. It was a notch in our travelogue, but it had been a vacuous experience.

We returned by way of the SS118 and Ficcuzza, where the Mafia had used the ravine to hide bodies. We passed through Marineo and Misilmeri on far better roads, and fine mountainous scenery. As we descended, the depressing clouds cleared and we had an exceptional view of the Bay of Palermo and a crystal-blue sea. Taking the motorway east along a rocky coastline, we by-passed Cefalù, nestled under a huge castle-bearing cliff, to a proper campsite at Finale.

---

[12] *Into the Heart of the Mafia*, David Lane, Profile Books

Finale

When we arrived at the reception for the Rais Gerbi campsite at Finale it felt like a homecoming – not that we had been there before, but with the exception of two nights at Sferracavallo (which was more like a *sosta*) and the unoccupied sites at Petrosina and Agrigento, we had not been in the warm folds of the camping community for some weeks. As we went through the familiar check-in routine and drove down the road to the lower terraces, there were motorhomes big and small from Germany, Switzerland, France, and later, we would discover from the UK and USA. Normal camping folk watching curiously as we arrived, but later found an excuse to pass by so they could say,

'Hello. Where are you from? Where have you been? How long are you staying?' Of course we had no idea how long we would be staying, but many of them had been there for months and so any new arrival was of great interest.

We started out lazily, sitting outside reading, relaxing, and lunching in a gorgeously warm sun with an occasional wander to check out the site. It was marvellously manicured, with many trees, and arranged as wide, double-ranked terraces with large, mainly concrete pitches on a cliff-side that went down to a blue sea and had the Madonie Mountains as a backdrop. The railway ran right through the middle, but in such a deep cutting it was near impossible to see the trains and we were hardly conscious of it. Later, we walked the three hundred metres to shop in Finale and found it to be smart and clean with two small supermarkets, butchers, greengrocers, and other shops as well as café-bars and a restaurant or two. Re-energised by the second day, Gail did the laundry and I washed the van, shamed by the mud-spattered state of ours and the pristine ones around us. Needless to say it rained immediately afterwards and into the evening.

January 16th was Gail's birthday, and we decided to spend it in Cefalù. As we prepared to depart, Ingrid (a Swiss lady who'd had a brief conversation with us previously as she wheeled the toilet cassette past) came over to tell us there was a better pitch available next to theirs and we should move. Such invitations, nay more instructions, always induce a mixed reaction in me (and I suspect Gail as well). We always tend to park away from the group, so why are people so keen to have us as neighbours on the basis of one conversation? Is it curiosity, or that we look clean and wholesome (well some days we do – and we'd made an effort for Gail's birthday!), are they swingers, do they simply want to have a small van on the next pitch to prevent a big one parking there, or do they simply realise we don't have dogs or children and seem to behave quietly? We diplomatically explained we were going out, but would have a look later.

Judging by the frantic tooting and waving of motorists on the slip of a road round the northern side of the massive rock, Cefalù appeared to be only accessible by one route and I had to reverse half a mile back up the hill above the marina. We parked by the *lungomare* and were surprised to see a meter maid for the first time in Sicily – an encouragement to use a one Euro per hour parking meter.

FINALE

Cefalù proved to be an interesting and historic town crammed onto a small, western peninsula jutting into the sea and squashed back against a two hundred and seventy metres high rounded rock, which in turn is surmounted by a castle and its walls. (We visited it a number of times and enjoyed it greatly.) Once in town, we found it was busy with locals and some fellow tourists. It had many café-bars, one of which served us the worst coffee we had tasted in the whole of our journey (I have no shame in saying it was Café Antico in Piazza Garibaldi!). Ancient gates led to narrow, cobbled streets running up the hill from the sea, and interlaced by alleys, and a main street bounded by elegant historical buildings in an arrangement retained through Greek, Byzantine and Norman conquests. There was a Baroque state pawn shop, a medieval washing grotto where clear waters gushed out of lions-head spouts, numerous churches, and an old waterside fort where teenagers were carousing and one singing into a mobile phone. Down by the harbour fishermen had dragged their brightly-coloured boats ashore and were mending nets, probably having sold their catch under the arches of the defensive houses edging the water. Saved from a shipwreck there, Roger II ordered construction of the Basilica-Cathedral in 1193 and it is recorded as 'one of the most precious examples of medieval architecture in Sicily…' Its creamy stone, square twin towers stood sentinel-like, glowing in the morning sun against the unlit limestone of the mass behind, whilst in front the steps dropped down to a pretty, palm-fringed main square surrounded by historic civic buildings with many tables for outside eating, drinking, gathering and conversation. Inside the cathedral, Christ Pantocrater (the oldest in Sicily) beckoned from the end of a long, columned apse. There were reminiscences of Monreale, near Palermo, and the latter may have been a grandiose copy.

We walked through the town, and from Piazza Garibaldi accessed a steep track up the cliff to view Roger II's castle and walls that surmount it. I was distinctly lacking in energy and blamed the previous day's exertions cleaning the van, but with Gail's goading I managed to struggle up. Only one other couple seemed to have made it. Recovery afforded me views down to the harmonious, pastel pink-red roofs of the town's buildings huddled below, compact and regular and crammed into every inch of the limited space available, as though all were on tip-toe and each not wishing to be the one that unbalanced and stepped off into the sea. In contrast, immediately below the cliffs, and taking up half the space of the old town, were the massively solid, interconnected Basilica-Cathedral buildings with their ochreous roofs. Within the castle's perimeter walls, which run round the circumference of the rock, we found the small, unprotected, two roomed, ivy-covered ruins and megalithic construction of the Temple of Diana and nearby water sources or *cisterna*, dating back to the ninth century BC. We wanted it to have magical powers on our special day, and with a little imagination and light-headiness from the climb, that area of ancient rituals captivated us.

From our Rough Guide we selected two of the recommended restaurants to find the first had changed its name and was closed, and the second was simply closed, so we settled on a touristy restaurant on the seafront. Further along the beach there was a more modern area where, from a glass and chrome American bar, we spotted a large Sidi Supermarket and subsequently used it on occasion, but the limited SPAR in Finale won on customer service, because we were always greeted by the blonde checkout girl there with a cheery '*Buongiorno*' as we entered, as though we had lived there all our lives (plus the man at the delicatessen counter knew which cheeses we wanted and how to slice the meats for us).

When we got back later that afternoon, Ingrid told us that unfortunately the pitch she'd wanted us to have had been taken.

'You would like to come over for a drink later?'

Ingrid was married to Felix – a tall, thin, shaved-head man who we had seen go past at regular intervals on his electric bike. In true Swiss fashion, their Knaus van was perfectly organised and tidy. Over drinks of instant coffee they told us they spent six months of each year in Sicily and were studying Italian in Cefalù twice a week. Later, Ingrid brought some Swiss chocolate over as a birthday present for Gail.

Felix stopped off on his way back from the toilets on his bike – a sturdy silver job. It was impressive, with pedal or electric power, and the electric motor cut in at the press of a button. It had Sturmey Archer gears that I remember from my first childhood bike, along with hub brakes that looked like modern disc brakes. We discussed the Swiss Army and National Service, and whether it induces discipline and respect in the population at large, and also learnt that Switzerland has a Navy to patrol the lakes, which sounded like an excellent posting. I invited Felix to fetch Ingrid and have tea with us, since we had already benefited from their hospitality, and we had chocolate chip cookies. He returned to say,

'We won't come to you, but Ingrid says to come to our van.' I was at something of a loss how to respond, but simply said we would be pleased to. It turned out Ingrid already had the kettle on, and a first-rate array of coconut dainties elegantly arranged on a cake stand and fine china, as opposed to our chocolate chips on a plate. We also discovered that their haste to get us to move to the pitch next to them had little to do with love for us, but rather an adversity to a German couple (especially the husband) who they apparently thought moaned a lot, particularly about the weather.

'Did you get him like this, or did he become like this?' Ingrid had injudiciously asked the German lady of her husband.

'He came like this,' was the reply.

Ingrid then went on to tell us the Swiss version of the glass half full or half empty and how negative people were moaning about the weather and other campers – which was precisely what she was doing.

Apparently the pitch Ingrid and Felix were on had the best views of the sea and coastline (which it did), but was known to get muddy and trap unwary campers after rain. Having seen this in previous years, they had successfully asked the ground staff to bring a dumper load of stone chippings to the pitch and spread them around so they wouldn't sink. Oh, the consternation that caused amongst the other campers – the Swiss 'getting all the favours'. But as Ingrid rightly said,

'Anyone could have done it!' I began to admire her positive spirit, even more so when she confided in us that Felix had a progressive illness, hence his bicycling to and from the toilet block.

We were becoming immersed in campsite personalities. Roger and Rosemary in a double-axled Eurovan on the terrace below us were the only others from the UK when we arrived. A number of cats led by a large white tom scampered past us as we spoke.

'There's about fifteen of them,' advised Roger. Someone had put an enormous bone at the end of our pitch. I tried to palm it off on a passing Welsh Collie called Nixon, shepherded by a German who spoke good English, but the dog refused it. The German had a large Welsh flag flying from his substantive motorhome, so I was convinced it was in honour of his dog.

'No,' he said with a shrug. 'I like the dragon.'

Fellow campers Robert and his wife Dorian, Americans from Louisiana, were interested in languages. For six weeks they had been attending an intensive Italian language course in Cefalù for three hours a day, at a cost of one hundred and eighty Euros a week each. They had bought a maroon American Dodge Freightliner in the USA and Robert had converted it. They were very curious about our van, since theirs was a rebadged Sprinter, and Robert had engineered a number of conversations so they could take a closer look. Inviting us back to their van, we found it had that lived-in feel about it. Over drinks they told us they had been touring for about thirty years – initially coming across to Europe in a boat.

'We sailed all the way across the Atlantic then couldn't find anywhere to moor up,' said Dorian. 'Then when you do get somewhere, you're tied to your neighbours because there's so little space. We saw nothing but harbours and had to rent cars, so we decided a motorhome would be better for us.' Their van didn't have the high roof that we had, so their bed was fitted transversely at the back rather cramping their remaining space. Robert had cleverly fitted a sink, cooker, oven, ice-box, neat swivelling table, a bench seat, wooden floors, bathroom with toilet and shower, and an impressive array of dials and switches over the door that told him everything he needed to know about the functioning of the van's utilities down to the temperature of the fresh water tank.

'Do you have a water heater in yours?' he asked.

'Yes, it's part and parcel of the van's gas heating,' I replied. 'Don't you?' It came as something of a dampener to be told that he couldn't find and fit a suitable water heater, so for their showers they had to boil the water in a kettle on the hob and top up the tank.

Returning to our van full of motorhome gossip, I realised I'd received a text message from long-standing friends back in the UK: We're at a motorhome show. Any advice?

'What can I say to them?' I asked Gail. 'How do you condense all that we've learnt in the last five years into a cryptic message?' I telephoned instead. Inspired by our own trips, they had decided to do the same, and had already bought a new motorhome. I didn't know whether to be flattered or concerned, thinking of all the advice I could have given them.

After a few days of leisure, relaxation and gossip, we were ready to break out and explore. Overlooking the campsite was a range of mountains, and on a rocky spur we could see the isolated village of Pollina. As time went by we became curious as to what it might be like. It looked relatively easy – the road started opposite the campsite gate with a gentle incline. However, as we proceeded, the eleven kilometre, six hundred and forty-three metre climb soon became a series of hairpins on a narrower road. The view back to the coast was worth it though. On the advice of Robert, we parked in the lower village on a small area by the tennis courts. An old man peered out of his doorway as we reversed into the only space between a dark-green Piaggio mini-truck and a red Corsa.

'*Va bene qui*?' I shouted across. He scuttled back into the blackness of his house. It soon became apparent, looking up through the pines and to the walls, that Robert's advice on parking had left us a long way below the main village – one hundred and twenty near vertical metres, to be precise. The walk up round more hairpins was challenging, and Gail's continuing entreaties to enjoy the view to the Tyrrhenian Sea passed unheeded. Through an arch in the town's walls we entered a maze of narrow, hilly, cobbled medieval streets and passages, and passed through arches between stone houses, many of which were supported by rusty scaffolding. In some places substantial wooden beams had been used and intricately worked together to form an arched framework that would not disgrace a church or old barn and served to keep the walls of buildings on each side of alleyways upright and apart. Many properties had suspicious cracks. Was this village of 3,000 souls sliding down the steep hill? And was this perhaps a result of earthquake activity?[13]

We went past the cathedral and slipped down a narrow passage between old houses, emerging onto a grassy knoll at

[13] My later research suggests there may have been one in 1993.

the rear, where a goat track of a path led down the hillside. In the distance were superb views of inland, snow covered ridges. Back in the village we made further explorations. It was a step back in time. The dark streets were wide enough for a donkey and maybe a small cart, the houses clinging together as though seeking mutual protection from falling down the mountain. Old women clothed from head to toe in black shuffled along the cobbles and laboured up the hill to the little corner shop, finding respirational relief on its level entrance. Others sat on doorsteps in blind alleyways. In the church a small group bent in reverence and listened to a reading. An old, battered 4x4 light-green Fiat Panda, driven by an even older little man with three days beard growth, drove up the cobbled hill hopelessly slowly, its lack of inertia threatening a standstill and swift reversal of motion back down again. It turned into an impossibly narrow street, round an even more impossible right angle, under a ridiculously narrow arch between houses, and finally disappeared from view. Fiat Panda Rules!

We tagged along to find an unusually tall man for Italy in leather boots, jeans, and blue sweater coming down a hill leading a donkey loaded with hessian saddlebags, the corners tipped with leather. We tried to slow him for a photo but he didn't want to know, calling to a woman across the street – I envisaged something along the lines of 'Bloody tourists!' We grabbed what we could before he descended the cobbled hill out of view. We climbed further up to the castle, its walls set into the rock of the mountain, its rectangular, ill-fitting towers built for the Ventimiglia family so the astronomer Maurolico could stay there between 1548 and 1550 and observe the stars. Below the castle, and set into the hillside, the modern open-air 'Pinkstone Theatre' had been constructed in the style of a Greco-Roman theatre. And there was our Panda driver's car, along with dozens of old men. With the exception of Corleone we had never seen so many. Anoraks, sweaters, corduroy pants and flat caps were ubiquitous. They sat on the stone blocks of the theatre, immobile, a polite separation between each of them, their heads bowed and hands between their knees, probably asleep, or charitably at prayer. Another group leant back against a low protective wall, oblivious to the wondrous vista of the Madonie Mountains behind them. Our arrival caused no more than a lazily raised eyebrow.

By now we were desperate for coffee. We climbed up the theatre steps to re-enter the village at the uppermost part, then wound our way down, round and round the narrow streets to discover a bank, a butcher, and a tiny little shop with an old lady sat on a stool by a fire cracking pistachio nuts into jars, but no café-bar or hint of coffee. So we drove all the way to Cefalù. Later that evening we examined our pictures of the day. The ones of the donkey were not a success, but the background was interesting – at number twenty-seven, and immediately behind the donkey on a wooden board, was 'Bar San Antonio – Caffetteria' with painted pictures of a steaming cappuccino and glass of strawberry sundae. We had been so engrossed photographing the donkey we had missed it.

There was a wild storm in the night, with lashing rain and wind such that the sea became violent and brown from all the soil that had been washed down from the land or churned up. The day was unusually cold and grey and I didn't get to the showers until midday, by which time they weren't hot enough to stay. It remained cold into the evening, and we had to put the gas heating on. Lots of vans had arrived the day before, including four German vans on the top terrace above us, one more on our level, and a French van on our right. The next day I discovered it was occupied by Brits, Chris and Viv, who lived in France and were building and renovating property there. In gorgeous warm sunshine, Chris and I sat out chewing the fat and lunching late. Chris was tall with a slightly scruffy beard. A builder, smallholder, and market gardener, he could turn his hand to anything and had divorced his former wife because 'she did sod all apart from playing with her horses.' Their dog was rescued from a neighbouring French farmer because it barked all night and kept him awake.

'I told him, give it to me or bloody shoot it,' said Chris. I got the impression he was a man of impulse. Viv – small, pretty, and prim with glasses, was an ex-teacher and told me that Chris was irrational and she had to tidy up behind him, filling in his grand plans with workable details. Chris was all for doing three-hundred kilometres a day, but she had to focus on where they could stay. As a result of Chris wanting to do huge distances they missed a lot of sights, only realising later exactly what.

The sky was clear blue, and to shake off our entrenchment on the site, we decided to venture out. Rosalba was the pretty site receptionist and spoke fluent German and English impressively. We entered her office just as her four-year-old son, Federico, was singing Happy Birthday in English down the phone to his mother-in-law (an Italian). Rosalba thought it would be good to teach him languages early.

'You're not leaving?' she asked.

'No, just a day trip to Castelbuono and the Madonie Mountains,' Gail replied. 'Don't let our pitch go.' Behind Finale, the peaks of the Madonie National Park range up to nearly two thousand metres high, but our first target was Castelbuono at three hundred and seventy-four metres. The Madonie are an extension of the Nebrodi and Peloritan mountains to the east, and part of a rugged chain extending through Italy across Calabria and Sicily, and then into Tunisia. Many of the towns nestled into the Madonie are of Saracen Arab origin, dating from around the ninth century, and were subsequently developed into larger villages under the conquering Normans. Several are ancient, built upon the remains of Sicanian, Greek, and Roman settlements. The road from Finale wound up the foothills and into the mountains, revealing wonderful big sky scenery of hills clothed in Holm Oak and beech forests, chestnut, and holly trees. I also discovered that there was a unique crop called *manna* that comes not from heaven, but from a species of ash tree, *Fraxinus ornus*. Found uniquely in the areas surrounding Castelbuono and Pollina, there was much history and ritual to its collection as stalactites of crystallized sap from gashes in the trees. It was apparently sold in pharmacies and tobacco stores for its mild laxative effect, its natural sweetness allowed for its use in alcoholic drinks, and it was also used in the cosmetic industry.

In Castelbuono we parked under the fourteenth century (twelfth and thirteenth century origins) castle, climbed the long steps up to the impressive entrance, paid our entrance fees, and just as I was wondering whether I wanted to tour another ancient building, we entered the first room to find its walls festooned with large photographs of nude women. This continued throughout the castle, which was being put to very good use as an art gallery. I think the original owners, the Geraci family, would have approved, as their castle was richly embellished with ceilings made up of inlaid and decorated raised wooden beams, and the chapel, housing the skull of Saint Anne, a Baroque extravaganza.

We liked Castelbuono. It had the usual narrow streets, but these had women in them, some smart shops, and a pleasant square (Piazza Margherita) with a fountain, a 1316 prison (that became the State pawnshop and morphed into the Culture Office), and the old cathedral in it. After a thorough meander round the many notable buildings, a quick lunch and an ear-bursting salvo from a cement lorry that couldn't get down the street because of errant parkers, we returned to the van. We drove out of Castelbuono and further up the mountains to very special easterly views of Etna almost covered in snow from the recent rains, peaks and crags, remote villages perched on summits with no visible means of access, an occasional large farm, honey coloured cows with large bells leaning over roadside fences, and large birds riding the winds above. The Madonie impressed us, and continued to do so as we climbed to Geraci Siculo at 1,112 metres and looped back before finally joining the A19 to descend to the coast and wonder why it was necessary to build the motorway on stilts to cross the final valley to the sea.

Later that day Chris asked me if I could get their satellite TV working.

'I'm not sure if I'll be able to get anything,' I cautioned.

'Anything on the screen will do,' he pleaded. 'Why have it if we can't get anything on it?' I fiddled about with the dish on the roof and the set controls, when suddenly 'Red Hot TV' appeared.

'I don't think so,' said Viv. Then I got Sky TV, but with no sound.

'Well, what good is that?' said Chris.

'I thought anything would do – and you've got captions.' Then the sound came on and I was sure he'd be pleased.

'I hate Sky News,' decided Chris. 'They just keep repeating and repeating.' I flicked through the other channels – they were all German, so our broadcasting adventure was over. They nevertheless invited us over for a pasta dinner, and we spent a delightful evening swapping stories. The next morning I saw Chris and thanked him for their hospitality but noticed he was clearing up.

'We're leaving for Sardinia tomorrow,' he replied.

'Nothing we said, I hope?'

'No, can't sit in one place for too long.' The next day they were ready to leave by 9 a.m. 'Sardinia, ho!' he shouted from the driver's window as they set off up the hill to the top terrace and exit. Later, I wandered up to the reception to use the Internet and was amazed to find Chris and Viv sitting outside in their van.

'What's the problem?'

'Rosalba hasn't arrived yet.'

'She's normally here at ten – that's why I've come up.'

'Anyway, we're not going to Sardinia.'

'No?'

'No – we're going further east, along the coast to Oliveri. Don't ask.' So I didn't.

I had a couple of dispiriting conversations with the young couple that parked next to us after Chris and Viv had left. They had a caravan, an older white Renault estate, and a pretty black and white cat. When they'd arrived the previous afternoon and were engaged by Chris I sensed the tenor of their conversation was that of complaints, and snatches of the ensuing hours of conversation confirmed their dissatisfaction with Southern Sicily, Sicilians, their dishonesty, dirty beaches, the price charged to go up Etna (they walked part way but it was windy so came down), the weather, and various other deprecations, although 'the stones' (or ancient Greek temples), came in for favourable mention. I decided I didn't like them, but the next day, in an attempt to be communicative and neighbourly, I offered informational help should they need it.

'Is there a decent supermarket?'

'There's one in Finale,' I replied.

'No, we've been there, it's pah!' It had served our (and most of the site's other) inhabitants adequately, but not sumptuously.

'It's limited I agree, but we use it for essentials.'

'We want one where we can get beer.' I was sure they had some beer in there.

'You could try Cefalù,' and I tried to explain the approximate location. Later in the day, after their visit to Cefalù, another conversation full of complaints ensued. They would only spend another week on Sicily and couldn't wait to get to Frejus via Pompeii and Rome. I impartially explained that although much of what they said did happen, it was part of life – different to what we were used to, certainly, but that was why we enjoyed travel. It seemed to make little difference, and they simply launched into another round of complaints, which was a great shame since our fellow campers, be they Austrian, Swiss, Italian, or the jolly, smiling old German couple next to us (their only complaint, as far as we knew, was the weather), were great.

On Rosalba's recommendation we went on one more trip back along the coast then inland through the western Madonie Mountains to Piano Battagliala. The sky was clear, and as we progressed inland, great mountains arose around us. With no other traffic, the wildness of the Madonie exerted itself. As we progressed, we realised that the peaks were covered in snow and snow markers appeared at the roadside, along with patches of snow in sheltered spots. As we pulled into Piano Zucchi (that appeared to comprise of two closed but magnificently positioned hotels), the roadside and verges were completely covered. Six majestic snow ploughs sat waiting to be called to action. As clouds descended and mist drifted across the road we debated whether to go on. The road had been ploughed – there were snow piles to each side and the rivulets of water running down suggested it was melting so we ploughed on. The snow at the roadside deepened and a thick white blanket lay in the forest. The pass was only a few kilometres away. We rounded more hairpins, many packed with uncleared snow, and there was no sign of habitation should we need help, but a 'just one more bend' attitude drove us on to Piano Battaglia, a 'No Motorhomes Beyond This Point' sign, and deep snow. Fortunately, there was also a sign for a '*Refugio*', and what welcoming strong coffee they served for their only guests, along with 'just one synthetic, packeted, cream *cornetto*.' The log fire roared and crackled as we sat in the well-type seating around it, and the chef and assistant came to say '*Ciao*' and see who could possibly have been mad enough to venture up here. Looking out the window, the clouds looked pregnant with snow so we decided our adventure up to 1,552 metres was over and slid back down the mountain to Isnello, a charming village in a deep gorge with a protective castle and church on a rocky crag, but no food left in any of the cafés. We set off along a road that wound round and round and never seemed to leave the village, and then finally broke away for a descent into brilliant sunshine, wonderful views of Cefalù, and the coast.

Towards the end of January, after three weeks at Rais Gerbi, we enjoyed consistently hot days, and sitting out sea-gazing was *de rigueur*. Gail even talked of having 'built a nest.' Roger and Sue had moved opposite us because the groundsman had started to lop all the pine trees around them, and rather than a trimming job, had completely denuded them. Roger was tall and lanky, and with his front teeth reminded me of the British comedian, Cardew Robinson. Their van, which they'd bought new, had been a nightmare for them.

'Need to be a permanent handyman, Keith,' complained Roger as their grey cat nuzzled his ankle. I helped them out with some places they could visit and sites they could use. I was getting restless.

'Robert and Dorian are thinking of going to the Carnival in Acireale,' I announced to Gail out of the blue. 'It's about a hundred and forty miles over the mountains – we could think of it as a few days away.'

'We've done the east coast, so it would mean going back, and I'm not sure I fancy watching a parade,' said Gail unenthusiastically. I snuck down to Robert and Dorian's van and perused *Carnevale* on their computer – it looked exciting. The next morning, Gail pronounced at breakfast that she could 'build a nest anywhere now that we had the small van.' We were on the move again.

Carnevale

We set off in bright sunshine west along the coast road beyond Cefalù to pick up the motorway to Catania. We commented on the necessity of building it on stilts and tried to apply the logic of the simplicity of construction with factory pre-formed sections but thought it more likely that it was down to Mafia contracts. We had been told they controlled concrete production in Sicily.

The valley, flushed by the River Grande, was wonderfully green, and provided a fertile soil resulting in row after row of perfectly planted vegetables along the valley and up the lower slopes. Lonely pickers bent over double, extracting crops by hand. Higher up, the mountains became craggy and bare, with a few herds of long-horned cattle and an isolated farmhouse swathed in the low cloud. We stopped for fuel, LPG, and coffees at an Esso service station and realised we had drunk our excellent cappuccinos nearly as fast as the Italians drank their espressos. We passed over the top of the mountains, and around Enna the land softened. Upon entering Catania province it became one huge citrus grove under the watchful gaze of an almost snow-capped Etna. The dearth at the peak was no doubt due to the warm under-soil. Finding the Panorama campsite in Acireale was a challenge (as was their twenty-seven Euro a night price and indifference to whether we stayed or not), so we headed for Santa Maria La Scala and the La Timpa campsite, set on a rocky crag looking out to sea below Acireale. There we received the warmest of welcomes. 'Whatever you need, just ask.' We were sited on our own in a sea-facing citrus grove of oranges, lemons, grapefruit, and banana palms, the Villa Belvedere at Acireale way above us.

I didn't know what to expect of Carnevale – a celebration of winter's ending and spring's coming. Maybe some floats, religious processions, a pageant or parade, marching bands, circus animals and beauty queens, lightly-clad pretty dancing girls, dancing in the streets, masks, and costumes? Would there be suffocating crushing crowds, marshals, high-spirited, riotous, and noisy behaviour, pickpockets, crime, or officious police? We were about to find out. Crowds were already funnelling up the hill into Piazza Indirizzo when the owner ran us up in the camp minibus around 4:30 p.m. From there we walked down the pedestrianised Corso Umberto, the lampposts supporting a profusion of graceful and stylish festive lighting, below which lay a black lava stone street covered in multi-coloured confetti and plastic-squirted streamers. Everyone was enjoying the sun, and many were in fancy dress – a jester's hat, a witch's outfit, ghouls and crones, Dalmatians, and even a pair of lovers dressed as a chicken and cockerel walked the streets. Children were free to throw confetti over anyone passing, unbridled in their use of squirt-cans of plastic streamers bought by encouraging and occasionally over-enthusiastic parents. It was certainly a party, but there was no sign of any floats. By the time we reached the Piazza Duomo there was a good throng of people milling around the stage, where a band was warming up, and even more over in the corner where young majorettes in blue and red were preparing (along with a group of older folks in similar uniforms but without the short skirts!). Scheduled to start at 4:00 p.m., we were already late. We found a tourist office and got the programme from the untroubled official who had been quietly reading the financial pink papers. When he checked his watch against the published schedule and realised that it should have already been well under way, he shrugged his shoulders and waved his arm in that 'maybe later' sort of way. After admiring the cathedral and the Baroque buildings in the square we walked up the narrower Corso Savoia, one of the other sides of the triangle that comprised the route.

Approaching Corso Italia, the first float appeared – a colossus on wheels pulled by an orange tractor. It was a two-storey high assembly of about a dozen colourful, comical and monster male figures – a huge, papier-mâché head with furrowed brow and red wavy hair, Crocodile Dundee characters riding green crocodiles out of a jungle, giant blue ostrich-like birds and other jungle creatures hidden within. There was a complete blue, open-top jeep projecting from the front – it was a jungle adventure, a Jurassic Park on a trailer about forty-foot long. That there was a trailer underneath was only evident by the tractor at the front and the smell of exhaust from the generators hidden under the trailer. We were amazed by the float's characters, but mainly by the immensity of it. It passed within inches of balconies on each side and cables overhead, occasionally brushing a central hanging street lamp above.

Behind it was another with a huge, central, sombrero-wearing plastic Mexican accompanied by a host of others, green parrots, and other unknown creatures. At the junction with Corso Italia we watched as an even bigger float with the name 'Hollywood' and an Oscar Awards theme arrived and attempted to turn the corner. Papier-mâché buxom froufrou girl dancers stared down at us as skilled tractor driving brought it within inches of making the turn, but not without the ghoulish movie figures at the top left colliding with the second floor balcony and the huge car with two movie stars aboard colliding with the vendor's stall on the right. Men in shiny-black blouson jackets ran backwards and forwards shouting directions. The blue tractor was turned violently, but unsuccessfully, to this angle then another in an attempt to get the massive creation round the corner. The driver reversed it backwards but to no avail. After twenty minutes of mutual driver fascination I was tugged away myself. We returned to Piazza Duomo with the light now fading into evening.

We stood a little way into the square so we could see the floats arriving. With the natural light now gone, the floats were lit with powerful rear-facing floodlights on the front of the tractors, but each was also a panoply of internal and external lights, bulb illuminations beyond imagination, colour luminosity gone mad, Las Vegas on wheels. Each figure had a changing pattern, and a change in music would herald a new event. Figures to the side of a float swung out to double its width. The figures were moving, a huge car at the front rocking and rolling, two giant figures riding and waving from it. There were boats sailing the seven seas, sails aloft, cannons out of the gun ports; giant animal figures on seesaws going up and down, and a huge, sea-snake-like creature leering out at you – its monster jaws opening and closing as though they could take your head off. But these were just to warm you up. Something was opening. A colossal figure was emerging and rising up from the float – it was now three storeys high. Animation was rife – streamers of lights were flashing, eyes were winking, arms waving, and legs bending. We were witnessing gigantic, illuminated works of moving art. We watched in awe – fascinated and mesmerised as each came into the square for its themed performance. Dads lifted youngsters in fancy dress onto their shoulders for a better view. The crowd clapped and cheered, pointing frantically to the children in case they missed one of the many simultaneous events.

One float had a circus theme. At the front a huge male figure, I would guess thirty-feet high, in a showman's outfit of a bright red and yellow diamond patterned jacket with blue edging to the lapels, yellow trousers, luminescent green dress shirt, all with blue Catherine-wheel-spinning buttons, green boots, a crimson hat adorned with beads of lighting, the detail amazing. The face, a boozers-red with magnificent white teeth and blonde-streaked green hair and moustache, piercing blue eyes all lit internally and externally, the lighting changing constantly. The whole figure was on a trapeze attached solely by his hands, behind other circus creatures twirled but all focus was on the man. His face said 'watch me, watch me.' The human circus master dwarfed by the creatures on the float conducted 'the orchestra,' his choir sang along, his showgirls gyrated to the music. At the front the technical maestro conducted the technicians; tiny human Lilliputian-figures scuttling around on the float switching on this, pulling that. The music changed from a crescendo to a drum roll. We knew what was coming. The giant figure did a complete headstand on the trapeze the back of his red and yellow-coat-tailed jacket streamers of flashing bulbs. Then a quarter rotation so its head was in the crowd leering at us 'I told you to watch me' and then it was back down. Could there be any more? The music lifted again, the lighting became more moody, another drum roll and he was up again and the trapeze was rotating round at the same time, lights were flashing his face was changing colour other figures on the float were doing their own thing a worthy climax to an amazing show

'Hollywood' spectacularly produced a giant car from the front with Abbott and Costello aboard. The car rose out and above the crowd, lurching from side to side, as though bumping along a country road. The music was upbeat – 'We Will Rock You'. The float 'grew' a scarlet, curtained theatre stage high into the starlit night sky, above which appeared a golden, roaring, MGM lion. The curtains then opened to show a blue *Phantom of the Opera* figure, only to close again as that piece of music subsided. The lights were subdued, and into the night, Pavarotti's voice rose above everything. The crowd quietened as the stage opened again to reveal his image, the crowd clapping in appreciation of the remembrance. Some may have had lumps in their throats, but as the singing progressed and the lights came up, their approval gave rise to cheering as the stage curtains closed and the music moved to Tina Turner's foot-stomping 'Simply the Best'.

Other floats drove into the piazza, miraculously turned and then squeezed past others that had just entered, the crowd sandwiched between them, not knowing which way to look. After the *carri allegorico-grotteschi* (grotesque-allegorical floats) came the *carri infiorati* (flower floats). Not quite as large, but still brushing the second storeys and passing within inches of the buildings on each side of the street, they were beautifully illuminated, and despite the complexity of creating creatures of flowers, also highly animated. There was a giant lottery ladybird with stunning red, expanding wings, accompanied by a trailer of white-flowered winged insects and exquisitely detailed roulette tables. Only when they were close could you see the thousands of carnations they were made from – even the soles of their feet. A variety of floats followed, and between them, a bevy of beauties in an extravaganza of dresses well beyond description by this mere male! Suffice to say that the pink ensemble that platformed out from the waist to provide a Mad Hatter's Tea Party was fun, but not as beautiful as the highly-coloured, similarly full-skirted, living examples of the more traditional Carnival type. Encouraged by Gail to photograph a line of these, I pushed through the crowd to find myself asking a couple of old drag queens to pose, and how well they did! I looked more closely at the rest but was never sure (except for the couple at the back in the white and gold outfits with gigantic wings who posed and pouted so well, I was certain!), they all looked beautiful, so I took photos of them in their enormous orange taffeta creations anyway.

We attended the carnival on the Saturday evening, Sunday morning and afternoon, and the finale on the Tuesday evening. Sunday was pleasant in the sun and it struck us as highly incongruous that whilst the grotesque-allegorical floats paraded in front of the cathedral to a packed crowd and parked there for viewing, there was simultaneously a packed house inside receiving God's word. Some managed both, moving in and out of the entrance in their jesters' hats or other carnival attire. The finale on Tuesday was heaving in the piazza, and it was a miracle that the floats managed to manoeuvre through the crowd without anyone getting crushed. It was a pleasing feature that there was no crowd control, and the increase in police presence to two vans was discreetly hidden away. Everyone was free to move around and between floats and in and out of cafés or shops (they all stayed open) as they wished, and there was no drunkeness or aggressive behaviour. Butchers in the narrow back streets had set up barbecues outside their shops with steaming grills of steaks, pork, sausages, and fish, and the smells of roasting flesh were intoxicating.

We won't forget our Saturday evening, because nothing could surpass the sheer delight of our first exposure to the moving-theatre art of Acireale's magical Carnevale. When we revisited on Thursday, there were only traces of confetti and streamers left, and the central stage was being loaded onto trucks.

'I wonder where they store those massive floats?'

'Perhaps there are new ones every year.'

'And how did they keep those flowers fresh for the duration of the carnival?'

'I don't know. Let's have a coffee in here.'

'*Due cappuccino per favore*.'

'What? There's no water in town. Even for a coffee?' Nor for the toilets, as we later found.

Santa Maria La Scala (where we were camped) was a haven of tranquillity below the hubbub of Acireale and its carnival. The orchard we were in produced bountiful crops for us, and breakfast grapefruit along with fresh bread from the baker who delivered to us every day was a pleasure. We were his only customers, so how the purchase of two rolls for half a Euro was going to sustain him we didn't know. We hadn't the heart to refuse, even when we didn't want any. The village of Santa Maria La Scala, a short walk down the hill, was a tiny, picturesque fishing village with a few houses, some pretty restaurants, and a church huddled at the base of the rocky coast round the quay. As we walked into the village on the Monday to shop at the tiny store and buy green groceries off the travelling man with the overloaded Piaggio, we found Robert and Dorian parked in front of the church, wild camping. They had already completed their grand tour of Sicily and were about to head off up the east coast of Italy.

'How did they possibly get round Sicily in such a short time?' I asked Gail. 'They've been to every place we mentioned!'

'They're American.' We invited them back to the van, but the campsite girl wanted to charge them for their visit and we were the only people there. The site also had another quirk. I had read in our guide that the only cassette emptying point was at a garage up the road. Since it was a long walk up a steep hill, I didn't fancy carrying the cassette up or moving the van. I approached the helpful owner, who got a key and led me down the terraces on the cliff-side to a small, ramshackle cabin set into the rock with a rusting iron door, corrugated iron roof, and a 'Disabled Toilet' sign. It was exactly what it said on the sign – disabled – with a toilet blocked with dried faeces and soiled walls. The Black Hole of Calcutta and the hothouse torture pen in *Bridge over the River Kwai* immediately sprang to mind. The place was a shit hole in every sense of the word. He slid a cover back on the mucky concrete floor under the basin and pointed to a roughly cut hole in a brown plastic pipe traversing it – the cassette emptying point – disgusting. Strangely, they never trusted me with the key and I had to be accompanied on both the visits made. God help anyone who was disabled.

After seven days and a one day discount we decided to return to Finale. The owner beseeched us to stay longer, or to return, with promises of even more fruit from the orchard and discounts whilst stuffing brochures through the van window for our '*amici.*' I told him I was writing a book and we had already been in Sicily since November, but he misunderstood and thought I meant until November, so he ran back to the office for more brochures and asked us to tell all the other campers we met about his site. Yes, a wonderful site, but what about the waste hole? Even as I write I can see and smell it!

Final days at Finale

As we left Acireale, Etna was crystal clear in an unusually cloudless sky, with a snow covering down to the lower slopes and smoke issuing from two craters. Although we could have returned to Finale via the motorway, we decided to take small 'interregional' mountain and 'less congested roads' coloured yellow on our map and edged with green to indicate a 'scenic route'. We passed the modern shopping complex of Etnapolis, and whilst discussing whether to stop at the immense 'Cathedral of Commercialism' we missed our turn into Paterno. Taking the next exit, we found ourselves descending a ramp that halfway down warned of a three metre height limit under a tunnel, and so we had to reverse back up onto the main road to the accompaniment of Italian horns and unhelpful gestures. After a detour to appreciate the countryside we finally found our route – the S121 – a country road through orange groves to the north of Paterno, and under Etna's by-then cloudy gaze.

The landscape changed to grassland with large-horned cattle, then became even more impressive with a lake below, and mountains surrounding us. The town of Agira rose up spectacularly ahead of us. With its castle, it was like another Erice perched on a precipitous hilltop. We climbed and climbed, expecting to reach it, but at the last minute the road veered off to the right and passed below. The scenery became dramatic, but the twisting roads were crumbling and in many places had given way to become van-sized potholes. Close to Nicosia, an incongruous stretch of new road had been constructed through a series of tunnels. Beyond that we encountered wild roads, occasional cattle, isolated windswept farms, and snow covered mountains. The skies were leaden grey with snow filled clouds – a contrast to the crisp blue, sun filled sky of coastal Acireale. We climbed to 1,130 metres, and the lonely road continued to deteriorate until we came to a section where half the road had disintegrated. I have to confess to a frisson of concern at the remote, inhospitable landscape and danger that snow might fall and trap us. A considerable interval had passed since we had seen either another vehicle or a farm. Another side of Sicily was showing itself to us.

Getting down the hill to Mistretta and squeezing into the only parking place outside a restaurant was a tension reliever. After lunch and a review of the dismal weather forecast in the papers, we descended to the sunbathed coast and back to the Rais Gerbi campsite. In the office we eagerly told Rosalba about our enjoyment of Carnevale at Acireale.

'*E 'fantastico, magnifico, spettacolare!*'

'I also went to a festival with my family,' she responded.

'Oh, where was that?'

'Agrigento. The dancers were also spectacular.'

'What sort of dancers?'

'Irish River Dancers.'

The site was busy and we had to take a less favoured pitch. Our German friend with the Welsh Collie dog came over and looked at it.

'You should move. Too much dove shit.' The weather forecast proved to be correct and it rained for two days. Gail saw someone pulling out of our old pitch and ran over with a chair to reserve it, but the camper next to it told her they had already reserved it for their friends who would be coming the next day. We didn't believe them. We spent a week at Rais Gerbi doing chores, shopping, and walking to Finale for coffee.

'What day is it?' I asked Gail.

'It's Wednesday. Or is it Tuesday?'

'Is that the thirteenth or the twelfth?'

'I have no idea – do you want me to get my diary out?' There comes a time when you lose track. Without the discipline of getting up to go to work and the fixed routine of Monday to Friday followed by weekends, every day is the same. The only reference point was that the campsite office was closed on Sundays, but you would only notice that if you went up there to use the Internet or get a wash token (which you shouldn't be doing on a Sunday, anyway). The sun rose, the sun set. Only writing my notes up in the evenings gave me a clue, but I had skipped a few days as there had been little activity, scintillating conversations, or significant events to record. We decided to move on before lethargy became our downfall.

We left on Saturday 16th February. A number of others left at the same time – if we'd stayed we could have had their pitches! Rosalba was profuse with her goodbyes.

'Your book – what is it called?'

'*How Katie Pulled Boris*.'

'What does that mean?'

'It's a double meaning. Like when a boy picks up a girl at a dance.'

'*Uff*! *Remorchio*!'

'Exactly! Like pulling a trailer.'

A grey day ensued for our journey east along the thin strip of coast that struggled to be big enough for both our road and the railway, but couldn't contain the motorway that soared above us on stilts, the twin-tunnel mouths gaping open. Sometimes there wasn't enough room for our road either, and we climbed inland to see the mountains darkened with rain clouds. At one point, half the hillside had been cut away and we had to divert onto an unsurfaced road. The town of Caronia appeared on a hilltop, but was uninviting with blocks of modern flats crowding up to the edge of the cliff face and no relieving Duomo dome. We tried to turn into Capo d'Orlando, but were defeated by two low bridges under the railway, then suffered a major diversion round Gioiosa Marea up one-in-five gradient hills and sharp hairpin roads, so were pleased to finally stop for coffees in a modern, non-descript café in an unmemorable place. We ate the last two croissants and watched the local boys playing table football as they sheltered from the drizzle outside.

We diverted slightly to climb up to the Santuario della Madonna Nera, 'a lavishly kitsch temple built in the 1960s, where pilgrims come for the black Madonna,' but as we entered the otherwise empty complex of outside car parks and saw the extortionate fees and paraphernalia of mass tourism, our interest waned and we set off back down towards the coast and the campsite at Oliveri. Maria was just closing for the 1:00 p.m. lunch and told us the weather was the worst in living memory. The site was depressingly gloomy, and the rail side toilets and showers depressing. I spoke to one of the few other campers, a Brit gentleman from Penrith who had recently arrived in Sicily and driven from Messina, a short distance to the east. He sat outside repairing his bicycle.

'How's it going?' I asked, as cheerily as one can on what was turning out to be a cold and damp day. 'Enjoying the trip?'

'Just been here a few days, and only arrived in Sicily this week. I'm on my own – it's my first trip, and a new van.'

'It looks a nice one.'

'It was. I've already hit the roof on a road sign and scraped the front trying to make sharp hairpin turns on diversions. The roads from Messina have been dreadful.'

'Have you considered using the motorway?' I suggested, knowing what he was going to face.

'No, I think it'll get better from here, and I'd miss a lot.'

Umm, like a few road signs, was my immediate thought, but I kept it to myself.

'Well, I admire what you're doing. It can't be easy on your own.'

Gail and I walked along the windy beach into town to find a café-bar. A few brave souls were casting lines out into the waves. The town was in an 'out-of-season, not bothering' mode. The old men huddled under a café-bar awning, sheltered from the wind and drizzle, playing cards. We went inside, the only customers. After a while a man came in who looked like he had been sleeping rough. He had unkempt hair and beard, an old gabardine raincoat, wore woollen mitts with no fingers, and walked slowly with a walking stick. I watched, fascinated, as he sat at a table near us and emptied a pocket full of small change onto it. His hands had the tremors, but he methodically counted the coins into piles of the same denomination until he had what he wanted. He replaced the unwanted ones in his pocket, scooped up those on the table, made his way slowly to the bar, and handed them over to the young girl serving. She seemed to know what he wanted without asking.

'Going to get a shot of alcohol,' I whispered to Gail. The girl took down a glass from the shelf and they both moved to the display. He came away with a Knickerbocker Glory. He edged his way back to the table, his eyes never leaving the precious cargo. Sat down, he scooped a glistening load of pistachio and chocolate *gelato* with his spoon, savoured the moment as he held it up in front of him, then slowly slid it into his mouth. His eyes closed with the pleasure. With each spoonful he went through the same procedure, transported to his own *gelato* heaven. We got up to leave, and chastened by my rush to judgement I asked him,

'*Il gelato, è bene*?' A big smile broke out, revealing a set of broken brown teeth.

'*Si, si.*'

'*Ma è freddo oggi,*' I shivered. He laughed, and we left him and his twinkling eyes relishing every spoonful. *Gelato* is a way of life in Italy.

That night was noisy, with strong winds ripping bits off the trees that fell onto the van roof. In the morning Gail tried the showers and said they weren't very good. When I set off for them, it started snowing. As they were partially exposed to the elements, water only dribbled out of those I tried, and the doors wouldn't lock, so I didn't bother. Over breakfast, we made the decision to leave.

We drove to Milazzo, 'not a place you're likely to make a beeline for,' and agreed there were a lot of oil refineries on approaching the peninsula, however, the views of the city, its Duomo, and castle on the eastern arch of the spit of land, were good. Furthermore, as we parked by the port and watched the empty ferries to the Aeolian Islands waiting for anyone to come aboard, the sun broke through. Milazzo has a massive hilltop castle built by Frederic II and extended by the Spanish in the fifteenth and sixteenth centuries, with its own walled city and old Duomo. We paused on the hill in front to take in the view. The narrow spit of land containing the city is bordered on each side by the Tyrrhenian Sea. It sparkled in the shafts of light streaming down from gaps between the heavy clouds that encompassed the sombre mountain peaks beyond. It was well worth the climb up, but difficult to encompass photographically. We walked back down to the city along a pleasant cobbled street bordered by palaces.

Thinking of where we might camp, we drove out of Milazzo and further along the eastern side of the steeply rising peninsula, towards Capo di Milazzo. The two campsites along the road were closed, and we debated whether it was ethical to wild camp outside an existing campsite and what we would do if the owner came by.

'We could say we were waiting for him to open,' I volunteered, but lost the argument. We continued round the coast through seaside towns that merged and were non-descript with the exception of Spadafora, where we caught sight of a fine, sixteenth century square, fortified palace, and piazza in front. We ignored the main road and motorway that rounded to Messina in favour of a country road that ran to the northeast tip of Sicily, anxious not to miss any part now that our tour was coming to a close. Our first sight was a flock of sheep on the road. Once cleared, we spotted what appeared to be a small campsite down a track to the right. Gail went to ask and met a delightful, slim lady, Patrizia, with curly black hair, and smiling eyes who spoke good English. She explained that they were closed.

'We don't need anything – could we just park for one night?' Gail pleaded, crestfallen at the thought of more searching.

'Of course,' said Patrizia.

'How much?'

'There is no charge.' What a lovely site. Set in a hundred year old olive grove below hills, two hundred metres from the sea, and not in any of our books – finding a little gem like Peloritano Camping made it all worthwhile for what would be our last night in Sicily. We hoped the weather would continue to improve.

Leaving Sicily

Our initial landscape was gulches and ravines, but as we rounded the northernmost tip of Sicily, mainland Italy came into sight. After Mortelle and Cap Faro, and along the thin strip of coastal land, it all became a blur of inland lakes with buoys, fishing boons, coloured boats, birds, and nature reserves. The places became crowded and vibrant and traffic was heavy – Sicilian style. Sant'Agata had a big-top circus, beautiful bay, and *Pace a Duomo* by the sea. There was a hubbub of roadside vendors with stalls selling an abundance of fresh vegetables. We had not seen such activity since Palermo, and there was no doubt we were in the environs of a major city. Before we knew it there were huge ships alongside the road and we counted ourselves lucky to see the 'Villa San Giovanni' ferry sign and be able to turn across the traffic into the port for a swift embarkation.

On board, there were a group of teenagers from a coach party – most were outside on the smoking deck having fun. Without exception, they wore black tops inscribed with '*Gela*', jeans, and sunglasses. One of the boys produced a camera and two of the girls standing by the rail instinctively transformed themselves into a pose that could have graced the front cover of any trendy fashion magazine. For a moment they looked like chic young women, and seconds later they were young girls again, laughing and enjoying themselves. There was another fashion statement further down the deck, where a man had a fluffy white dog partly inside his coat, and was cradling it like a baby. He put it down on the deck in front of his wife. It wore a tight-fitting, tartan coat and denim trousers that were so tight that it couldn't walk properly. It looked like one of those Japanese robotic dogs as it waddled around the deck, and whenever anyone approached, it immediately lay on its back in submission. Just as I was imagining it sliding down the deck and through the railings into the sea, the man spookily scooped it up and put it back into his coat.

As we leant over the guardrail and looked across at Sicily disappearing in the white wake of the boat, I reflected on our fourteen week visit. We had chosen Sicily because we saw it as remote and different from mainland Europe – not without risk, yet having European order and systems. The trip had been an exciting challenge for us in our new van. There were many emotions swirling round – Sicily had amused, fascinated, baffled, gripped, confounded, frightened, and welcomed us. The people had bestowed kindness and friendship on us beyond measure – like the offers of free camping from Patrizia, and over Christmas from Federico, and the Boxing Day repairs by Montalto Caravan. We would never forget Michele and his sister in Noto. The scenery had been varied, challenging, and magnificent, and the history and culture overwhelming. It was with a lump in my throat and moist eyes that we reluctantly left.

Our confidence as to where we could go in the van was now unchecked, and rather than sticking to the coastal strip, I suggested to Gail that we head into the Aspromonte Mountains to Gambarie and then cut across the tops to the southern coast at Melito di Porto Salvo, thereby missing Reggio di Calabria (of which the Rough Guide had said 'there is little to detain you…' and the Calabrian Mafia or 'Ndrangheta have an octopus grip on the town.')

The twisting drive round blind corners went up through scenic gorges, small villages with their houses huddled at the roadside, and citrus orchards. Terraced olive groves banked up from the road, orange coloured collecting nets rolled and stuffed into their branches. As we twisted and turned, there were glimpses of mountain through the forest of trees, and if we managed to look back, steep drops to the coast. We drove past a small fountain and entered Santo Stefano – the village birthplace of the Calabreses' Robin Hood hero, Mussolini, who led the *Carabinieri* (Italian military) a merry dance up and down the Aspromonte, only to spend his last thirty years between jail and a lunatic asylum before being laid to rest in the village. It was not hard to imagine this as a tough area to live, and the stimulus for the mass migration to America by so many from small villages in Calabria. As we climbed higher, there was a noticeable temperature drop and we could see that the mountain tops were covered in snow.

Gambarie is situated on a plateau at an altitude of 1,310 metres, a small winter-sports village with fantastic views down to the Straits of Messina, the Tyrrhenian and Ionian seas, Etna, and the Aeolian Islands. What we took to be an artist's masterpiece of an ice sculpture in the square beyond the Esso station was the frozen waters of the central fountain. After a precautionary fill with diesel, we kept warm over lunch in a snug café and asked the proprietor in our limited Italian about our plans to cross the mountain. He looked out of the window into the square deep in snow, and nodded questioningly in the direction of our van:

'*Impossibile*!' He then advised us to return by another route (S670) that looked even more secondary. Initially, we drove on straight stretches across the plateau, the sun breaking out for us, before the descent began round steep hairpins. After fantastic scenic views of Sicily, we came to San Roberto on the valley floor at two hundred and eighty metres, a profusion of mimosa abounding amongst the half-finished, grey brick buildings, and eventually returned to the coast to continue south. (When I later did some research on San Roberto I found it to be a Calabrian village snapshot: Its 2,668 population had declined to 1,985 between 1991-2001, and only one hundred and sixty-three of these were recorded as being in employment – fifty-six working in 'administrative offices' [my guess is these were government related]. Only twelve people were recorded as working in four factories, and interestingly, no companies were registered on the website for the town.)

I sat no more than thirty feet from the main railway line. I could see the passengers crowded onto their ancient, blue-grey commuter carriages, the diesel engine changing to a higher gear as it passed. Moments later, a non-stop modern express train literally whistled by, thundering along the electrified track, then another commuter train passed in the opposite direction. A short distance beyond, forty tonne trucks worked their way up a raised section of the main SS106, travelling south from Reggio di Calabria. A promising sign, '*Villaggio Magna Grecia*', had caught our attention as we ran along the coastal road south of Regio beyond Pellaro. We dipped off the road, down onto a dirt track then under a new railway bridge and to the sea. Turning left, we ran behind a street of poor quality concrete houses on the seashore that had great views to Sicily. (In other parts of the world they would have been considered desirable and been refurbished by city types for idyllic weekends away). Another turn left, then right, and we arrived at a terracotta coloured building with an overabundance of white, faux Doric columns. Further along lay some sort of plaza, and then a gateway with more terracotta buildings and Doric columns. A man came out and said we could stay for fifteen Euros. He lead us past the emptied swimming pool to a concrete base between two grassy olive groves lined with small, tarpaulin covered caravans and an occasional motorhome that hadn't moved in years. He showed us the sinks behind us where pots could be washed, and the washrooms where we could wash whilst watching trains go by. There was one electric post but no electric. This was a residential, rather than a touring site, and no one else was touring or residing. He had to turn the electric on for us in the offices. I went to the sinks to get some water and the bottoms of the long rectangular basins were covered in thick brown slime like I had never seen before. (Well I had, but I couldn't think that people had been emptying their toilet cassettes down the sinks). I tried a tap. The water that emerged was brown Windsor soup. *Just run it off a while*, I thought. It got no better – clearly the reason for the brown slime, and I saw that many taps had brown, dangling stalactites. I tried another tap clearly intended for drinking water, and my bucket was filled with brown water, not as bad as the others, but revolting nonetheless. Thank goodness we still had our own supplies. He came over to check we were okay with the electric, and noticed the right-hand-drive, which he deemed to be 'very dangerous.' I thought of all the things I could say about Italian driving and his site, but desisted.

'Normal for me. No problem,' I said. I would love to have seen the site brochure, but knew only too well the photographer would have been standing with his back to the railway and road. We thought that such a huge complex would have its own beach access, and wanting a pleasant walk in the afternoon sun, headed in that direction, but access was obstructed by the road and more cottages. Only after we had got to the end of the run and avoided the black, barking dog chained strategically to a wall mounting length, did we find a few painted boats and a rocky foreshore. Intrigued as to how we were going to exit the campsite and get back on the main road, and seeing a bridge of potentially sufficient height under the railway, we continued, only to be met by a sewage smell so overpowering that we turned around. Back at the site, we asked how to get out because of the one-way system, although we knew the answer – under the sewage bridge. I have never before enjoyed a shower in the van so much! Then the electric cut out. What a contrast to the site we had stayed on in Sicily – could it really only have been the night before?

Round the Toe

We rose to a beautifully sunny day and left Lazzaro via the back road, with splendid views of Etna across the Straits, a splash through the stinking overflow, up through town and past the English named 'Greasy Pole Restaurant' onto the main coastal road south, soon to pass a colossal but rusting industrial plant. Escaping, we turned inland past citrus groves of bergamot, then olive and almond groves up to the tiny, mountain-top village of Pentedattilo, so called because of the Greek name for the striking five-fingered rock formation of Mount Calvary that it sits below, and close to a torrent. Edward Lear, who travelled to the remoter parts of Italy in 1847, described the isolated village as 'perfectly magical' and we shared that feeling. Old Pentedattilo is a ghost village that from a distance almost merges with the grey crags around it, and like its boulders, looks as though it could cascade down the steep mountainside should any disturbance occur above.

We parked below. As we made our way up the stiff climb, a black cat came out to befriend and follow us as we walked the crazy-paved Byzantine alleys and up flights of steps past houses stacked on top of each other until reaching the steepled Saint Peter and Paul Church. Overhead wires, rustic fences, pergolas, and many of the buildings, including the church, appeared surprisingly intact. There were occasional signs of attempted rehabitation – an artist's name above a door, marble floor tiles laid in the shell of a building, a communal plaque. But apart from hillocks of grass, plants, shrubs, and previously cultivated trees that poked out from walls and steps, succulent plants that grew in abundance on the rocks, and thick hedges of Indian fig that lined the paths, it was lifeless. When we looked down on the tiled roofs below, most had collapsed, the walls preserving only the pretence of a building, and nature was well into its repossession. In amongst the rocky crags and the bulbous and spiny cacti, the last remains of the 'three hundred door castle' and monastery sat as though suspended, waiting to fall on anyone who dared to re-settle below. Landslides, earthquakes, floods, and disintegration of the rock on which it stands had forced residents to leave Pentedattilo to return to the coastal Melito di Porto Salvo, from where they had once fled to escape pirate raids.

Lifting our eyes across the mountain brought spectacular views of a smoking Etna across the Ionian Sea, its base all but invisible whilst the snow covered top floated like a cloud. Whichever direction we looked, the scenery was magnificent. However, as we sat on some steps in the morning sun, the black cat nuzzling against our legs appealing for our attention, I read that Pentedattilo hid a dark secret. Founded in 640 BC, it was a strategic point for the Greeks and Romans crossing the Aspromonte Mountains. In 1510, it passed into the hands of the Abenavoli family, who subsequently lost it in 1589 to the Alberti family from Messina, causing much friction between the now neighbouring clans. As all good stories go (and there is more than one version), the displaced young Baron, Bernadino of Abenavoli, secretly fell in love with Antionetta, daughter of the Marquis Domenico Alberti. He wished to marry her, but the Marquis died and his successor (his son Lorenzo) forbade the marriage, causing bitter resentment with the Abenavolis.

Lorenzo then married Catherine Cortez, daughter of the Viceroy of Naples. During the wedding celebrations, the Viceroy of Naples son, Don Petrillo Cortez, took a liking to Antoinetta and their engagement was subsequently announced. Baron Bernadino was enraged at being usurped, and the old feud rose again. On Easter night 1686, with the aid of a betraying servant, Scufari, Baron Bernadino led a band of fourteen men into the Pentedattilo Castle and massacred most of the castle's occupants, but saved Antionetta and her fiancé, Don Petrillo Cortez. An army was despatched and took Baron Bernadino's castle, freeing Don Petrillo Cortez and capturing seven of the fourteen who had carried out the massacre. Their heads were hung from the battlements of Pentedattilo Castle. Bernadino escaped with Antoinetta and forced her to marry him, eventually putting her in a convent while he travelled via Malta to Austria, where he joined their army and was fatally shot. Antoinette's marriage was annulled and she spent the rest of her days in the Convent of Reggio Calabria believing she was the cause of her family's demise. It is said by the old folks recounting the story that on a windy day you can still hear the cries of the Alberti family – Lorenzo having been repeatedly stabbed by Bernadino as he lay in his bed with his wife Catherine. Their son's head was smashed against a rock. A chill breeze blew across the village, the black cat looked up and tumbleweed drifted down the path – our visit to Pentedattilo was over.

Further along the coast, we turned inland hoping to reach another mountain village, Bova. We set off confidently, but couldn't find a signed turn and we eventually got lost. At the back of our minds was the warning the Rough Guide had planted within us that the Aspromonte was not a tourist destination, with warnings of kidnappings, because it was a 'stronghold of the

'Ndrangheta, the Calabrian Mafia, and as such most Italians would think you insane for going there… ' Eventually, after retreating to the coast, we found our way back up along a narrow road on the ridge, then climbed steeply to Bova. We parked by a terrace on the entrance road, watched carefully by shopkeepers sitting outside in the morning sun, and walked into the town.

'Come and look at this,' I yelled. 'It's amazing.' Gail ran to where I was standing.

'How on earth did that get here?'

'I have no idea.' In this remote, two thousand year old town, population four hundred and seventy-one, perched on a craggy pinnacle, nothing could have come as more of a surprise than the huge black locomotive and tender on a piece of track the same length. Never in history had railways approached this mountain peak – there wasn't even a hotel in Bova – yet there was an iron horse befitting a wild-west movie! Black, as though it had come out of the night, but with eight bright red driving wheels and couplings. I was soon climbing into the cab, imagining it shaking and vibrating to the power induced by a roaring fire and belching steam – it was every boy's dream. Why it was there and how it was transported up that mountain road remains a mystery.

Much of Bova was derelict (it was bombed by the Allies in 1943), and it had suffered a sharp fall in population. Many of the older generation still speak with a Greek-Byzantine dialect. We wandered up narrow winding lanes, their names preserving their Greek heritage, and through tiny passages between buildings built into the rock, before arriving at a remarkable property inset into a Norman tower, with wondrous views down the rooftops and mountain across to Etna. Inland, the ridges of the Aspromonte were wild, moody and magnificent.

Above the church there was a modern concrete monstrosity of a building, and then a castle, but the plain concrete of the piazza was being pounded by a yellow JCB digger to be replaced by something more aesthetically pleasing, and lower down, buildings were being sympathetically restored. Bova was a gem, with views described by Lear as 'truly magnificent.'

The Polish girl serving in the café-bar in Palizzi Marina where we stopped for lunch didn't know there was an engine in Bova, but had been to Pentedattilo. (Her colleague tried to explain that some of the monstrous workings we had seen earlier in the day were coal mines, but we're still not sure.) We followed the coast, and as it turned north round the toe of Italy, it had a different feel to it. The area was undeveloped, the beaches were blocked by the ever-present railway, the towns more open, and the buildings were no more than three storeys. Each seaside town had built a long *lungomare* alongside the sea, but with little after-development. Magnificent white chalk cliffs dipped into a deep-blue sea and inland moody mountains hid the remote villages of San Luca, Plati, and Ciminà – the alleged homes of the 'Ndrangheta and Brancaleone on the coast, where prosecutor Emilio Siranni told author, David Lane, 'Here you can feel the 'Ndrangheta's presence, touch it with your hands.'[14]

We continued up the coast and started looking for a place to stay overnight, exploring a terrible woodland track to a closed campsite. With no others to be found, we ended up on a town's *lungomare* that stretched for about two miles along the seafront. Sitting relaxed in the van, we watched families and couples enjoying the *passeggiata*, the slow walk in the early evening sun, some with children on scooters or roller blades, others savouring *gelato*. I was conscious that a new black Fiat Bravo had driven past a couple of times, then it came from behind and pulled in immediately ahead of us. It reversed so close to our front bumper that I couldn't have pulled out if I'd wanted to. The *lungomare* was almost empty of cars, so why had this guy chosen to do that? I could

[14] *Into the Heart of the Mafia*; David Lane.

see that there were two people in the car. The driver got out. He was small, tanned, thick-set with thinning hair, and wearing jeans, a black leather jacket, open-necked denim shirt, and sunglasses. I mentally checked that we had locked all the doors. But what could go wrong out in the open? He knocked on the passenger window. I wound it down an inch.

'Hi there. How are you?' he said in English.

'Fine, thanks.'

'You're a long way from home.'

'Yes, we are.'

'You have a nice motorhome.'

'Thanks.'

'You are enjoying your visit?'

'Yes, thank you.'

'Where will you stay for the night?'

'Here. We have everything. Is it okay?'

'Oh yes, but I have a nice place in the mountains, you could park there.'

'We'll be fine here, we're settled now.'

'You can follow me and my friend in my car – we will show the way because it's difficult to find.'

'No, it's very kind of you.'

'At my place you will have water, electric and views of the sea, and you will be locked in and secure.' Red lights were flashing in my brain. Then again, he could genuinely want to help.

'Perhaps another day, we may stay longer.'

'Okay. My name is Giuseppe.' And he drove away.

'Do you think I've misjudged?' I said to Gail.

'Better safe than sorry,' she replied. 'With all the warnings, it's hard to know what to think.'

After an undisturbed night, and setting all thoughts of our visitor aside, we set off inland to Gerace, named from the Greek *Ierace*, or sparrowhawk, that supposedly led Greeks to the safety of the mountain when fleeing a Saracen attack. We parked in the lower part and sat outside a café-bar whilst the owner went to a great deal of trouble bringing out a table with a fresh maroon cloth simply to serve us coffees and a *cornetto*. The lower part was tiny, but had interesting old houses and a small, impressive tenth century church with a round, wooden roof tower. Although the upper part was clearly visible, the way up wasn't.

'*E possibile ascendere*?' I asked an old lady soaking up the sun on her porch.

'*Si, si. A destra*,' she said, indicating a narrow passage between two houses, with a right turn at the top. The approach was steep, and the whole town above seemed to be supported by a monstrous concrete wall curving round the cliffside like a dam, the only relief being some sculpted arches. The original, massively thick, protective city walls were originally breached by twelve gates, but only four remain.

Standing at the top by the Porta del Sole, the seaward view was the usual spectacular panorama we had come to expect, but it was so crisp and clear that every detail of the tiled roofs, the verandas, and back yards of the tightly-jammed lower town's houses could be seen, before falling away to the bright green fields, olive groves, and deep blue sea. Photographs taken through the arch were travel-poster perfect, but I doubt that Gerace is a tourist hot-spot.

Inside the walls, the centre is medieval, with cobbled streets, small squares, balconied houses, ancient wooden doors, archways (one resplendent with a sundial), and many old churches (it once had one hundred and twenty-eight), as well as a huge Norman cathedral – the largest religious building in Calabria, with thirteen columns from the ancient temples of Locri, on the coast. It was undergoing extensive and detailed restoration, but I doubt that the rest of Gerace has changed in centuries. I became fascinated by a man in a beige puffa ski-jacket, brown trousers, and black woollen peaked hat wandering slowly and deliberately back and forth along a line of darker bricks in front of the cathedral. His head bowed, he leant to the left as he picked up his right leg, then to the right when he picked up his left leg. As a car squeezed through an arch and slipped past him, he waved. Others occasionally wandered past and each got a wave, but he never deviated from his mesmerising path – he was as much a part of the town as the cathedral behind him. Gerace is not a fast moving town, more the village I wanted to call it. There are few people, and no one is in a hurry.

At the top of the town was a fine, but partly-ruined, eleventh-century castle standing on a Greco-Roman site. It was a perfect spot for a couple of old men to lean over the walls, take in the awe-inspiring picture beyond the cliff edge to the Aspromonte mountain ridges and toy-like dwellings dotted in the valleys below, and chat the day away. It would be hard to tire of the views, but could I ever see myself doing that? Wouldn't conversation run out on the third day? Would the simplicity itself become stressful?

The Magna-Grecia mountain villages had turned out to be captivating places to visit, and it was a shame about the concrete mass propping up Gerace – 'the Florence of the South' – surely they could have blended it into the surrounding rocks?

We drove back to the coast in search of the museum at Locri, hoping to see the ancient Greek site. Things were very relaxed in a 'suit yourself' sort of way, and after seeing many fine exhibits we ventured outside to try and find the Greek Theatre. Traipsing through long grass that I'm sure would soon be full of springtime flowers, we found many fallen stones and part walls, but nothing to suggest an ancient theatre. Back in the museum, we sought help from the young lady in charge.

'Oh no! It's not here. You must drive one kilometre up the little road to the side of the *museo*, park, then walk one hundred metres.' And that's what we did. Parking the van, we walked down a track, scrumping oranges that had fallen to the side of it. We got to a theatre, but it was a wooden one. Bemused, we walked up onto the stage and spotted the ancient one behind, but the access was locked. Perhaps she could have told us.

We chose to park back on the *lungomare*. After showering, and with Gail drying her hair, the black Fiat returned once again, reversing up to the front of the van. This time we let Giuseppe in. He was a fascinating man. Born locally, he had subsequently emigrated, married, and got a job that took him round the world. He had always wanted to return to his birthplace and build a house.

'Let's go in my car. I'll show you around.' We drove to the impressive castle sitting above his town, but it was closed. We went off again, further into the mountains, and then onto a scrubby plateau.

'My grandparents lived in that little house,' he said, pointing to a remote white building some distance away. 'They had no money and lived off the land. They swapped surpluses with others for things they couldn't grow or make. There was no water. We had to go to the next valley, walking or by donkey, and carry it back.'

'Here's the only water tap for miles,' he said as we stared at a remote, galvanised zinc pipe at the roadside a long way from where he had said his grandparents had lived. We stopped at an isolated house with glorious views across the mountain to the sea. 'It was built years ago by a rich family as a summer house, but they never used it. Many build houses in the hills but the young people aren't interested.'

'Why are so many buildings in southern Italy not finished and often falling down?' Gail asked.

'Ha! It's the cement. They don't know how to make it. They put too much sand in, leave the buildings open, and they disintegrate. They build everywhere and never finish the houses. The top floors are left for their children, but they're not interested. Nobody cares – today, tomorrow, ten years. They don't worry about the outside. But the inside – very clean.'

'But even the by-pass flyover and tunnels have been abandoned,' I added.

'It will never be finished.'

'Why?'

'Nobody wants it. They obstruct it. Every year, money comes from the EU. They do a bit more, this year a few railings went up, then the money ran out. Each year they get new money, then it strangely runs out. It will never be finished – the locals won't allow it – but the money keeps coming.'

We drove down a winding hill to the edge of town, and Giuseppe pointed to elegant palaces being restored. One with a grand entrance had been recently repainted in pale yellow. It looked overdone. Another in natural stone, but wedged between lesser houses, was more pleasing to the eye. We parked the car and walked to a smart café. (The first chapter of the book relates the rest of our conversation there with Giuseppe, our insight into the real Italy, and his brush with local officialdom and 'friends' who might help getting the permission for his house-building project.)

Giuseppe wanted us to park on his land and it was hard to think of another excuse, so much against our judgement, we apprehensively followed him in the van up a narrow lane behind some houses, then up another even narrower one, and we were soon climbing up the mountain, the light fading, to where, we knew not. Twisting and turning round blind corners, I worked hard to keep up with him as he threw the car from one side of the road to the other. If we changed our minds we couldn't turn round – we had to keep going. There were no signposts at T-junctions, and I had no idea how we would get back if we wanted to. We arrived at a padlocked, double steel gate set in high walls and Giuseppe jumped out to slide the gates back, beckoning us to follow him in.

There were views to the sea and marina, clear signs of building in progress, and he did have a motorhome, a *Portakabin*, and a small, new breeze-block building. What a relief!

Trumping in the Tower

The next morning we had coffee with Giuseppe in his motorhome, looking through photographs of his other motorhomes and presenting him with one of my few remaining copies of *How Katie Pulled Boris*. He told us more of his life and the time he was, like us, parked on the *lungomare* and had to take his waste cassette in a black bag to the marina to empty it. After a few times, Customs got suspicious of what he was doing, apprehended him on arrival, and asked him to open the bag only to investigate a cassette full of poo.

'Are you going to Bari?' asked Giuseppe.

'We don't know. Why?'

'You should avoid it at all cost. Brindisi is not much better. They turn the signs round so visitors end up in remote places and get robbed. Garages will do things to your van so it will break down, then charge you for recovery and repair.'

We decided to skip Bari and Brindisi. We set off in mist and drizzle up the coast, to turn inland once more to the mountain town of Stilo. By now you should have a picture of a narrow, bland, coastal strip with road, rail, and sea. Inland, there are interesting places which can only be accessed by narrow, twisting, rivulet-like roads up the sides of the mountains, or along river valleys. In this case, the rugged Monte Consolino. Few roads or tracks cross-link the towns. The draw in Stilo was a tenth century Byzantine temple, the Cattólica, with a reputation as the best-preserved monument of its type. With a population of around 3,000, it had a rich historical complement of a castle, palaces, churches, and a cathedral, and had been a Greek settlement in ancient times. The Cattólica was a steep walk to the top of the town, where a lonely priest, looking commendably Greek in his black robes and hat with a bountiful greying beard, welcomed the intrusion into his otherwise boring day. The church is in the shape of a Greek cross, and is so small that it only took a few minutes to examine the remaining frescoes. The outside, with five circular, raised, pepper-pot towers (imitated by many a modern Spanish Costa housing developer) and rectangular base had been repointed so extensively that it all appeared very neat. The obligatory photographs taken of the building and the landscape laid out below, we scooted round the rest of the town, saw the carved pair of feet climbing the wall outside the cathedral (they were taken from a pagan temple), and with all the café-bars looking a tad unsavoury and the day rather dull, we departed.

The coast from here on was flat, and the inland mountains fell away. Off on a side road to Borgia that should have been the SS198 (or even the Rough Guide's SS106) but seemed to be the SS384, we found the easily overlooked, ruined Basilica of Santa Maria della Rocella (or La Roccelletta), an impressively high, red brick ruin of a building, with round towers said to be Norman in origin and built from material obtained from the remains of the Roman town adjacent – the theatre abandoned in AD 350 still visible. It was all tucked away in an olive grove, with gardeners busying themselves digging drainage trenches.

The next guidebook stop (and if you get the impression we were working through it you would be correct) was le

Castella, situated much further up the coast on the ball of Italy's foot, close to Capo Rizzuto. At the far end of the town, which was ghostly quiet, a small island in the sea is totally occupied by a mellow, stone, high walled Aragonese Castle. A thin isthmus of land provides access. It's the stuff of Crusader films, and has been fortified since the fourth century BC. A strategic stronghold, it has witnessed bloody battles between Aragonese and Angevins, violent bombardments from Barbarossa (the Turkish scourge of the Mediterranean), pillage, capture, and slavery. The inhabitants spent so much money reinforcing the castle that they became impoverished, and in 1558 Alfonso made the suggestion that the way to stop the Turkish attacks was to pull it down: no castle, no attacks – an interesting plan. Nó-one agreed, but he almost got his way, because it was subsequently sold. The purchasers themselves then went into debt, and the last owners were the Filomarinos in 1644. In 1799, there was a final battle between the French and Bourbons.

No one was about apart for two young men on the isthmus trying to jump-start a car, so we marched boldly through the front gate, full of enthusiasm, only to be hailed by one of them.

'*É chiuso*! *Lavori in Corso*.' The dreaded 'works in progress'. As we returned to the van, the reason for the deadly quiet became apparent. What appeared to be the whole village had turned out for a funeral procession. A silver Mercedes hearse with white buckets of lilac, yellow, and white flowers hanging from it led the white-robed clergy, family members with huge sprays of flowers, the pall bearers with the coffin, and then finally, what we thought might be a never-ending congregation. After a decent interval, we drove back to the main road to get to Isola de Cappo Rizzuto and down to Capo Rizzutto itself. With Gypsies parked on a stretch of grass, a dead cat with a fresh pool of blood, and a depressing entrance to Camping Manusco, we were not enamoured and returned towards

Isola di Capo Rizzuto. About halfway along, we pulled into a large open car park surrounded by undeveloped land apart from a modern church and an aquarium, and decided we would spend the rest of the day there and wild camp for the night. It was good to stop for a rest as the day, and the two hundred and seventy kilometres had become a fusion of unremarkable towns linked by open spaces. We were missing the mountains, but every time I looked at places of interest they were at an altitude that probably put them above the snow line.

Inland Santa Severina, on the eastern fringes of the Sila Piccola, was our target for the following day.

'You have travelled where?' asked the young pump attendant, fascinated by us as he filled the van with diesel and *Gasauto* at the API station.

'*Sei mesi – Francia, Italia, Sicilia e adesso a Londra*,' I tried.

'Kilometres?' Now he had me. *Let's round it up to ten thousand*, I thought, but what is that in Italian? I was stuck with hundreds and thousands.

'*Dieci mille*,' I said slowly, and deliberately holding up ten fingers. He drew breath, and appeared mightily impressed, shouting to his mate over on the other pump, who discussed it with the driver of the car he was filling. *Oh God, I hope I got it right*, I thought. More and more questions were fired at me, but were way beyond my Italian. We went for a coffee and a *crema cornetto*.

Once more a winding country road bordered by swathes of wild flowers led us up. But then, parked outside a remote farm, the beautiful sight of four little, working Piaggio three-wheeler trucks – a green one, and three pale, dusty-blue ones. Is it only me, or do they bring a smile to everyone? I especially love it when there's a husband and wife duo squashed in the front!

Views across the rolling rippling hills had a Tuscan drama to them below a huge, wispy cloud sky, and soon we could see the roofs of the Cathedral Campanile and Castle of Santa Severina sitting on top of a cowpat of a hill that, despite my description, enticed us in. One local guidebook said that when the valleys are full of mist from the Neto River, it 'resembles a large stone ship. A ship in a vast sea of history, in which the presence of the past still glitters.'

We managed to park below the splendid, crenulated Norman castle, 'the most beautiful in Calabria,' where much road renovation was underway, and set off enthusiastically and excitedly to explore. Through the sliding glass doors of the castle entrance sat a young girl at a desk intently reading a magazine.

'*Cinque Euro ogni persona.*'

'That's a bit steep,' I said to Gail, 'but we're here now.' The girl tried to explain something about the tickets that had one Euro, and four Euro for

'*Mostre e Esposizione.*' I looked it up – Exhibitions and Exposure, and 'Visitors are required to study the regulations and observe them.' She carried on at great speed in Italian, and we were lost and my head hurt.

'*Inglesi*?'

'*Si, si.*' But we were perplexed – had she mentioned 11:15?

'Let's just pay and go in,' I said to Gail. The girl came out to direct us to a small theatre, where a video with birds-eye views of the castle was showing, but the commentary was in Italian – so what happened to the English? We were bemused, bewildered, and frankly, I was getting a bit fed up, and after five more minutes of '*bella vista*', very restless!

'If the castle closes at eleven fifteen then we'd better get a move on – there's less than forty-five minutes left.' We abandoned the theatre and marched up the ramp to the castle.

'No. No. Stop,' yelled the girl, launching herself through the glass doors. After explaining in broken Italian that all we wanted to do was wander round (and as no one else was visiting that day, why not?), we finally deduced that we had to wait for a guide. One had been sent for, and would arrive at 11:15 a.m. We went into the village.

Beyond the castle, over a deep defensive moat, was a beautiful cobbled square known by the locals as 'the Field,' bordered with elegant buildings and restaurants. The cathedral was at the opposite end to the castle, and at the edge were excellent views from the observation points across the Sila mountains to the Ionian sea. Much attention had been paid to the pathways and plantings, with a mini-maze of snake-like paths lined with benches. The pavings were decorated with patterns from the zodiac. The thirteenth century cathedral was wonderfully light and bright inside, with religious scenes painted on the pillars and walls framed in Wedgewood-blue majolica. The altar was a Baroque elaboration gone too far and out of keeping with the rest of the church, although I suspect that was the intention.

We were back in the castle five minutes ahead of schedule. A young woman with black hair and strange mouse-coloured streaks, square rimless glasses, a long black puffa coat worn by so many Italians, and brown plastic boots, was chatting with the girl receptionist as they warmed themselves over the heater.

'You can wait outside,' she said rather abruptly. We stood like idiots waiting while she finished her conversation. Finally she came out and I noticed she was showing the first signs of pregnancy. There was not a hint of introduction, none of the expected, 'I'm Maria. I'm your guide for the day…' She walked past us and up the ramp, slowly, oh so slowly. We followed like two obedient dogs.

Room by room down into the catacombs and up again she quietly, almost inaudibly, explained the castle's history, right up to the twentieth century, when the castle was acquired by the municipality and restored. Although built by the Normans in 1076, floors and fortifications were added in the late fifteenth and sixteenth centuries by feudal lords.

'If you would like to sew a dress?' she asked Gail, who was nonplussed by the statement until she was shown a sixth century sewing kit. 'If you would like to spend some money?' and a coin collection followed. In passing, I noted all the information boards had English on them – we could have just wandered round ourselves. We went up the towers, through the later apartments that had elaborately painted ceilings, and exited rather thankfully onto the walls, where the construction of the different periods was evident. It wasn't a relaxed experience.

'You can see by yourselves.'

Oh yippee! I thought as we bounded up the steps.

'Which eye are you looking at?' asked Gail.

'What do you mean? I haven't been making eye contact. In fact, she won't make eye contact with me!'

'That's because one is a glass eye.'

'No! I never saw that.' We returned, rather hoping the slow ordeal was over.

'Now we go to the museum.' We were despondent as we climbed the steps to the Armorial and Archaeological Museum in the tower, but then she let out a ripping fart, and it was all we could do to maintain our composure.

'Trumping in the tower,' I whispered to Gail as we viewed the reproduction suits of armour. She turned to Gail (I still didn't know which eye):

'Would you like to wash your clothes?' For a moment we thought she was being rude about our state of dress – didn't she know we had been on the road for five months? Gail was speechless, in case she made a *faux pas*. We descended a circular iron staircase to an underground laundry room. Gail tried to laugh at what was supposedly the final jokey highlight of the tour. We bought some postcards in the souvenir shop to show willing, Gail wrote some complementary comments in the guest book, and we ran out of the back gate, simply to have a change of pace.

The coastline did little to imprint itself on our memory – it was flat up to Punta Alice, a few hills emerging thereafter. We stopped on a *lungomare* of one of the many non-descript out-of-season resorts to eat sandwiches, as we were ravenous. Because of the intricacies of the adjacent railway, the many little streets and low bridges, (and probably our as yet unabated hypoglycaemia), we argued over which way we could get back across the railway, and drove three miles out of our way. A revolting power station complex and tall Enel chimney puthering out smoke put us off camping at Lido San Angelo near Rossano, so we settled for the seaside pine forest of Camping Il Salice at Corigliano Calabro, approaching through an Industrial Estate.

'Do you recognise those vans?' I asked Gail.

'No. Should I?'

'There are people here from Punta Braccetto. Look, there's the perfect German lady who was parked behind us.' As we eyed up a vacant pitch, Welsh Brian, his wife (I never did catch her name), and Taff the dog ran out from the caravan next door.

'It's taken, move on,' they shouted in jest. The usual conversations ensued.

'So where have you folks been?' I asked.

'We drove straight from Punta Braccetto using the motorway. The wife didn't like it in Sicily.'

'Oh that's a shame. Where did you go, then?'

'We just stayed at Punta Braccetto. The site here isn't that good either, there's too many cats and they smell,' moaned Brian. 'We've moved pitch once already, but now we think the site down the road may be better.' I looked across at his pitch. Attached to his large caravan was a massive, blue-grey awning that had windows with country-cottage drapes, and was fully furnished and reminiscent of a conservatory. There was a large TV satellite dish, and a fenced off backyard of outdoor barbecue and other paraphernalia. It must have taken him a week to move.

'We're here until April now,' continued Brian as Taff eyed up my left leg.

'What's there to see?' Gail asked.

'Oh, the beach is okay for walking the dog, but mostly we go up to the big shopping centre on the main road.'

Over a cup of tea, Gail and I discussed our travel plans, the time we had left, the distance still to be covered, places we wanted to see, and thoughts about having a rest. We were happy doing what we were doing. I decided that as we were paying for the facilities and after a long day, I'd use the campsite showers.

'Off for a shower then,' volunteered Brian's wife as I emerged from the van towel over arm. 'They're communial [sic].'

That's a worry, I thought. *Do they mean all in together, or separate, cubicle type of communal?* It was cubicles. Two were in use, and judging by the frilly-edged, pink dressing gowns hanging over the doors, occupied by females. I couldn't find one with a working lock. *Even more worrying*, I thought. Two more ladies arrived, conversing in what I took to be German, and started trying doors. I was suddenly struck by the notion that the Welsh lady had got it wrong, or had decided to play some huge joke, and I was in the women's showers with an unlocked door. I panicked, stuck my leg out of the shower, and shoved my shoes under the gap in the door, hoping the door tryers would see them. But they might also realise they were men's shoes... They took cubicles each side of me, and shouted and laughed to one another as they audibly lathered up. How was I going to get out without being seen, and cries of 'Pervert' ringing in my ears? I gave up on the shower, dressed quickly, and waited until I couldn't hear anyone outside before making a dash for it, bumping into a man at the entrance.

'Hello, in a hurry?'

'Think I'll shower in the van from now on,' I said to Gail.

A Beautiful Book

We left the next day – it wasn't for us, staying in one place visiting the shopping centre, endlessly walking the beach and speculating on who was leaving or arriving.

We retraced our route back down the coast to drive up the winding hairpins to the hilltop town of Rossano, where we missed the main Corso Umberto, but managed to approach from the northern side.

Again, I struggle whether to call it a town or a city, so I looked it up on Wikipedia: 'Rossano is a town and commune in southern Italy, in the province of Cosenza (Calabria)… known for its marble and alabaster quarries.'

After a short walk we gained the main cobbled square, Piazza San Anargiri, a busy area festooned with triangular bunting, and surrounded by sandstone-pink buildings, many with shuttered windows. Next door to the Town Hall was the inviting Café Tagliaferri. A smart waiter in a cream jacket, white shirt, and white gloves ushered us past a glorious display of pastry delicacies to a wood panelled area with small tables covered in white linen. I swivelled around, looking at the many sepia photos of Rossano in olden times, and was particularly taken by one showing two young men at a table having drinks outside the café we were sat in. They were dressed in stylish suits and sat in a self-assured way, legs outstretched in front of them, getting envious looks from the small crowd of other young men gathered around. I wondered who they were to command such respect. The steaming coffees and two *cornetti* arrived.

The morning sun was warming the square as we asked one of the many men for directions to the cathedral. Rossano, like all other hilltop towns, has a cathedral to be proud of. He pointed down a hill.

'*Francese*?'

'No. *Inglese*.'

'At least he didn't ask if we were German,' I said to Gail. The cream painted cathedral sat in a small square at the edge of the hill and had been restored, but it wasn't what we had gone to see. Next door was a small museum, Museo Diocesano. A lone girl sat at the desk and took the six Euros for our entrance before directing us into a room of religious artefacts while she rushed away to unlock the rest. I generally have no hankering to examine such things, however, in a wooden box with a glass top there is a prize exhibit: one hundred and eighty-eight of the original four hundred pages of the famed Codex Purpureus Rossanensis. The unique manuscript, on reddish-purple parchment, illustrates fifteen Miracle and Passion scenes from the life of Christ taken from the gospel of Matthew, and partly, Mark. It is said to be the oldest pictorial gospel known, and it was discovered in Rossano in 1879. Interestingly, although the judgement of Pilate and the release of Barabus are shown, there is no crucifixion scene. The colours are bright, the drawings detailed, the text in silver, and the whole thing charming. We were so enamoured that after completing the tour of the museum, we had to go back and look at it again. The Rough Guide makes a point: '…see Christ and all his disciples not seated but reclining on cushions round the table, and all eating from the same plate,' as distinct from the later depictions of them all sat at a long table. (Schaff-Herzog saw it as the first transition in Christian art from the incorporation of pagan elements to conventional Christian motifs.)

What bowled us over was the Rough Guide's evocative story that, 'The book was brought from Palestine by monks fleeing the Muslim invasions...' It added vision and romance to a wonderful physical entity. The true history appears lost in the sands of time, although the preponderance of opinion seems to lean towards it being a sixth century Byzantine-Greek work, possibly composed in a monastery in Syria or Asia Minor (now Turkey). It was then brought to Calabria in the seventh century by monks, either because they were fleeing from Arabs, or escaping the edicts of Byzantine Emperor Leo III Isauricus to destroy religious idols. The monks may have found refuge in the sandstone caves that gave Rossano its name.

Rossano is a town full of history. The refurbished cathedral, reminiscent of many Spanish or Mexican churches, had a carved wooden ceiling, and was heavily into grey-green majolica with brown marble-panelled pillars and arches. As we walked past each of the side chapels, lights were automatically triggered. There were landscape paintings on the ceilings and pillars, and behind the altar was a Byzantine fresco. We also tried to find the 'diminutive church of San Marco' but it was so diminutive that we couldn't. Exasperated, Gail asked two men where it might be – they pointed behind us. It was very similar to the one we had seen at Gerace, except it was locked up.

There was probably more to see in Rossano, but our sensory acceptance of history was diminishing. We were momentarily relieved by a shop selling washing machines and other white goods – '*Eletric [sic] Shock*.' The Italians love using English words, but so often get it wrong. One motorhome had '*Garage Living*' emblazoned across it. We drove back down the mountain to the coast, straight past 'the world's largest archaeological site' at Sybaris, and what remains of a city said to have had a population of 100,000 and much myth and legend. Like the excavations in Locri, there appeared to be little to see.

The coast road north was flat, and rather boringly agricultural. It appeared poorer than many, with a continuum of unfinished buildings and vegetable plots, so I'll transport you forward through the endless orange groves of Metaponto (a strange village with two cafés but no food) and a poorly signed archaeological site and museum that were both closed, to an inland minor road to the Masseria Serra Marina.

Masserias are large farmhouses, and many offer places to stay for tourists under the *Agriturismo* banner. We picked it simply from a roadside sign. On arrival, the gate swung open automatically and we had soon made arrangements to stay in a paddock with commanding views as far as the eye could see across the plains (including an AGIP station down below whose car park would probably have saved us the seventeen Euros we had just paid.) It was bliss to sit out on the grass alone with ourselves and soak up some afternoon sun, contemplating our five month journey thus far, and the distance we had covered. I couldn't sit still for long though, and I was soon washing the van while Gail cleaned inside and lent a hand with drying the van before we made use of the excellent facilities and piping hot showers.

Fifteen thousand diseased people were forced out of the squalor of Matera's prehistoric troglodyte cave dwellings known as the s*assi* during the 1950s and 1960s, but the area subsequently became a World Heritage Site and the backdrop for biblical films, including Mel Gibson's *The Passion of Christ*. It was a 'must do' on our list, and the hot early morning sun lifted our spirits as we drove from the *masseria* along excellent, white-surfaced roads bordered by large agricultural plots and gently rolling hills. Our first stop, however, was the Café Ridola on Via Ridola for coffees and a cream-oozing *cornetto*.

Matera allegedly originated as a Roman town, and was then subjected to a long history of conquest, serial owners, earthquake, squalor and pestilence, before becoming the region's capital. On 21st September 1943, it distinguished itself as the first Italian city to fight against the Germans. Men in smart overcoats and trilby hats ambled along in two's or three's in front of the majestic Convent dell'Annunziata and Governor's Palace, stopping occasionally so that the speaker could emphasise his point with vigorous hand gestures – maybe a goal-scoring opportunity missed in Saturday's football? Following the 'Second Itinerary' of our tourist map, we moved along Via San Biagio to San Agostino (a church perched on a cliff edge), then down the lower slopes to the road running above the ravine itself. From there, we could look up at the maze of the *sassi* houses clinging to the wall of the gorge and the openings into the cave dwellings.

'Do we want to look round a cave?' I asked Gail, spotting a sign to an entrance.

'I don't know. What do you think?'

'Oh, let's do it. We're unlikely to come again.' Incongruously, the two girls taking the four Euros admission were Goth devotees, but had taken just enough of the sub-culture's influence to be fascinatingly attractive, and proved helpful answering the many questions I suddenly thought of asking. The warren of caves was far more extensive than we imagined – rough-hewn stone passages twisted and turned and ran up and down to more than one level, they had water pits, smoke burned roofs and green-stained walls, housed two churches with faded wall paintings, and looked out onto the dribble of a river in the gorge below, making the visit well worth the fee. The bareness required some imagination to picture them inhabited, but this was alleviated by a visit to the restored cave house of Vico Solitario. Dating back to the eighteenth century, it was surprisingly habitable, organised and homely, with a separate room for the mule, pig, and their fodder. The matrimonial bed, built high off the ground to avoid humidity, provided room for a mother hen and her chicks below. The chests of drawers doubled as a night-time bed for the usual six children. There was a large weaving loom and, vitally, a cistern bringing rainwater to the cave, as there were no springs or aquifers. The kitchen was bigger than that in our van, and just as well organised. Life in that cave survived to 1952. Sanitation relied on a *cantero* or painted chamber pot – a similar mechanism to that in our van.

When the heat of the day and pangs of hunger came upon us, we climbed back up the main square to a Lowry scene of a mass of smartly-dressed, over-coated people milling around on their Sunday *passeggiata*, greeting each other in air-kiss embraces as though they hadn't seen each other for, well, at least since the week before, and intensively discussing matters of great interest. Occasionally a young child would break free and have to be run after and gathered up by a parent to be taken off for an ice-cream.

There was an absence of restaurants, and we had to settle for a ham and cheese *foccacio* in Via A. Perso café. The owner started to pack things into his car and was clearly anxious to close, but couldn't resist our Euros, so we ate with indigestion-inducing speed. When we returned to the main square everyone had gone – there was not a soul to be seen save for a blue and white police car driving slowly through the pedestrianised zone as though ready to question anyone still lingering there. Had someone blown a whistle, sounded a bell? No wonder our café owner had been keen to depart! We returned to the van and, like everyone else, left town.

We drove back to the coast through Latera to a *sosta* at Metaponto, and joined in the setting sun *passeggiata* along the seafront, observing the delicate boy-girl, parent-accompanied relationships in contrast to the young couples favouring a lie down on the beach. What a beautiful way to end a perfect day – shame some idiot had to leave his car engine running behind us at 11:30 p.m. whilst he bade his lengthy farewells to friends in the camp and local restaurant.

New Italian Friends

We took the motorway to enter Taranto from the north. A Quatermass experiment of giant chemical and steel works, chimneys belching polluted gaseous clouds, pylons, cranes, containers, sheet metal stacked like piles of black Polo Mints, steel tubing, and oil refineries flaring-off waste, it was not an edifying spectacle. The acrid smell found its way into the van, and then off to our left, a great noxious white cloud erupted as though an atomic bomb had exploded.

The next part of Taranto is a small, ancient island, and leads across another inlet to the southern, more modern section. We did the scenic bus route before crossing the Ponte Girevole to the southern end of town and slotting into a metered bay on Via Regina Margheritta, but the machines for dispensing tickets didn't accept coins. The news vendor leant out of his stall on the square to indicate the *Tabacchi* across the street, where the old lady helpfully completed the complex forms so that we didn't pay for parking beyond 1:30 p.m. (when it became free until 3:00 p.m.). I watched as a motley pack of six wild dogs lolloped along the pavement ahead of me to a pedestrian crossing. They paused as the large black lead dog stepped out a little and the traffic stopped, then they eased their way across and went on their way. I tried to do the same – it didn't work.

The central island contained the old town, and in ancient times, Greek temples and an acropolis. On the bridge to it, we came across an unusual phenomenon. The wire mesh preventing people clambering over the railings to dive into the water (or commit suicide?) that leads to an inner sea, was adorned with hundreds of padlocks – each with an enduring Pentel message of love: '*Uniti X Sempre*', '*Ciccio & Nica*', '*Kekko E Minia X Sempre*' – some more rusty than others, some where the permanency of the Pentel ink was being challenged. Maybe an idea on a night of alcohol-fuelled romance, locked together for life, the keys thrown into the briny below?

On the island, the Crusader-style castle that we discovered was inaccessible, being owned by the Navy. Beyond was a labyrinth of tiny streets between tall, decrepit buildings with heavy wooden doors, a court where shady looking men waited outside (and some of them were police), and a cathedral with a crypt that houses the bones of Taranto's Patron Saint, Cataldo, an Irish monk. Once we reached the fish market, we returned along a palm-planted promenade and the inland sea (where oysters are apparently abundant) and partook of coffees and a particularly oozy chocolate *cornetto*.

After a walk through the fine, pedestrianised piazzas and streets on the southern part, some supermarket shopping and a late lunch, we left in a positive mood about Taranto (if you ignored the northern industrial zone and, as we discovered, the boring and spread-out southern end).

The coast running east from Taranto was rocky at first, and then became flat with occasional sand dunes. We passed white-painted marinas and lidos, all devoid of customers. As the coast turned down towards the heel of Italy, beyond Porto Cesareo at Torre San Isidoro, we spotted two motorhomes parked on the dunes. It was a rare event – we couldn't recollect having seen another motorhome since leaving Sicily. In that bond that brings fellow motorhomers together, and needing somewhere to stay, we drove over to find that they were Italian.

'*Buon giorno.*'

'*Buon giorno,*' replied a small bespectacled man in blue corduroy trousers, pale fleece, and baseball cap.

'*E possibile stare qui?*' I tried.

'*Si, mangiare.*' It was okay to stay, but I didn't understand the bit about eating. We set up the van pointing out over the sea and looking towards the defensive tower, and sat out watching a reddening sun dip through the wispy clouds, silhouetting a couple of fisherman out in their small boat. With our Italian neighbours alongside we felt safe and relaxed – a perfect situation.

'They're packing up next door,' I whispered to Gail.

'Why?'

'Maybe they were only stopping to eat.'

'*Dove va?*' I asked the guy in the brown corduroys and speckled grey sweater.

'We go. Don't stay here.'

'No?'

'Not good – police.'

'*Dove va*?' I asked again.

'Porto Cesareo.' After more exchanges we asked if we could go with them.

'*La passeggiata è bello,*' explained the other man's wife. And that was it. After a couple of false starts, and lots of discussion between the drivers, we were in the middle of a fast moving convoy back to the harbour-side car park at Porto Cesareo.

Our new friends were Felice and Rosa, and Carmelo and Annina, a jolly set of two retired couples. They were determined to show us the evening *passeggiata*, but there was some confusion, as when we got there the streets were almost empty and what they had enjoyed the previous Sunday evening with 'thousands of people' was not repeated on a chilly Monday evening when all the weekend visitors had gone home. Undaunted, they were determined we should be shown the shops so they could show off their English friends to the shopkeepers, who they encouraged to try out their school English, generating much shyness, silence, and eventually, embarrassed laughter (and for us, the price of two new sweaters).

'Goodbye,' was all we got.

As we entered a street where every other shop was a fishmonger and the mood was one of word banter and hilarity, I seized the chance to ask a question that had puzzled us. Whenever the astrological forecasts were given on the radio in Italian and they got to Pisces, they always said 'Feeesh.' Trying to explain this to our friends was something akin to the saying, 'When you're in a hole, stop digging.' Rosa spent the rest of the evening shouting,

'Feeeeeesh,' and bursting out laughing. She was prompted to tell us that the fish came straight from the harbour, and were so fresh that one she bought was still wriggling when she got it home and was ready to cook it. More laughter ensued as she demonstrated the wriggling of the dead 'feeeesh.'

Later, I was grateful for the purchase of the sweater as we made a post-prandial visit to Carmelo and Annina's unheated van and watched them play what looked like snap but was called *Scopa*, examined wedding photos of their divorced children (Carmelo and Annina had five, and Felice and Rosa three), and not get their joke about the three B's: Bush, Blair and Berlusconi. Strangely, they were keen to establish our ages and weights, making suitable '*impossibile*' noises. Rosa plied everyone, save me, with homemade *fragola*, a sweet, strawberry after-dinner liqueur or aperitif. As the mood glowed (and I regretted not having had some *fragola* to warm me up), so did our confidences in each other's language, and this led to more adventures trying to discover the difference in the pronunciation of '*carne*' (meat) compared to '*cane*' (dog). None was discernible, but I still have Annina's little dog drawing in my notebook.

We had heard an Italian song being incessantly played on the radio and assumed it must be top of the pops, but couldn't catch the title. Our best guess was '*Niente pa ora*' but that didn't translate beyond 'Nothing pa hours.' Six minds worked feverishly on the problem and a 'Eureka' moment was reached when Annina shouted,

'*Niente paura!* Don't worry!' So, we didn't.

The next morning we rose to a sea mist and Felice knocking at the door with fresh *cornetti*. Two huge orange construction trucks drove around the square followed by a tiny green Piaggio, like two elephants leading their baby. Next to us, a man was setting up his vegetable and fruit stall, not allowing us to purchase until the display was perfected. Our new friends wanted us to go to the 'feeeesh' market with them (the joke wearing a bit thin by that stage), but we declined. Wanting to push on, we all took photographs of each other, exchanged email addresses, and at some point they discovered I was not only writing a book, but had published one. Rosa, feeling she was in the presence of a celebrity, immediately took out her mobile and phoned her sister-in-law in England so she could get a copy for her. (As it would have been around 7:30 a.m. in the UK, her sister-in-law's confusion was understandable). Carmelo was anxious to know our route, and drew me aside to tell me that the women in Lecce were 'out-of-this-world' beauties.

We set off back down the coast, along deserted sand-strewn roads, and nearly ran over an attacking black dog with a white eye-patch (perhaps my mind was already on those Lecce goddesses). We soon arrived at Gallipoli, heading straight for the furthest point on the island and the old town and parking at the port. The castle was under restoration, so we entertained ourselves walking the narrow streets of the squat old town with their whitewashed houses reminiscent of Spanish Andalucian villages, even to the extent of having old men and women sitting in doorways and windows watching passers-by. There were arcades and patios, but none of the expected drying tomatoes – only washing lines of clothes. The cathedral was wide and dark, and had some huge paintings, with everything undergoing restoration. In the café, the topic for men and women was football and a match involving Liverpool. Opposite, a wonderful old pharmacy had shelves full of apothecary jars, and in the fish market we were shown that the stallholder's octopi were full of life.

From Gallipoli, the countryside was limestone walled fields, and where we touched the shore, rocky and craggy with umbrella pines and an occasional sandy beach. We stopped at the southernmost point of the heel, turning off at Puenta Ristola between some enviously large modern villas and a small, cliff-top park of modern statues. No doubt an EU grant bore some responsibility, and once again lamps were missing, a building was unfinished, grass was growing through the blocks on the pathway, and rubbish abounded. Nevertheless, the sun was shining and there was a deep-green sea gently lapping on the shore below as we ate our lunch at the Italian Land's End.

Turning north, round the heel, olive groves in stony fields were occasionally interspersed with a neatly tilled field of deep brown earth or a scrubby one awaiting the plough. The road dropped into rocky coves, with many signs for grottoes, and then it climbed out and they disappeared. It was exhilarating to drive. Men repaired walls with wooden lathes to guide the selection, chipping and placement of the rough stones. The area was different to any other we had encountered in Italy. It was sparsely populated, with long gaps between small white villages, all asleep in the early afternoon sun. Down below, the water was crystal clear, with only a rare fishing dinghy causing a ripple as the men splayed out their nets from the rear. There were one or two high-quality houses hanging onto the rocks with splendid sea views. We passed ancient, stone-built towers defending prominent points. In the olive groves we saw small, round, stone uninhabited buildings and wondered whether they were *trulli* (traditional dry stone huts or houses with conical roofs) or simply for animals or storage. There were no cars or people for long stretches – only a few signs pointing down dirt tracks to lidos.

Passing by countless small ports and marinas, the rocks got bigger and appeared as cliffs above us as we moved inland. At Porto Badisco, the road took us away from the sea to approach Otranto from the south-west, where we woke the owner of Oasis Parking from his siesta and parked amongst the overwintering boats. The Alsatian guard dog lying in the sun had teats like a cow's udder and was responsible for the little four-week-old bundle of fur squeaking in the rockery garden. We took showers in the unadjustable, scalding-hot water and relaxed, contented in the continuing sun. Well, I tell a lie. Five months and 5,400 miles of travel in a small van with two hundred and fifty kilometre long days brought one of those moments when the male (me) doesn't know what he's done wrong and the female (Gail) gets mad because he can't see what is so blindingly obvious to her. Since there is nowhere to hide in such a van, resolution is the only option. We agreed that alternate days would be like birthdays – when the celebrant could do, and say, nothing wrong. But who would go first?

'Happy Driver's Day!'

Capo d'Otranto, being the most easterly point on the Italian peninsula (and a target landfall for illegal immigrants), sees the sun first, so we were pleased to enjoy the early warmth before paying our thirteen Euros and departing for Otranto. Vincenzo, the camp labourer, told us Otranto's population grew from five to ninety thousand in the holiday season, making me wonder whether his English wasn't as good as he thought, or whether he was exaggerating, as the Rough Guide said that 'it tripled'. How could Oasis Parking possibly cope with a population increase on that scale? Going from one (that is us), to eighteen might prove tricky. Vincenzo also took great delight in telling us, with much graphic detail, of the nearly 12,000 people (and the Rough Guide confirmed the number) who were starved to death by Turks who laid siege to the walled town in 1480, the archbishop who was sawn in half, and the eight hundred survivors who were led up the hill and beheaded.

Once again the parking meter was jammed, and I wondered what remote and secret shop was guardian of the tickets this time – the butchers, dry-cleaners, or a pet shop? (Although, come to think about it, I had never seen a pet shop.) A girl putting her key in the lock of a house across the street assured me it was '*libro*', despite all the warning signs to the contrary and our fear that foreigners might get a different treatment to locals. At the bottom of the hill from where we had parked was the impressive, high-walled castle jutting out into a harbour, and the subject of the siege, and on the left, a small market in full swing. We passed through the walls and along the narrow alleyways, seeking the cathedral. A man lingered, hoping to practice his English, and with a 'to the right' pointed us towards the entrance.

Oh, not another cathedral – I hear you echoing my own thoughts, but this one had a couple of surprises (other than the ceiling that was adorned with a series of dark blue and white patterned, gold-embellished dinner plates). The twelfth century mosaic floor was a Disneyland of mythical and real characters and animals, and we twisted and turned limbo fashion to try and recognise them, impeded by the red rope barrier. We descended some broad steps to the crypt. It was pitch black down there, and however much we played with the audio machine and donated our loose change, light was not forthcoming. It began to get creepy. Gail went off and found a speechless man, who came and threw the necessary switch. It was a crypt with frescoes, but not what we had come for. Back upstairs into the main body of the church and off to the right, we found our way to a side chapel with a modest marble altar surmounted by a diminutive, long-haired Mary in a brown cloak, the baby Jesus on her lap. It took a moment to realise that we were surrounded by glass-fronted bookcases running to the ceiling and round the room. They were crammed full of an orderly arrangement of the skulls and bones of the eight hundred who were beheaded. Someone had made sure all the skulls looked outwards into the chapel and were equally spaced.

The road to Lecce was every open-top sports-car driver's dream, except where it went through a town or village and the road disintegrated into potholes. In addition, there had obviously been a grant for traffic light installation, as on one country stretch they occurred every three hundred yards. San Cataldo, according to the Rough Guide, had 'come alive in the last couple of seasons…' I have news – the resurrection was short-lived.

The road from San Cataldo to Lecce was straight as a die, a ten kilometre race track, with solid concrete centre blocks and advertising hoardings. One can only imagine the speeding traffic at the start of a weekend or holiday period racing from Lecce to the coast – 'Last one there buys the drinks...'

We were lucky to find parking right in the centre of town near the castle walls. Although we discovered Lecce had much to offer in the way of wide open spaces and fine buildings, I took so few photographs that the urge to be in a sunny town with busy people must have taken over. There's a great pleasure in simply being with other human beings, even though you're not in any sort of direct communication with them. Wandering round the market was good fun, and provided a new pair of socks – although, as I subsequently discovered from their length, 'stockings' would have been a more appropriate label. We spent time in a bookshop and bought a campsite guide that we never used and a British Sunday paper. It was a relief that the cathedral and adjacent campanile were closed. The Baroque Basilica di Santa Croce and its extravagantly decorated rose window, the Roman theatre and amphitheatre were sufficiently diverting to stimulate photography. Finally, we went for a pizza lunch in a small take away.

'*Due Pizza Margheritas per favore e due capuccinos*,' I asked confidently. The girl stared at me blankly.

'*Due Pizza Margheritas per favore e due capuccini*,' I tried again. The girl, an increasingly helpless look on her face, turned towards her companion to assist us.

'I'm sorry, she doesn't speak English.'

The name of a camping site in Lecce included the words '*Le Mura*', so any idiot with a smattering of Italian or French would know that it has to be something to do with 'walls.' Lecce had walls all the way round, and we drove round all of them without there being a hint of a campsite, even returning to view some sections twice. With frustration reaching new heights, I was thankful it was 'Happy Driver's Day.' I stopped and bought a map, but it didn't help – there was no site within the city. I finally decided to be guided by the GPS. It took us six kilometres outside the city, and down a lane to the campsite in a garden of a young man's private house. It was surrounded by walls.

Tony Blair's Friend?

We had a quiet night and woke to dew dripping from the trees onto the van.

'Where was that church that had skeletons over the doorway?' I asked Gail as I wrote up my notes.

'Do you know, I can't remember. Was it Matera, or Santa Severina?'

'Santa Severina – where was that? I can't remember a thing about it.' In the ten days since we had left Sicily, we had stayed at ten different places and probably visited twenty, as though we were on an intensive two week tour. There comes a point when the lack of things to see and explore is a relief and the mundane a pleasure. At breakfast, despite my careful logs, we were having difficulty remembering where we were a week ago (and this wasn't due to huge distances, because we had only been averaging a hundred and forty kilometres a day). Our minds were becoming numb with churches and cathedrals, castles and palaces, walls and theatres, Roman and Greek, Baroque and medieval. Every one in isolation was an architectural wonder, hundreds of years of labour and artistry, but at the same time, the scenes had begun to fuse together like a film being run too fast. Even the Michelin Italia map had become like Italy: fractured, disjointed, and a law unto itself – because of the shape of the heel and toe, many pages had to be turned for small distances. However, the urge to see places is inherent, and the guidebook sucks one in with more 'must see' places, so like a child in a sweetshop or a crazed druggie with a dealer, I found it difficult to resist. There was a huge chunk of unexplored Italy and the weather was being kind, but had the fact that we had turned north and left the heel of Italy brought a feeling of returning home, despite the 2,200 kilometres distance?

'Happy Navigator's Day.'

'Thanks.'

'Look at that magnificent castle.'

'It's Lecce cemetery.'

We decided to make the day easier for ourselves, and opted for the motorway from Lecce to Brindisi, passing through a flat, uninteresting area with olive trees, scrubland, and a shepherd or two tending flocks of brown sheep. Taking the ring road, and momentarily absorbing the industrial smells of Brindisi, we got to the coast before turning inland to see the spectacularly stunning and tempting sight of Ostuni, a Greco-Roman glistening white town perched on three hilltops, above green olive groves. How could we resist? We had to feed the addiction.

It was a great place to have coffee, opposite a twenty-one metre high obelisk dedicated to Saint Oronzo and the City Hall-fronted piazza. The winding streets and steps, fortified towered walls, palaces, courts, arches, alleys and houses of the old medieval town were lime-washed like a Moorish town. Many of the houses were dug into the rock with buttresses and supports. The palaces, Venetian-style bridge, and rose-windowed cathedral made a delightful little square.

'*Tercera de Marzo*,' said the man helpfully as he tidied his display of postcards outside his shop, hoping we would buy one or two.

'The cathedral is closed until the third of March.'

'We've missed it by four days.'

'That's a relief then.' We set off to find another treasure, but it took forever. We knew we were close, but there was a maze of streets and little alleys, and the Rough Guide's information was wrong. When we eventually found the museum, it was closed.

'What did we miss?'

'Delia, the skeleton of a pregnant young woman found in a crouched position, her bones decorated before burial,' I read from the Rough Guide.

'How old is it?'

'It doesn't say.' (I subsequently found it to be 25,000 years old.)

At 11:42 a.m. we tried to use the handheld GPS to get out of Ostuni, but set off in the wrong direction. By 11:47 a.m. we had failed miserably and were doing a three-point turn in an impossible street.

'Can't you see where to go on the GPS?' I pleaded.

'Fuck the GPS!' exclaimed Gail – a word I had never heard her use before. By 11:57 a.m. we had done a complete circle of the town, ending up where we came in. Ten minutes that seemed to drag to ten hours. Then we saw a sign to 'Locorotondo'.

'Happy Navigator's Day.' The road was a *trulli* road – the conical stone houses were scattered near and far, blending perfectly with the dry-stone walls, olive groves, knobbly vines, and almond blossom. It was a scene change, a rural idyll, an Italian Cotswolds – above which rose Locorotondo, another hilltop, white town. Parking in the circular town was, for once, easy. It was a delightful place to walk around, like an Andalucian village, but the whitewashed houses have 'saddle roofs of calcar tile', and contrasted with the sand coloured Baroque churches (I counted ten) and palaces. The streets were narrow, with steps up to doorways, iron railings, and ornate balconies bedecked with flowers. The 'Mother Church', dedicated to Saint George and showing the dragon-slaying scene in bas-relief, was having the floor attacked by workmen with pneumatic drills. (Strangely, down one alleyway we came across a doll-like figure in a black pinafore, a grey and black shawl, and a bonnet resembling a wicked witch strung between the tops of two houses. What was that about?) After a lunch of *orecchiette* served with meat sauce and creamy white cheese, a local speciality, we took a post-prandial walk to the belvedere, and looked out over the panoramic vista of the Istria valley and a tapestry of green fields, olive groves bounded by stone walls, dotted with *trulli* and pink and white almond blossom. All was well in our world.

We found our way out easily and were soon entering Martina Franca, which offered no obvious parking, and then before we knew it, we were out the other side on the SS172. We searched for a *masseria* but were thwarted by a low railway bridge, had to turn around, and finally managed to get under the railway and down narrowing country lanes to find Masseria Il Vignaletto. Was it the one we were looking for? We didn't care, it looked fine. We drove up the grand driveway and parked near the extensive whitewashed, fortified farmhouse.

'*Buon giorno*.' Gail cheerfully greeted the lady who had come out to see what the dog pack was barking at. 'Can we stay here?'

'It is closed.'

'For one night?'

'All is closed.'

'But we have everything. To park only,' Gail pleaded.

'*Benissimo*,' relented the lady. Gail looked back at me questioningly.

'*Quanto*?' I asked.

'*Gratuito*.'

'*Mille grazie*.' What a result – free parking.

TONY BLAIR'S FRIEND?

On Friday 29th February we woke early to a bright sunny day with a misty dampness creeping across the fields surrounding the *masseria*. We drove into Martina Franca, where, after a couple of low bridge avoidances, we parked on Via della Stazione, unsurprisingly, close to the station.

'Ah, Engleesh,' announced a man returning to his car parked alongside. I was worried we had parked too close.

'*E va bene qui*?'

'*Si, si.*' He then asked where we were from, and where we were going. 'Do you know Tonee Blair?'

'We know *of* Tony Blair, but don't know him personally.'

'I know Tonee Blair.'

'Really?' we chorused.

'Me and Tonee Blair we are like theeese,' he said, emphasising the point by holding his hands in front of him and rubbing the index fingers together, mimicking a scout starting a fire from wooden sticks. We looked at him incredulously.

'When Tonee comes to Italy, I look after him. We are like theese,' he said, re-enacting the finger rubbing.

Our looks must have suggested there was a doubt in our minds. The situation was unreal. We were talking to Tony's friend in a back street in Martina Franca? He had a mid-size car, and didn't look like the owner of a magnificent villa or super-yacht like Berlusconi. He flipped through his wallet, desperately seeking some supporting documentary evidence, but couldn't find what he was looking for. Then he dived into his car and pulled out a dark blue and white uniform cap covered in gold braid, waving it in front of us as though it was sufficient. In Italy, anyone in uniform has an elaborate cap, be they parking wardens or naval attaches! Registering continued confusion on our faces, he was back into the car's glove compartment, finally producing an official looking identity card.

'*Navale*,' he announced, pointing to his name, Corallo Martino, and proffering his handshake. I reciprocated by showing my driving licence and pointing to my name.

'Cheess?' Oh why did I bother? I've simply got to get myself another name for visiting Italy.

'Keith,' I tried. He shrugged in that 'whatever' way.

'Where are you going now?'

'Centro Storico.'

'I take you, get in my car.'

'Thank you, we like to walk and see the town,' I replied, glancing at Gail. The Rough Guide's kidnap warning was flashing red lights in my mind – he couldn't be for real.

'No, no, ees too far. Get in. Get in. *Andiamo*,' he said, leading Gail to the door. Neither of us could come up with an excuse as to why not. He drove speedily round the back streets, pointing sights out as they flashed past. Flung against the back seat, I tried desperately to remember street names and buildings. Finally he parked in a square and we got out.

'*Grazie mille*,' I said, in an effort to say goodbye.

'*No. No. Andiamo. Un bellissimo Palazzo*, *no*?' he said, pointing to an ornate Baroque building. 'You take a photo?' He continued to point out medieval masterpieces until we arrived outside his bank, where he asked us to wait while he went in to draw some money. Knowing how long banks could take, we insisted on making our own way and he suddenly changed tack.

'I have much time these days. The Italian defence force eese quiet.' He struggled to find a pen and paper so Gail rummaged in her handbag and found one. He wrote his name, and a home and mobile phone number on the back page of her diary. 'If you or your friends want to buy property – call me. Eees very quiet in defence. I have much time.' We bid goodbye.

'Do you think he was for real?'

'Who knows?'

'Maybe Tony and Cheri are planning to retire to a *trullo*?'

The morning grouping of smartly-dressed men were gathering as we entered the Piazza Roma and medieval quarter through the Porto di Santo Stefano. We walked along clean, balconied streets with limestone paving, marvelling at the palaces, the unusual pitched roofs, and the Baroque façade and light, fresh, cream and blue pastel interior of the Chiesa di San Martino with its new, out-of-place bench seating. As we exited, a man was putting out a pavement sign of Jesus on the cross, like one of those aproned waiters holding a restaurant menu with the dish of the day – 'enter for a religious treat.' I noticed he was chaining it to a railing on the church wall to prevent religious groupies or souvenir hunters walking off with it. We liked Martina Franca – they had managed to slot modern bijou shops into old medieval buildings – there were no visible McDonalds, building societies, or estate agents. There was no graffiti or litter, and this part of Italy was showing a difference to many of the other unfinished, crumbling, litter-strewn places we had been to. Arched, double, solid wood doors with ornate knockers protected closed shops, houses and garages – so much more pleasing than steel roller shutters – and probably as effective.

We were so keen to enjoy the shopping experience we went into an *Electrico Domestico* to get a fuse for the car-charger part of the GPS (not expecting them to have one). Ten minutes of rummaging through an assorted collection of boxes and bits and double-checking against our sample led to a pronouncement of satisfied expertise, and the vital part being handed over to us by a proud shop owner. To celebrate, we stopped for coffees and one very creamy and light pastry *cornetto* in the Music-Arts bar. The lounge would not disgrace the poshest of London's West End eateries. The walls were covered with pseudo paintings of the likes of BB King and Pink Floyd's *Dark Side of the Moon* album, and an Enya CD was playing. It was one of those places where you could while the day away having coffee after coffee and reading papers. We returned to the van through the more modern part of Martina Franca and found it equally as good – all in all, an hour and twenty minutes well spent.

The roads out of, and immediately beyond, Martina Franca proved challenging. Once more we came up against low bridges and had to retrace our route, and as I look back on our recorded track, I wonder why we weren't dizzy with the twist and turns as the GPS subjected us to another round of physical abuse. Finally we escaped towards Locorotondo. When we saw it on the top of a hill to our right, we turned off into a small lane bounded by restored white *trulli* with grey stone roof tiles to get the perfect picture. It appeared as a stunning, circular, white complex of buildings crested by a pale church dome and bell tower, a jewel reflected in the morning sun above the scrubby, yellow-flowered olive groves below. As Gail walked back and forth down the lane to avoid telegraph posts and lines (of which there were a surprising number, as though some giant spider had spun its way across the land), I couldn't help feeling that I had seen it all before – on adverts for modern Spanish villa complexes.

We were truly in the depths of *trulli* country. Walled fields were tilled to expose the brownest of brown earth, or contained olive groves, almond and peach blossom danced in the light breeze, and fluffy white clouds and blue skies added to the picturesque scene. It was moments like this that made us wonder why we had toured in the winter and hadn't set off in the spring. Our arrival in Alberobello was unheralded – most people seemed to have deserted the main streets for lunch with the family, the *sosta* was empty, and the little wooden cabin closed. The fifteen Euros charge looked expensive, as there were no facilities other than dumping and water, but knowing we needed both we rushed the van down the site to use them. The *sosta* was set in an olive grove close to the middle of town and sloped appreciably down the hill to the street, making a street-side spot the only sensible choice.

A short walk up the hill behind the *sosta* we found the *trullo* church of San Antonio (it's a cheat – it was built in the twentieth century and not very appealing) and narrow street after narrow street of the Rione Monti district, where freshly-painted *trulli* posed for the few digital camera-bearing tourists. With a postcard-perfect blue sky, how much money had Kodak and Fuji lost on those little streets since digital had arrived? However, that didn't stop *trullo* owners carrying the familiar signs for films for those who were still in the bygone photographic age, as well as souvenirs of glass-domed *trulli* in snow, *trullo*-shaped money boxes, ceramic *trulli*, plastic *trulli*, and all manner of *trulli* souvenirs. Owners, or more correctly, shopkeepers, sat outside on chairs hawking their wares, wishing they were enjoying a steaming pasta lunch, but languorously trying to entice the few punters in. One had colourful clothes lines of washing with pink sheets and striped towels hanging from the wall outside for those photographers seeking an authentic touch (or perhaps real people lived in that one?).

One gimmick was the draw of a rooftop vista – the only access being a narrow passage through a shop so stuffed with souvenirs of the breakable variety that there was a better-than-even chance that anyone squeezing through would catch one of the shelves and have to pay for the breakage. The odds rose dramatically when those leaving (having seen the so-called vista of a few rooftops in the next street and examined close-up how the famous tiles don't have any mortar and had symbolic decorations painted in lime) then had to edge back through the new arrivals in a 'No, after you,' manner. Rucksack wearers were condemned to a double bout of breakage, since on turning to see what they had upskittled the first time, were destined to repeat the act, and unless they stopped spinning, would quickly acquire 'bull in a souvenir-shop' status, and a large entry on their next credit card statement.

Another striking feature of Alberobello was its cafés – they were devoid of food apart from one that had two curly, white bread, salad sandwiches of the 'is that all you've got?' 'grab a bite at the Esso station' variety. Even the standby request for 'toast?' yielded nothing.

'Where are the *pizzetas*, *arancini*, *panini*, *focaccia*, or even just one *cornetto*?' I muttered.

'We'll have to go back to the van,' said Gail. We walked through lots of pretty, residential *trulli* in pleasant, uncommercialised, narrow streets down to a small park, where our hopes were lifted when we found a delightful log cabin restaurant with an 'Open' sign. Like someone on the third week of a starvation diet, I dementedly attacked the doors – but it was closed. The town seemed to have banned eating in cafés – I began dreaming of McDonalds, and for once it wasn't a nightmare.

Hunger satisfied in the van, I took a post-prandial walk around the *sosta*, hardly believing that there were no electric, showers, toilets or security, but thinking it might explain why we were the sole occupiers. We were parked by a bushy border and small wall away from a street where overnight parking would have been free and no less noisy than where we were. Since there were no gates or other impediments to access, cars sporadically took a shortcut through the site, until one drove over more purposefully and a man got out and requested fifteen Euros. Of course we paid up, and he gave us a little scribbled note. Effortless money, particularly if you have nothing to do with the camping but need some money for a quick fix.

Alberobello is the trouble-free option for viewing the conical-roofed *trulli*, and in summer must be jammed with tour buses, guides, and camera-swinging tourists (although I have seen suggestions that it is only just getting into the tourist swing of things – there's certainly an opportunity for anyone wishing to open a café-bar serving food…) The *trulli* are en-masse everywhere, or pop up between regular buildings when you least expect them, creating a unique Tinky Winky, Dipsy, Laa-Laa, and Po *Teletubbies* pixie-world.

The evening brought out the townsfolk, and we joined in the walking about with no particular purpose past the upmarket and expensive clothes shops. The Casa D'Amore, or House of Love, was not a brothel, but the tourist office, and the first *trullo* to go to two storeys using mortar. It was, of course, closed. More intriguing was the information on the history board outside that the development had been opposed by local Counts – one in particular who ended up having his view to the square blocked by the structure. Part of the building (if my memory serves) was an art gallery, so we went in just for the joy of going in to somewhere that was open. The pony-tailed Russian artist and Bond-movie style girlfriend watched us as we circled past the modern art. As we left, they rushed to lock the doors and walked down the street arm-in-arm to wherever Russian couples go in the evening.

It wasn't to a restaurant, as these didn't open until after 8:00 p.m. With an early evening chill setting in, we ended up in a small gelateria for coffees, which I know Italians don't do. Looking through a door, I saw a girl with a fetching net hat, like they wear in food-processing factories. Her tan was of such a deep hue that she couldn't have spent her winter in Alberobello (or she'd had a good going-over with the St Tropez spray tan). She was working away with some stainless steel mixing machines, and emerged from the 'laboratory' beaming triumphantly and supporting a huge tray of freshly prepared *cassata* that she inserted into the cool cabinet. There are those moments where the visual senses are overcome and lead to involuntary action, and before I knew it I was being served the cake with white, pink, chocolate, yellow-vanilla and trifle layers – it was a six Euros multi-coloured heaven on a plate. Gail had a tart, and the pretty girl, having by then taken a fancy to me, ('in your dreams') brought us scoops of yoghurt ice-cream to go with it. I nearly went for the *Zupa Inglese*, imagining a hot, steamy bowl of Heinz 57 Oxtail soup, but found it was only another form of trifle (possibly brought over by nineteenth century tourists but now enjoyed by Italians with a chilled local white wine).

On our walk home (for the van had become that long ago) we passed a furniture shop of unbelievable dimensions – way beyond anything Heal's could dream of. It went on for shop after shop, block after block, round corners and street after street. The furniture was modern and stunning, and as I pressed my face against the window-glass I noticed they had my favourite kitchen made by Snaidero – a sleek, polished, assemblage in Ferrari red or blue that in a mad moment in our past life I had nearly bought for our apartment.

'Will you be cooking in your kitchen?' the salesman of the upmarket Surrey kitchen shop had asked.

'Not me personally, but I've married someone who's very good at that sort of thing,' I'd replied, wondering where else you might cook other than a kitchen.

'If you're going to cook then I wouldn't buy this kitchen.'

'You wouldn't?'

'No, it's more for show.' But it still looked good in D'Oria Arredi – the displays were dazzling whether you wanted a lounge or a bedroom furnishing – it was our idea of a modern furniture paradise, and I went into a momentary fantasy of shipping stuff home.

'Don't be so ridiculous.'

A Quiet Night?

We set off early across country towards Altamura, and then Gravina In Puglia (probably so named in case any of the local population forgets they are very close to the border with Basilicata). And for those of you following on a map, although I have no reason to believe you would, you will also see that being very close to Matera (which isn't in Puglia), we had circled the heel of Italy.

The landscape was one of order and tidiness. The area is known as Le Murge on account of the limestone plateau that rises up as you travel inland from the Bari coast. Unlike in Sicily, houses were finished, and we passed substantial farmhouses with grand roadside entrances. The parcels of land were more impressive, with acres of winter wheat or seas of pink and white almond blossoms. Apart from the fact that somebody must have sown and be harvesting the crops, it was a time-stood-still, rural landscape. We were shocked out of it to the east of Gravina (forgive me for leaving off the 'In Puglia' bit but we all know where we are now) by a new hospital so impressively large that there must have been a bed for each of the 42,000 population – just in case a plague should strike. The road whisked us into town and we parked on Via Orsini, which competes with Corso Vitorio Emmanuel to be the main street. It was the Orsini family which settled the town after a particularly brutal episode in its history, and held it from around 1380 to 1816. Pope Benedict VIII was born there in 1649.

A young, dark-haired guy was standing in a narrow doorway with one of those '*i*' for information signs over it. I grabbed Gail and marched over – it was unusual to see one, and even rarer to see one open. Our new best friend (whose name I failed to record) was studying seventeenth century history in London. He wanted to show us something special – I unconsciously started fingering the coins in my trouser pocket. He led us through back streets of dilapidated houses and down some steps where he unlocked a padlock on a chainlink gate to take us into an open, grassy area running to the edge of a ravine, with the backs of decaying houses up on the ridge opposite. An Alsatian dog stood on the wall of one and barked incessantly.

There was a light mist as we moved off at a quick pace to the left and down a slope to the face of the ravine, which was pot-marked with cave entrances. Another gate unlocked and he led us along narrow passages into the grottoes. These, he explained, served as bolt-holes for the population in times of barbarian attack as far back as Neolithic times, and later, when it was under Greek influence prior to capture by the Romans in 305 BC. He asked us to look out of one of the caves across the far side of the T-shaped spectacular ravine, where we could see an impressive and near-intact Roman, two-level stone bridge – or was it an aqueduct? He led us through more grottoes to finally unlock another gate, and explained that we had arrived at the church of San Michele delle Grotte – a remarkable structure of five interconnecting naves with apses and monolithic arched columns all cut out of the rock. He showed us decaying frescoes from the eleventh and fourteenth centuries on the walls and pillars, and how they could be distinguished by the faces – first flat, and then more rounded. He ran his finger round a Christ with blonde wavy hair, blue tunic, and brown cloak. The grotto, he said, probably dated back to the early Christian's worship of Saint Michael the Archangel (which was propagated in the fifth century), as a statue of Saint Michael had been found in a grotto. Various pilgrims would apparently wait in an outer hall for baptism, and many came from Canterbury. The population who first lived in the caves later built houses, but still regarded the church as their cathedral. In AD 999 they had to retreat there when Saracens attacked, but it was to no avail and they were massacred. Our guide showed us the site of the ossuary where the bones were found.

We emerged from the dark, dank caves and made our way back up the town. All twenty thousand men of the population seemed to have assembled in the square, and the small, round café-kiosk we chose for coffee was packed with them.

On the way out of Gravina, we passed Frederick II's thirteenth century castle sitting on a mound north of the town, but were in no mood to stop as we were on our way to the supposedly 'finest' of the string of castles he had built across Puglia at Castel del Monte, some fifty-five kilometres away. We realised we were climbing and the area was the High Murge, but the appearance of snow poles on the verges was still surprising. The landscape was barren, with scrubland and pine forests, and the rocky strata became the walls.

When we turned for Castel del Monte, we debated whether it was the castle we were seeing or an industrial complex, so out of keeping was it with the surrounding terrain. On arrival, it's a steep windy walk up to what looks like an octagonal, eight-towered folly in cream stone, or possibly something restored to modernity, rather than a battered old castle – and in that respect, hugely disappointing.

'It's got windows. Why would anyone build a castle with windows?' I pondered.

'There aren't any battlements, either,' added Gail.

'I'm wondering what it defended. There's nothing for miles around.'

'Let's go and see.'

'Probably going to charge and arm and a leg to get in!'

'Well we've come this far, so don't grumble.'

The inside was set out as a museum. We walked the circular route and there were explicatory boards in Italian and English. There was much ornate marble, and the wind rattled the glass in the windows (yes, a double-glazed castle). The arrowslits don't provide any view of the ground (where an enemy might be assembling), but do light the staircases very nicely.

'What are you doing?'

'Taking photos of the message boards – there's so many, and the wordiness of them is doing my head in.'

'Photography isn't allowed.'

'I know, but I'm not using a flash.'

The first board told us it was built for the Emperor in 1240, but as it has no military embellishments like a moat, probably wasn't a castle, but a hunting lodge or house of pleasure. There are fanciful theories about the eight towers, the octagonal shape, the eight rooms on each floor ringed around the central courtyard, and astrological connections – but let's face it guys, nobody has a bloody clue what he, or the 'Wonder of the World' as he was known, wanted it for – maybe it was a work creation programme. Strange that the Italians chose a building that has no known purpose to use on their one-cent coin. (I later read that the Italian government had acquired it as a ruin in 1876 and had involved 'replacement of the stonework.' Is that a euphemism for 'rebuilt'?) I'm sorry I can't bring you more from the signboards, but moving close enough so I could read the print in the camera viewfinder resulted in only one-quarter of each being digitalised. What a relief.

After a lunch in the van we set off for the 'cosmopolitan and atmospheric' coastal town of Trani along a straight as a die road raised above the endless olive groves. We drove through the town until we reached the harbour wall, and were greeted by a delightful scene of pontoon-moored boats bobbing in the green water and larger working boats undergoing repair against a backdrop of a pale, sand-coloured medieval town built of Trani stone. On the far side of the U-shaped harbour was a sturdy, eleventh century Romanesque cathedral with a tall bell tower. The scene was totally uplifting – we had chanced upon a gem of a place. Parked in a bay outside a swanky hotel and with no one about, we decided it was an ideal spot to spend a quiet night. We were simply another vehicle in a line of parked cars along the harbour wall.

'It will open at four,' a small man in a thick coat told us in perfect English as we stood surveying the cathedral. 'Would you like to see the Jewish Synagogue?'

'Not at the moment, thank you,' I replied.

'*Prego*,' he replied, shaking my hand warmly before he moved on.

The cathedral was an arresting, severe building – it had a rose window and, standing over an archway, a tall bell tower threading its way sixty metres to the sky. I couldn't help thinking that the cathedral set against the edge of the sea and at the mouth of the harbour looked better from a defensive point of view than Castel del Monte. It's an unusually tall building because there are apparently three churches inside, each on top of the other, with vaulted crypts and the remains of a sixth century early Christian chamber. Round the corner we found the castle built by Frederick II in 1233 – oh, how he loved his castle building! Water lapped against the plain, rectangular walls and towers.

The sun was lower in the sky and we felt the chill, so retired for coffees at a harbour-side café. As I paid, I admired the ice-cream display and voiced my approval, but resisted temptation. In no time at all the man at the till had served us '*gratuito*' with yoghurt ice-cream and *panatone*. Around 6:30 p.m. the centre of town came alive, and we joined in the *passagiatta* along the streets, admiring the attractively designed shop windows. Deciding to eat out, we selected a pleasant restaurant at the far end of the harbour, where we were greeted as an intrusion and asked to go upstairs where another couple were dining. We discreetly elected a table away from them. The waiter appeared with their food and started grumbling at us, energetically waving his arms after he had put the food down.

'It's something about the table, maybe it's only got three legs,' I whispered to Gail as we selected another.

'Sorry, I don't understand, *non capisco*.' But the waiter (who I'm sure spoke English) couldn't be bothered as we struggled with our Italian and his interpretation of the menu, which clearly hindered the choices we wanted to make.

'*Uno di pesce. Uni di carne*,' he pronounced, swirling around with a haughty air and marching off to the stairs.

'We're one of the first here and they're already limited on food,' I sighed. Our romantic meal in an upmarket restaurant wasn't going well. Our *antipasto* arrived to the tune of the chef beating my veal to death in the kitchen. He didn't do a good job and it tasted dire.

'*La carne non è buona*.' The waiter had suddenly gone deaf, and bore an air that suggested we were lucky he was serving us.

'They should be grateful *we* came in – only one other couple has bothered,' said Gail. Then, as an afterthought, 'Is it possible he thought you said *cane* rather than *carne*?'

'Probably spitting in the desert as we speak,' I muttered. 'Let's have coffee in the van.' We walked back along a near-empty harbour lacking any semblance of a 'cosmopolitan air' and thinking that an early night might be in order.

'What did you do?' asked Gail from the bed as I sat at the table a little later.

'Nothing. There's a half a dozen boys and girls outside sitting on the harbour wall chatting. One of them bumped against the van. I'll try and get them to move.' I opened the van's sliding door. It must be quite a surprise if you're standing next to a van and someone's head suddenly emerges from it. I made ridiculous gestures and they, thinking a madman was on the loose, moved off. They were replaced ten minutes later by a couple in their twenties having a very serious discussion that, judging by the body language, was about their relationship (or soon not-to-be). I was observing this by looking out of the small rooftop window in the kitchen. They were oblivious to me. The problem was that people speaking so passionately less than three feet from the van is hard to ignore, and there was no chance of sleeping. I started the generator and they moved away, he still full of entreaties.

'That's a relief – I might come to bed now. I can't understand why everyone is choosing the spot outside our van, the wall runs for miles!'

Another group of around six arrived. We opened the blinds and stared out. They stared back unbelievingly – wondering what a couple would be doing in a small van at that time of night. I tried the genny trick again and they slowly drifted away, but as I looked out of the bathroom window at the rear there were still a lot of people coming and going.

'I'm going back to bed,' announced Gail. 'Are you coming?'

'In a moment.' It was now 00:30 a.m., the crowds were swelling, I couldn't settle and I felt cooped up.

'Are you coming to bed? It's bound to subside soon.'

'I think I'll take a walk.'

'Whatever for?'

'Can't stand the claustrophobia anymore.' I walked around the harbour towards the town, or more correctly, I pushed my way through the crowds – a seething mass of young and beautiful people packing out every bar and restaurant and spilling out onto the streets. Every parking place was taken, and cars buried in the swirling crowd had drivers and passengers leaning out of the windows to josh with passers-by as they sought an escape in vain. These young folks were having fun, but not in a lager loutish way. They were boisterous, but well-mannered, and I didn't feel any unease, I simply wished I was thirty years younger! If only our twenty-four hour drinking culture was as amiable as this. At 1:00 a.m. I passed the restaurant we had eaten in earlier – it was packed and people were queuing to get in. Restaurants and bars we had thought were closing now had crowds of people outside drinking and talking. At the far side of the harbour, away from the crowds and near the cathedral and fish market, I found three motorhomes tucked away in a quiet parking area. There was salvation.

'I'm going to move the van to the other side of the harbour – it's quieter over there. Do you want to stay in bed or get up?'

'Well I'm not staying up here.'

'It's going to be tricky – the road is solid with people.'

'Keith, look at them – you'll never get out, and there are cars in amongst them coming the other way.'

'Close your eyes if you're worried.'

'But where are you going to turn? It's a cul-de-sac.'

'Going to do a three-pointer right here.'

'Oh no!'

I made the turn, but was then head to head with an oncoming car and the people in between. He moved closer. I moved closer.

'You'll have to give way – he's not going to budge.'

'I've nowhere to go to.' He drove closer. The passenger doors opened and three guys got out and walked towards the van. 'Oh bugger!'

'Hello, English. I am the only one who speaks English. You need to let me help you.'

'Okay.'

'Drive on the pavement so my friend can get by.'

'Tell your friend he can drive on the pavement,' I said, thinking that there was no chance of me bumping up a three-inch kerb.

'Keith, please don't upset them.'

'We're fine, and the van is lot bigger than they are,' I said, going another inch forward to emphasise the point.

'Okay, wait while I tell him what to do,' the English speaker said. Eventually, with everyone joining in good-naturedly, we were released to join the next crowd and queue of cars crawling round the harbour-front road. By 1:30 a.m. we had made it to our tranquil haven and I flopped into bed and dozed fitfully in some transient land between oblivion, exhaustion, and security-minded wakefulness.

'Oh, for a quiet night from now on. Goodnight.'

'Goodnight.'

'You know what?

'No, what?'

'The guidebook was right. Trani does have a cosmopolitan air.'

'What a night. Did you sleep at all,' I asked, a blacksmith working at his anvil in my head.

'No. People parked alongside us in a car and then started partying outside so I was keeping an eye on them. Didn't you hear them?'

'Mustn't have done. Although I didn't sleep well.'

'Well, enough to be snoring all the way through!' We showered and slowly breakfasted, looking out on a peaceful Sunday, sunlit harbour, but couldn't muster the energy to set off. A big refuse truck arrived and men with fluorescent orange jackets busied themselves emptying the large skips by the fish market whilst spilling a new a trail of rubbish as they went along. Ten minutes later a little mechanical sweeper arrived and spent ten minutes running backwards and forwards clearing it all up.

Must be another work creation scheme, I thought.

We wandered round the harbour to our favourite little café and sat outside on comfy steel and blue wicker chairs, the table set with a crisp white cloth, drinking coffees, popping paracetamol, making duty phone calls to family, and pretending to read Italian newspapers. It could have been St Tropez. If only we didn't feel so knackered. People started coming out of the cathedral and the harbour was getting lively again.

'One minute partying, the next, praying. How do they do it?'

Nearly a Bull's Eye

'Look at all those cars and people; it's a huge Sunday market.'

'It's a cemetery.'

We had followed '*Tutti Direzione*' out of Trani, down narrow medieval streets, under a low arch, and round a ninety-degree bend between overhanging buildings – breathing audible sighs of relief when we got onto a main road alongside the railway and spotted the crowds. We drove past fields of fennel, olive orchards, grapevines, and an impressive castle before entering Barletta, where the lack of sleep, poor directions, and construction of a new hospital led to tetchy moments and a double-Windsor knot of a route on and off the motorway before we were finally back on the coastal road and passing through the salt pans at Margharita di Savoia.

Expecting to see thousands of overwintering cranes (of the feathered variety), flamingos and kingfishers, we scanned the sea to our right and Italy's oldest working salt pans to our left before finally convincing ourselves that a flash of pink was a group of flamingos – but it could just as easily have been seagulls or our neuronal synapses still sparking off. The road was, frankly, boring. Based on our in-town Barletta routing experience, we by-passed Manfredonia. The sun was shining, the sea below the rocky coastline was turquoise, the bare mountains of the Gargano promontory rose up steeply, and someone was hammering to get out of my head. We stopped in a lay-by for a picnic lunch, knowing we had to climb those mountains.

Avoiding the route with the worst hairpins, we settled for the S89b, which didn't let us off very lightly. Our destination was Monte Sant'Angelo, 'the highest and coldest settlement in the Gargano', and a place of ancient pilgrimage. On arrival, we unexpectedly came across block after block of depressing grey apartment buildings and the *sosta* we were seeking seemed to have been subsumed into one of them. It was not uplifting. Simply to be able to stop, we settled for a large, open-air car and coach park at the eight hundred and twenty-nine metre peak of the hill, by the imposing castle. Many tourist coaches were already parked, and across the road a fairground of tat stalls played loud, irreverent music. The man in the booth said we could stay the night.

Monte Sant'Angelo is a 'Top Ten' pilgrimage site. The story varies, but we have to imagine, around the year 490, a rich nobleman losing the best bull of his herd and then, after a search, finding it in a cave atop the mountain. Angered by the bull, he (or one of his servants) shoots an arrow at it (making me wonder why he bothered to look for the bull in the first place – perhaps it was a warning shot?). But no bull's eye was to be scored: the wind blows the arrow back like a boomerang and it hits the archer. Much trouble ensues in town as the bishop considers these strange events, but fortunately, the Archangel Saint Michael appears to him and tells him it was *his* sign, and the bishop should get up to the cave and dedicate it to God. But the bishop needs more persuading, so only when Saint Michael has helped them win a battle with neighbours on the hill, appeared for another persuasive chat, left a cloth suitable for an altar, a footprint in the rock, and pre-consecrated the site, does the bishop get down to some serious chapel building.

During the seventh century, the site was adopted by the Lombards, thereby spurring the development of Mont Saint Michel in France. Anyone who was anyone in the Christian and Royal world (along with lesser mortals) visited what was (and still is) one of the most important western shrines – with the added attraction that it absolves all sin and is en-route to the Holy Land. From the sixth century pilgrims have scratched their names and prayers into the rocks including five in the Runic alphabet of early Anglo Saxons and thereby antedates pilgrimages to Compostela.

We were not prepared for the transition from a plain, exterior portal and a dim, modern, unsigned stairway through the impressive brass doors from Constantinople (1076), into the drama of the cave church. I am not religious, but I see from my notes that I struggled for words to describe the feeling the grotto church stirred up. I think it was the mass of bare rock emphasising we were underground and vulnerable, and the simplicity of the main and side altar (if you excuse the balustrade of plaster columns bought from B&Q). Sadly, it was lessened by a group of posing tourists who lost their religious piety and, contrary to notices, flashed away with their cameras.

The main street that pilgrims had struggled up for centuries was lined with stalls designed to lessen your monetary load, with sellers of bread, *orecchiette* pasta and other packeted regional products that all looked identical. After a nap in the van, we watched the ranks of coaches from as far away as Cefalu and Palermo in Sicily depart with their souvenir-laden tourists. Against the flow of locals hurrying up the hill to answer the call of the church bells, we took a final walk down to the male dominated piazza. Returning up the hill, we marvelled at the blood-red sunset and discussed how much we were looking forward to sleep.

I spent the night dreaming about a conversation between an ancient traveller who met a shepherd sitting with his flock on a hill. After the usual greetings and 'where are you travelling from and to,' the traveller asked,

'And in your village, who is your Patron Saint?'

'We don't have a Patron Saint.'

'But every place I have visited has a Patron Saint.'

'Nothing has happened in our village.'

'What? No Christ weeping, virgins with visions, hands with stigmata?'

'No, none of those.'

'But what effigy do you carry round on Saint's day?'

'We don't have a Saint's day.'

'No carnival, drinking, feasting or dancing? Who's going to visit your village if you don't have a Saint's day? There'll be no pilgrims to fleece – think of the money.'

'Mmm. I feel a vision coming on… Would you testify for me?'

A burning sun rose and started to melt the pervading chill. We drove back over the top of the hill and hair-pinned five hundred metres down the other side, dropping into a valley before winding our way steeply up the other side into a dense forest. Our plan was to cut diagonally across the Gargano National Park and to hit the coast at Vieste – the easternmost point of the peninsula. Spring had not arrived yet, so the rising sun had no trouble penetrating the trees with broad shafts of light. We climbed back up to seven hundred and ninety-six metres. It was wild, and our only company grey-horned cattle with large bells donging. Once the descent began it was exhilarating, and even more so when the road was blocked by a large herd of grey cattle and calves being encouraged up the hill by a drover in a car. We stopped for a mid-morning break at a spot where the only sound was birdsong, and then careened down the final stretch, out of the beech and oak forest and across acres of newly planted olive groves to Vieste, where motorhomes were banned from entering town.

We parked in front of some shops opposite the harbour. After visiting the helpful tourist office, we were starving. I fancied some finger-food, but unfortunately, being Monday, none of the ten bars or cafés we entered appeared to have any. We finally found a *panineria* with cold pizza.

'Oh God, there's only three left,' I muttered to Gail as we queued behind a man and a woman. The man loaded up with bread, then as an afterthought, decided to buy pizza.

'Bloody hell.' He departed and my juices were flowing.

'Oh no, the woman has ordered pizza as well!' Gail whispered. The assistant removed a whole pizza, leaving just one. I felt sick inside. Another assistant arrived and I gave her my order at the same time that the woman decided to ask for more. There was a fight over the forceps and my girl won. She carved off one measly piece of pizza and was about to hand the forceps and the pizza back to the other girl when Gail shouted,

'*Encora*, *encora*!' We got our pizza slices and a withering look from the thwarted woman. I imagined her entreaties as we left:

'But I come here every day. How could you do that? What's my little Luigi gonna eat now?'

We sat on a bench in a sunny square. As I opened my mouth to eat, I developed aching lockjaw, so anxious was my mouth to have food put into it. I've never tasted better (well I have, but not at that moment).

We made a tour of the old town's narrow and steep whitewashed streets, saw another of Frederick II's castles (now owned by the Navy), spotted an intriguing spider's web of poles and ropes known as a *trabucco* jutting out into the sea to catch mullet, rattled the doors of the cathedral (prompting the lady across the street to shout '*chiusa*, *le cinque*'), but couldn't find the chopping block where five thousand local people were beheaded by Turks. On the way back to the van, we stopped for coffees and watched diners being served delightful meals at a café that offered no hint that it served food.

The coast north of Vieste provides for many 'Holiday Villages' amongst the white cliffs and pine trees. They were closed, and often undergoing refurbishment, with men in yellow JCBs having fun gouging away trees and earth. We slipped down the hill from Péschici to its port, hoping to park for the night, but Coastguard notices sounded as though the penalties imposed, should we decide to do so, would be life-threatening. We retreated back along the road, worrying we were out of town, when we spotted a motorhome in what looked like it might be a *sosta*, although there were no signs. We drove down the steep slope and into the sandy open area regardless.

An old boy dressed in scruffy trousers, a white, paint-stained blue-grey sweater, peaked brown corduroy hat, and carrying a black plastic bumbag like a handbag, shuffled over. He grabbed me by the forearm, intent on telling me something. I was at a loss and thought we were trespassing. The girl from the Italian motorhome came over to help.

'Dattoli.'

'Sorry?'

'*Si*, Dattoli!' he cried, squeezing my arm even harder.

'Sorry, *non capisco*.' I was even more bemused.

'Eeez hees name,' the Italian girl explained.

'Ah, *si*.'

'Antonio Dattoli,' he said, pounding his chest with a fist before opening his arms wide to acknowledge the blocks of white buildings, hen coop, outhouses with various pipes and sundry plumbing equipment outside, and the dented old 4x4 Fiat that had bee white, but was now a dust-covered grey belying its 'Young' insignia.

'*Benvenuto* Camping Residence *Dattoli!*' Feeling this called for some response I tried:

'*Bello, bello. Mio nome é* Keith.'

'*Cosa*?'

'Keith,' I said, pointing at myself, but knowing where it was going.

'Cate?'

'No, Keith.'

'Cheees?'

'Mia *moglie*, Gail,' I said, switching tack to introduce Gail.

'Gaaleh?'

'*Si, si.*'

The Italian campers decided to leave. I began to feel our staying there was a charitable act on our part. He carefully positioned us, his only campers, where he wanted and left reluctantly. We made ourselves at home and sat out drinking tea below a blazing sun. After 9,310 kilometres the weather had never been warmer – and just when we were heading home.

Antonio wandered over, a big tabby cat at his heels, and presented Gail with some lemons, insisting we smell them and pointing to the smallholding attached to the site with many fruit trees. He perched himself on a low breeze-block wall in front of us, ready for a conversation. *He must be lonely*, I thought. Now conversation was never going to be easy, and I won't bore you with the momentary misunderstandings, but we got on surprisingly well, considering Antonio had no English at all. I asked him why there were no signs for 'Camping Residence Dattoli' so he walked us over to a small utilities block. It had one of everything, but had either never been finished, or was being refurbished. Only the outside basin worked. At the back of the toilet were all the signs for his illustrious establishment. He would put them up at Easter. A phone rang and Antonio was soon deep in conversation, the latest model Nokia mobile to his ear – were appearances deceptive?

When he turned his attention back to us we discovered that 'poor bedraggled Antonio' was only there to do some painting. The series of buildings were his holiday cottages, beyond which Antonio had a villa. But he only used it during the summer. He lived in another villa during the winter. He turned me round and pointed to the top of the hill behind so that I could see a magnificent white villa nearly hidden amongst trees and enjoying far-reaching sea views. I asked Antonio about the weather and he demonstrated that it was going to be very dry over the next few days, emphasising it by running the dusty soil of the flower bed through his fingers.

Next day, on the basis of Antonio's forecast and the hot sun beating down from above, I donned T-shirt and shorts. He came over, tugged on my T-shirt and pointed at my shorts, and then gave a shiver and such a good imitation of a sneeze that I thought he was going to expectorate all over me. I wondered whether he could change a fifty Euros note, whereby with a wave of his hand and a 'why-ever not gesture?' produced a thick wad of notes from his shirt pocket. He kissed Gail goodbye and she wished he had shaved sometime in the previous three days.

A ball of flame leapt up from the hillside above us, followed by a mini atom bomb of a smoke cloud. It was the season for men to be chopping and burning piles of olive branches in the groves. Some still had a carpet of meadow grass with yellow and white spring flowers while others had already been tilled to a fine brown earth. The olives had either been collected or fallen to the floor and they lay in car parks and civic centres becoming a black pulp.

We left Antonio to his painting. Our objective was to run steadily up the eastern coast. The road climbed up to San Menaio, along a rocky shore and through pine forests. We craned over to photograph the primitive spider's web construction of *trabucchi* like giant stick insects stepping into the water. On some, the poles and rigging made a pointed headland appear to become a pirate ship sneaking out to sea. From Rodi Garganico, we eschewed the main road in favour of a slip road supposedly crossing between the Lago di Varano and the sea. Tall eucalyptus trees blocked our view to the right and wide agricultural land disappeared away to the left. We knew the lake should be there, but could see little sign of it, or the birds feeding on the eels. The road was a remote, straight, straight, straight twelve kilometres. It had been a malarial swamp – and proved about as interesting when we finally saw some of the shallow waters.

Even though we had nice views out to the Trémiti Islands (places of confinement throughout the ages, including a spell when Mussolini deported homosexuals there), we were unwilling to undergo a further twenty-seven kilometres to the next lake, Lago di Lesina, so opted to turn inland near Capoiale on a small road running along the west side of Lago di Varano. Much to our amazement, the water was now a rich blue colour, as though someone had tipped in Dolly Blue dye. The area was thinly populated, and what dwellings we saw, including a church, were run down, crumbling, or abandoned. At a junction at the end of the road that identified itself on our Michelin map as San Nicola Varano, we found nothing but a glorious, derelict brick building that could have been a hotel but probably had origins as a Benedictine Monastery. The road climbed and became worryingly narrow and more remote, with a few farms and cattle. We saw a sheep giving birth as we passed, a sheepdog laying close by and keeping watch.

We dropped down onto the main road, then onto a plateau to the south side of Lago Lesina, and stopped at an enormous garage sitting like an isolated island stronghold in a fen of agricultural swampland. But for all the isolation, it was full of parked trucks, coaches, cars and tractors. When we entered there was one man sitting at the bar in a café that probably ran to an acre. The man serving took great trouble to lay our table, even though we were only having two coffees and a *cornetto*.

It looked an excellent place to spend the night, but we moved on, along a straight flat road between the lake and fields. We passed little green three-wheeler Piaggios bouncing along tracks between ploughed furrows, ant-like gangs of crop pickers, little white huts, fields of fennel waving softly in the wind, giant pulsing water sprays, and bright orange tractors hauling stack upon stack of crates of harvested crops to the roadside entrances to the fields. We had entered the region of Molise, and the south of Termoli was a blush of pink and white cherry blossom.

Termoli port was busy with serious boats, cranes and gantries, but provided plenty of parking. We ascended the circular stairs to enter the quaint old town, imagining fisherman bent double with their catch, trudging up the cobbled alleys and through the arches and tunnels to their little whitewashed houses. Many had been prettily refurbished, and the work had been completed. The cathedral was open and a service for four people in a side chapel in full swing. It hid the bones of Saint Timothy so well that they forgot where they put them, and they were only rediscovered in 1945 during restoration. Our friend Frederick II built the castle to fill in the gap left in the walls, and it now has the honour of housing an observatory that sets Italian and Central European time and, fittingly, has a clock in the austere tower. (Disconcertingly, the clock shows 12:19 in the photo, whereas the camera has recorded it as being taken at 12:51 p.m.)

The castle and walls provided a fine viewing point for the many *trabucchi* that jutted out from the rocky foreshore. To the north, the sea gently lapped a deserted beach, its cafés and restaurants backed by modern resort buildings all curving away into the misty distance below a blue sky.

Our next stop was Vasto. The coast between comprised sleeping lidos and villages, and then nothing at all – even the railway gave up. Looping up from the coast to Vasto upper town, we were initially impressed by the solid Calderesco Castle and parked on a steeply inclined main street to have a look around. I spent ten minutes trying to photograph a little red Fiat 500 in a street with flower tubs, curvy art-deco lampposts, and some fine terraced houses with arched doorways, flower-decked balconies, climbing plants, and green shutters. We loved the Renaissance Palazzo d'Avalos and its courtyard where men were sweeping, and thought how nice it would be to have an apartment in such an elegant building. The street behind led to a belvedere with palm trees, coastal views, and relieving public toilets. Most disappointing was the pervading graffiti – even the ancient castle doors had been attacked with a blue spray can. What mindset thinks such things are worthy, and what tourism-hungry council allows it to stay there?

The coastline north of Vasto was a disheartening continuum of empty campgrounds that looked like refugee camps, and we became depressed thinking that the one we were heading for at Francavilla al Mare, near Pescara, might be the same. Entering Francavilla, we took a left turn to follow a '*Centro*' sign, and in so doing took a ten kilometre detour to a campsite that was where we had originally started. Or was it a campsite? It looked like a grand, modern, cream painted house. Gail ran across the road to ring the bell alongside the large metal gate, which swung open. The site was laid out in the orchard and bordered the sea. It was closed, but we were made very welcome, and could stay as long as we liked. Gail even got our washing started. We discovered a grass football pitch and an orange ball, and in a moment of childhood park-playing memory madness, I was Bobby Charlton unleashing a forty-yard cracker into the top left hand corner of the net.

'You old fool. You'll slip and then won't be able to drive.'

'Just get in goal and see if you can save it.' But it wasn't a shot of Champion's League quality, and soon the goalkeeper didn't want to play anymore (I think she'd noticed that the passengers in every bus that halted outside had nothing better to do than watch us over the garden wall).

It's Over

'It's pouring with rain, I'm off to get the washing in,' I shouted to Gail as she showered in the van.

It was wet and cold. We gathered in the undies with a salty spray whipped up by the crashing waves scalding our eyes and mouths. As the day progressed the rain became worse, and by evening we were being lashed by storm force winds and rain that rattled on the roof and rocked the van. The puddles outside developed into lakes and I developed Noah's Ark syndrome, thanking God we were alive but worrying about having to go out to empty the toilet cassette that was rapidly filling as a consequence of our constant tea and coffee drinking. The washing was all around the van in a futile attempt to dry it in the condensation laden atmosphere. Gail decided to do the ironing and made a mental calculation of the amps needed and what we had available.

'I'll put the genny on, then there's no problem,' I offered.

'No, we should be okay.' The little orange light came on as the iron started to heat, and the electrics blew.

'I'll have to go out and swap the plug onto another electric post – although I could put the genny on now like we should have done in the first place…'

'No, just leave it.'

'Which one do you want me to leave?'

'All of them.'

'But then you can't do the ironing. This could go on for days.'

'I don't think so.'

'How do you know that?'

'I don't.'

'So what now?'

'I don't care.' I went out dressed like the character on a Fisherman's Friend packet (except there isn't a character on a Fisherman's Friend packet, only a trawler in a stormy sea) and re-enacted one of those TV reports from the Caribbean islands with bent double palm trees when hurricane 'Ike' or 'Dolly' strike. Mission completed, I attended to the cassette and returned to the van, increasing the water and humidity content considerably.

It rained non-stop through the night and into the morning, and we were thankful we had parked on the concrete standing rather than in the orchard, which had become a boating lake. We drove the three hundred and eighty kilometres north to Bologna through constant rain and spray and alongside a filthy-grey, choppy Adriatic Sea, past many of the places we would liked to have seen. All the wonderful words we had read about Bologna were worthless – everywhere looked drab in the unceasing rain, and we were glad to find the Hotel Citta di Bologna campsite. It was surprisingly busy with German over-winterers. I discussed onward travel with a fellow Sprinter owner. He had heard from a colleague who was stuck in the Alps despite snow chains and tyres.

We left the next morning, heading towards Turin initially, and then down to the coast west of Genoa. A police car towing a rubber boat on a trailer went by.

'He's not taking any chances.' We passed through an area of Espalier fruit growing, Piacenza with its cathedral, churches, and towers, the surrounding industrial flatland, ploughed fields, and logging activities.

With over 9,500 kilometres completed, I reflected on the trip. The weather had deteriorated and 'interesting places' no longer appealed as they would involve trudging around burdened by thick clothes and face-stinging, cold, sleeting rain. Could it have been so hot and sunny just a few days ago? I watched the rear of trucks as we came up behind a long convoy of leviathans almost hidden by spray, then as we launched into the invisibility, glanced up at each of the drivers. I studied where they had come from and wondered where they might be bound for. A lot were from Greece, and probably aiming for an Alpine pass. How many days would the driver be aboard? With my HGV licence I pondered whether I would like the isolation of being in one's own cab world – only the mobile or CB radio to break the monotony. After a while do you become an automaton? Steering a forty-tonne monster between two white lines for mile after mile on cruise control, occasionally overtaking, but for the most part up the backside of another truck and in a convoy because your speed limiter won't let you have that five miles per hour extra to pass.

'They could join them all up and simply have one driver,' I said aloud.

'What?'

'Just thinking of all these trucks – why don't they join them all up and have one driver for these long, straight routes?'

'I think that's what a train is meant to be.' The wind suddenly caught us in a scary way and explained why Gail had been unusually quiet. We were high, flying across runways in the skyway above Lilliputian towns and villages, with a low, rusty barrier and my grip on the wheel the only things preventing a James Bond plunge over the edge to oblivion. I realised then that my palms were sweating, and I sensed Gail shift her grip on the armrest. We were in the business of covering kilometres safely, but there were lunatics about. Even when we had warnings for road works in a thousand metres and I had signalled my intention to pull out for them from three hundred metres, car drivers still thought they could squeeze through if they flattened the accelerator to the floor.

'Idiot!'

A BMW flashed past at high speed, just missing a bollard, and a Mercedes following closely behind was in a dilemma – stop or go? As I watched in my rear-view mirror, time appeared to be suspended: if he went for it, one of us would be collecting red and white bollards under the bumper. He braked furiously, his front end dipping down under the force. I hoped his tyres would hold in the sheeting rain and river of a road and watched in the mirror, transfixed as I proceeded steadily. The car disappeared behind the van.

'I hope he's scared himself to death and his passengers are giving him hell,' I muttered.

'What are you on about?'

'Some idiot behind. Probably blaming me for going at a hundred kph in these conditions.'

'You're doing fine – we're not in a hurry.'

I put an MP3 on:

'Oh Denis, doo-be-doo
I'm in love with you, doo-be-doo
I'm in love with you, doo-be-doo'

That's more like it – Blondie. Oh, the memories. I turned it up and pictured her on *Top of the Pops* giving out that sultry 'I know you fancy me but I don't care' look.

'You're my King and I'm in heaven every time I look at you
When you smile it's like a dream
And I'm so lucky because I found a boy like you
Oh Denis, doo-be doo'

Gail turned it off – she wanted me to concentrate. 'Denis.' It was an odd name for a boy – I guessed that Dennis just didn't work, but could she secretly have meant Denise? No – Blondie, a lesbian? It didn't bear thinking about.

Mountains came into view to the south and we stopped at an Autogrill for coffee and a *cornetto* (that was now called a croissant). Saying goodbye to the Alpine routes, we selected the A26 motorway through rugged mountain scenery with castles, palaces, and towers. Over a lunch of coffees and toasted Panini, the diners provided me with idle speculation as to who was with who, and where they might be going. I contemplated whether the toilets would be dry or, as I found, flooding my shoes after pissing into a urinal unconnected to any drainage system. The guy at the desk had a basket full of coins which I wasn't too anxious to add to, but did anyway – who needs the dirty look? I noticed the women's toilet had a queue of ladies from a coach party and judged that Gail would have a similar experience.

'Aren't they nice toilets,' Gail said emerging.

We were up in the sky again, supported by the thinnest of concrete legs, wind and rain lashing us like God was throwing buckets of water at the windscreen. The headlights were on, but the penetration was limited and exiting tunnels we would be suddenly buffeted by a crosswind, the van taking lunges towards the barrier. I hung on grimly.

'What does that flashing sign say?'

'Not sure. I think it means all trucks with trailers and caravans should get off.' But of course they didn't. We carried on, but conditions worsened and those coastal villages looked a long way down without a parachute.

'What do you think?' I asked.

'It's up to you, you're the driver.'

'But you'd be happier getting off here.'

'Yes. The wind is terrible and I can see you fighting with the steering wheel to keep control.' We exited the motorway and followed the diversions that took us spiralling down towards Savona and then Trieste to run along the seashore on Via Aurelia to Noli. It looked a pretty town – an interesting castle and walls flew past in the mist and rain that had fused with spray from a churning sea. On another day the scene would have drawn cries of 'Look!' but that day they only got brief glances. We were travelling – we didn't want things to look interesting, to feel we were missing something. Palm trees were on their knees, their fronds thrashing in the wind. A few motorhomes parked on a site nearly tempted us to take respite as the foreshore became rocky with frothy waves spewing over. The road was quiet, sensible people not venturing out. Beyond Noli, the road had been cut into the rock face and as we rounded the headland cliff and looked like we were about to be launched like a lifeboat, a barrier across the road and a '*Chiuso*' sign brought us to a sudden halt. We had no alternative but to go back five kilometres through Noli and climb back up to the motorway, invisible in swirling grey clouds. It was just as frightening the second time.

When we arrived in Imperia, the rain had become a dampening drizzle. We were looking forward to the two campsites because of their enticing descriptions in the Caravan Club Guide. A grand gateway and an even grander house boded well. It was a steep drive up the earth driveway amongst dense foliage to a property of faded, seventeenth century grandeur. A squatter camp of algae-covered caravans, the detritus of long-stay residents, cages of clucking hens, and a pungent farmyard odour made us glad that the 'pleasant owners' didn't come out to demand their twenty Euros low-season fee. We departed.

The next site had a villa, but little of the grandeur, and was overlooked by a block of flats, but we had little choice. The pitches had gardens set out on terraces in a woodland that I'm sure would be picturesque in summer. The rain set in for the night, and after we had searched in vain for someone from the site, we stayed in the van. I read that the owner was 'interesting,' which I interpreted as mad, so expected a knock and a scary face at the window at some unearthly hour, but none came.

As I sat back after our meal, Gail and I reflected on our trip, or, as usual, she let me ramble on:

'It seems a long time ago since we set off. Then again, it only seems a short time ago. I can't even remember some of the places on this list of where we stopped. Particularly this last – round the toe and heel of Italy.'

'Like where?'

'That place we met Tony Blair's friend?'

'Wasn't that Martina Franca?'

'You're amazing. I must be going senile – I can't picture any of them. The people, yes, but the places are blurred together. Where did we meet Felice and Rosa and the other couple?'

'That was Carmelo and Annina – at the port.'

'I knew it was a port – let me look on the list. Porto Cesareo!'

'That's it. Happy now?'

'Glad I won't have to write any more notes about Baroque churches and marble pillars. It's over, you know.'

'What is?'

'The trip. We've stayed in over sixty-five places and already covered 10,300 kilometres. It'll be another 1,600 by the time we get home. See, I'm not calling the van home anymore. Tomorrow we'll be hurrying along French motorways, and already I'm writing 'croissant' instead of '*cornetto*'.

'It's been good.'

'Okay if I put some music on?'

'Ooo-oo-oo-oo-oo, he speaks the languages of love
Ooo-oo-oo-oo-oo, amore, chiamami, chiamami
Ooo-oo-oo-oo-oo, appelle-moi mon chérie, appelle-moi
Any time, any place, anywhere, any way
Anytime, anyplace, anywhere, any way.'

Postscript

We made it home. The weather in Italy got worse, but was better in France. Driving through Liguria along the motorway raised on implausibly high stilts was like low-level flying through a thick cloud base. Down below, between the clouds, we got occasional glimpses of elegant mansions and inviting hamlets on the side of gorges that start at the sea and penetrate inland, or the other way round. Tunnels came and went, requiring constant starting and stopping of the wipers to prevent that awful dry, rubbing sound. The Italian roads were good, whereas, surprisingly, the tunnel into France had a poor surface. Menton and Cannes came and went and the rain abated to a drizzle, but by Frejus the overhead gantries warned of '*Vents dangereux*' (high winds). Fortunately, they blew the clouds away and released the sun (but didn't stop the ache in my arms from holding the van steady!).

France was neat, tidy, orderly and as always, spacious. It's hard to judge a country from a motorway but the road surfaces are good and unpatched, the signs clear – Chateaux and points of interest are marked, even a Crocodile Farm. There are picnic spots and aires with functioning, clean toilets, tables and chairs even elegant outside showers for extreme heat days, and no-hassle parking with wide bays. The areas are landscaped with trees and grassy banks. They want you to stop, to take a break, relax, enjoy the facilities whereas in the UK the only reason for you stopping is so a commercial organisation can squash you in with as many others as possible and lighten your wallet and don't dare hang around for too long if you're not spending.

Looking across the countryside, the villages looked neat, harmonized and integrated, with churches as central hubs. Fruit trees in the Rhône valley were ablaze with a pink fusillade of blossom, espaliered to order, nothing out of place, done with pride. Lyon approached – we had been warned of motorhome robberies on the motorway so we headed for Messimy, twenty kilometres east in the country. A delightful village, it has an area set aside for motorhomes and a new services station by the spanking new Sports Centre. We spent our Saturday night there – we had completed five hundred and sixty kilometres that day.

On Sundays there are few trucks on French motorways. Driving is orderly and calm – there are no middle-lane huggers as there are in the UK, and it's not frantic like Italy. *Péage* personnel are generally affable (although I can't say all, because of our prior experiences in *How Katie Pulled Boris*) and we did see a car towing a boat stuck in similar circumstances. Five customs officers had stopped a car and taken it to pieces, all the luggage was scattered in a circle around it like a bomb had exploded and blown it through the windows and their black sniffer dog sat, waiting to be called. But what can they be searching for this is the EU? We passed a giant yellow mushroom with a blue cartoon boy and we had a guess at what they grew locally. Villages with their green or red roofed houses float in oceans of green vegetables. Northern France is fields and more fields, some ploughed some sown, an occasional grain store looking like a rocket on a launch pad. I guess that's why they are each called silo's. The villages are bounded by the land, drawn in tightly by some invisible force or a forceful mayor.

In Calais there was a glimpse of the sun and we were hopeful, but wild storms were forecast and we found all sailings had stopped. We waited and waited, only to have our van cleaned by that great sky wash, and with the van rocking and rolling, we sought refuge in Le Tunnel.

By the time we reached home, we had covered 11,840 kilometres and stopped at sixty-seven different places and were still speaking fondly to each other. Our little van had run faultlessly. Italy and particularly Sicily had provided thousands of memories. Where should we go next?

From the same Author:

www.howkatiepulledboris.com

'*...highly entertaining read...*' Caravan Club Magazine

'*...the fun that is to be had reading about them...*'
Motorcaravan Motorhome Monthly

'*...It's a bit like having Keith in your own van as he recounts overcoming problems big and small...*' Practical Motorhome

Amazon reviews:

'It's entertaining, it's real and well worth a read.'
'...compelling and engaging right from the start.'
'Well observed and entertaining.'
'...informative, intelligent, fun, easy read.'
'This in short is a fantastic book...'
...well observed and splendidly written account of their travels.'
'The writing is excellent, it's refined to perfection and the author has done a great job of incorporating humor into each chapter...'

Lightning Source UK Ltd.
Milton Keynes UK
UKOW05f2027141113

221123UK00001B/5/P